Advanced Information and Knowledge Processing

Series Editors

Professor Lakhmi Jain
Lakhmi.jain@unisa.edu.au
Professor Xindong Wu
xmu@cs.uvm.edu

For further volumes:
http://www.springer.com/series/4738

Babak Akhgar • Simeon Yates
Editors

Intelligence Management

Knowledge Driven Frameworks for Combating Terrorism and Organized Crime

Springer

Editors
Babak Akhgar
Cultural, Communication
and Computing Research Institute
Sheffield Hallam University
Furnival Building
City Campus
Sheffield
United Kingdom
b.akhgar@shu.ac.uk

Simeon Yates
Director Cultural, Communication
and Computing Research Institute
Sheffield Hallam University
Furnival Building
City Campus
Sheffield
United Kingdom
s.yates@shu.ac.uk

ISSN 1610-3947
ISBN 978-1-4471-2682-9 ISBN 978-1-4471-2140-4 (eBook)
DOI 10.1007/978-1-4471-2140-4
Springer London Dordrecht Heidelberg New York

British Library Cataloguing in Publication Data
A catalogue record for this book is available from the British Library

Printed on acid-free paper

Springer is part of Springer Science+Business Media (www.springer.com)

Contents

Authors and Affiliations

Author		Affiliation
Babak	Akhgar	C3RI, Sheffield Hallam University, UK
Ameer	Al-Nemrat	University of East London, UK
Chris	Bates	C3RI, Sheffield Hallam University, UK
Amedeo	Cesta	Institute of Cognitive Science and Technology of the Italian National Research Council (ISTC-CNR), Italy
Mohammad	Dastbaz	Leeds Metropolitan University, UK
Sérgio	Felgueiras	Higher Institute of Police Sciences and Internal Security, Portugal
Gary	Herrington	West Midlands Police, UK
Hamid	Jahankhani	University of East London, UK
Lucasz	Jopek	C3RI, Sheffield Hallam University, UK
Samantha	Killick	C3RI, Sheffield Hallam University, UK
Nick	Kinsella	Rankin Kinsella Associates, UK
Richard	Leary	Forensic Pathways Limited, UK
Greg	Mann	Xanalys Ltd, UK
Kerry	McSeveny	C3RI, Sheffield Hallam University, UK
Mitra	Memarzia	PlayGen, UK
Sarah J.	Mitchell	C3RI, Sheffield Hallam University, UK
Glynn	Rankin	Rankin Kinsella Associates, UK
Alan	Robinson	C3RI, Sheffield Hallam University, UK
Marcos A.	Rodrigues	C3RI, Sheffield Hallam University, UK
Rodrigo Diaz	Rodriguez	Atos Research & Innovation – Atos Origin SAE, Spain
Kam	Star	PlayGen, UK
Jenny	Thomas	Forensic Pathways Limited, UK
David	Waddington	C3RI, Sheffield Hallam University, UK
Richard	Wilson	C3RI, Sheffield Hallam University, UK
Simeon J.	Yates	C3RI, Sheffield Hallam University, UK

Acknowledgements

We wish to thank to everyone who has contributed to this book and all of the various stages of Odyssey project. We would particularly like to acknowledge the following organisations and individuals:

Organisations

- European Commission
- EC, DG Enterprise and Industry "Aerospace, GMES, Security and Defence" Directorate "Security Research and Development"
- Europol
- Europol Homicide Working Group
- SAS
- Metropolitan Police
- Metropolitan Police - Homicide and Serious Crime Command
- SOCA
- UK Security NCP
- BKA
- ENFSI
- West Yorkshire Police
- Police Service of Northern Ireland

People

- Laurent Cabirol
- Commander Dave Johnston
- Commander Simon Foy
- Det Chief Insp Richard Moore
- Det Chief Insp Dave Fortune
- Det Chief Insp Tony Boxall (Rt)
- David Ellero
- Tim Crouch
- Geoffrey Taylor
- Alvise Grammatica
- Jose Cerecedo
- Maria Spulber

Acronyms

Acronym	Details
ACPO	Association Of Chief Police Officers
AHTU	Anti-Human Trafficking Unit (Ireland)
ANPRS	Automated Number Plate Recognition System
AWF	Analytical Work File
BIS	Business Information Systems
CEON	Central Odyssey Node
CEOP	Child Exploitation and Online Protection Centre
CONTEST	Government's counter-terrorism strategy
COTS	Commercial off the Shelf
CTCM	Conceptual Template for Construction of Methodology
DCIM	Data Collection and Information Management
DPA	Data Protection Act
DVE	Distributed Virtual Environment
ECHR	European Convention on Human Rights
ELINT	Electronic Intelligence.
ENFSI	European Network of Forensic Science Institutes
EPC	Cabinet Office's Emergency Planning College
EU	European Union
EU FP7	European Union Framework Program 7
FOIA	Freedom of Information Act
FSC	Formal Social Control
GMC	Group Mental Construct
HUMINT	Intelligence gathering through interpersonal/ informal contact between people
IMINT	Imagery Intelligence
INTEL	Intelligence
IOM	International Organisation for Migration
JAAS	Java Authentication and Authorization Service
JMS	Java Message Service
KM	Knowledge Management
LEA	Law Enforcement Agencies
LRAT	Life-style Routine Activity Theory
LRAT	Lifestyle Routine Activity Theory
MC	Mental Construct
NABIS	National Ballistics Intelligence Service
NIM	National Intelligence Model
NIR	Near Infrared

NRM	National Referral Mechanism
OCN	Organised Crime Network
OCTA	Organised Crime Threat Assessment
OSCE	Organization for Security and Co-operation in Europe
OSL	Odyssey Semantic Language
PVE	Preventing Violent Extremism
RBAC	Role Based Access Controls
RBN	Russian Business Network
REA	Research Executive Agency
RUP	Rational Unified Process
SEE	South Eastern Europe
SIEM	Security Information & Event Management
SIGINT	Signals intelligence
SIM	Strategic Intelligence Management
SIO	Senior Investigating Officer
SOA	Service Oriented Architecture
SOAP	Simple Object Access Protocol
SOCA	Serious and Organised Crime Agency
STA	Strategic Threat Assessment
SYP	South Yorkshire Police
THB	Trafficking in Human Beings
TIP	Trafficking in Persons
UNICEF	United Nations Children's Fund
UNODC	United Nations Office on Drugs and Crime
URN	Unique Reference Numbers
VE	Virtual Environment
WS	Web Services

Chapter 1: Introduction – Themes and Issues

Simeon J. Yates and Babak Akhgar

Introduction

This volume brings together a range of chapters which address the linkage between law enforcement, the uses of and developments in information and communication technologies (ICTs) and key ideas about the management of information, intelligence and knowledge in this domain. The book is split into three sections. Section 1 presents four chapters which address the details, outcomes, user needs and background theoretical ideas behind the Odyssey Project. The Odyssey Project was part-funded under the EU FP7 programme to explore the challenges of establishing a Pan-European ballistics and crime information intelligence network and to propose solutions, including a demonstrator prototype system. As such the Odyssey project represents an example of the type of system that is likely to become commonly used by Law Enforcement Agencies (LEAs) in the near future. The research goal of the Odyssey Project was that of understanding both the challenges in developing and potential opportunities provided to LEAs by systems that can securely integrate large volumes of crime data and then extract from this data, information, knowledge and intelligence of use at both an operational and strategic level.

The current rapid development in both computing power and the ability to mine and present in useful ways complex data sets provide the backdrop to both the Odyssey project and to this volume. As the work on the Odyssey Project demonstrated (see chapter 2) many of the challenges are not technical but organisational, legal, economic, social and political. Sections 2 and 3 therefore bring in chapters from other researchers, and wider commentaries from the Odyssey team. Section 2 explores other projects attempting to exploit the power of contemporary ICT systems to support LEAs in many aspects of their work including investigations, data analysis and presentation, identification, training and crime prevention. Section 3 takes a look at the social and organisational issues around aspects of crime prevention, crime detection, and policing – with a view to the role of ICTs in these contexts.

Lessons from Odyssey

Section 1 of this book is focused on the Odyssey Project. Chapter 2 discusses the overall results of the project and the key features of the prototype system developed. The Odyssey Project focused on data collection and exchange in the context of gun crime. Gun crime – that is potential and actual illegal events in which firearms, ammunition and other ballistic items are involved – happens widely across the EU, though the levels and definitions of such events vary between, among and within Member States. Such variations come from the multiple methods, systems and legal frameworks in EU member States. The majority LEAs believe that criminals actively use and move firearms across the EU. As a result criminals, guns and evidence travel across borders. Unfortunately comparable levels of data on gun crimes held by LEAs does not travel across borders, despite gun crime information being collected widely across the EU. The Odyssey Project was part-funded under the EU FP7 programme to explore the challenges of establishing a Pan-European ballistics and crime information intelligence network and to propose solutions, including a demonstrator prototype system.

A key concern for potential users of the Odyssey system was security. Chapter 3 explores the solutions to the problems of data security identified during the requirements research phase of the Odyssey project. Defining robust security architectures is vital for protecting IT infrastructures from cyber-attacks. This is especially true when the IT infrastructure is going to be used by investigators and law enforcement agencies to combat crime across EU. A compromise between the level of security and the level of acceptable risk must be found. Chapter 3 describes the analysis and the methodology followed in the Odyssey project (see chapter 2) to define a security-layered architecture able to support a secure Pan-European ballistics and crime information intelligence network designed to help tackle organized crime and terrorism.

Users were at the core of the Odyssey Project. Chapter 4 provides a user's view on why systems like Odyssey, and why interoperable data and systems in general, are needed by LEAs. The chapter looks at the impact of gun crime on communities and the ease with which such crime can cross physical and other boundaries, making it a signal crime that must be addressed through effective collaboration between LEAs across EU Member States. The chapter also considers the barriers that exist between the disparate disciplines of investigation, intelligence and scientific examination of evidence and potential changes to law that may be required to facilitate a true EU wide interoperable gun crime system.

The volume of data now available to LEAs in a variety of formats, systems and contexts presents considerable issues of complexity and the need to understand this complexity. Chapter 5 considers how the science of complexity provides some guidance on how to tackle these challenges. The science of complexity is primarily concerned with the examination and understanding of the workings of complex adaptive systems and it can be argued that crime and terrorism are examples of complex adaptive systems. Chapter 5 explores the implications of this for the detection and prevention of organised crime and the role information technology has to play in this.

Technologies and law enforcement

New technologies provide new solutions, new practices and new challenges to all organisations. In many cases the full implications of a new technology are far wider than those initially expected by the developers or first users. Very often new technologies, even ones designed to replicate existing organisational practice, can prove highly disruptive. Very often new technologies therefore open up new possibilities and methods by which LEAs can address their core activities from crime detection and prevention to training and outreach. Section 2 presents four chapters which address examples of other ICT solutions designed to support LEA activity.

Chapter 6 considers the use of ICT to support data representations of use to ongoing investigations. Good investigative practice should embody a consistent methodology and this methodology should emphasise accountability, standardized processes, and information sharing between investigations and agencies. It should also make use of appropriate tools to organise, manage, retrieve and analyse potentially large volumes of investigative data. However, an investigative methodology alone won't ensure that evidence is processed in a timely fashion. With greater amounts of data being available to investigators through public sources and data sharing initiatives, and improvements being made to data capture/entry facilities, bottle-necks may occur in the review of investigative data, potentially jeopardizing a successful outcome. Chapter 6 therefore explores how technologies such as text analysis, entity matching and resolution, and network analysis can be inserted into the investigative workflow to speed data processing, prioritise tasks, and facilitate search and analysis.

Both Odyssey and the systems described in Chapter 6 make use of data gathered during investigations. This data is most often collected after-the-fact of a crime. Chapter 7 explores how ICTs can support LEA activity in real time. The chapter explores how the development of advanced techniques for fast 3D reconstruction and recognition of human faces in unconstrained scenarios can significantly help the fight against crime and terrorism. The chapter describes a solution developed that satisfies a number of important requirements such as operating close to real-time, high accuracy in recognition rates, and robust to local illumination. The chapter considers two scenarios where the outcomes of this research could be exploited for forensic analysis and for flagging potential threats in counter-terrorism.

Chapters 8 and 9 consider how ICT systems can support changing social and organisational behaviour and systems. Chapter 8 explores how and ICT system can support the training of LEA staff. The recent tsunami and its aftermath in Japan to Icelandic volcanic ash, to terrorist instigated actions such as 9/11 and the 7th July bombings in London indicate there is a clear need for better training of strategic decision makers as well as the operational forces that need to deal with very complex and almost always multi agency operations. Quite often the difference between an emergency and a disaster is one or two critically wrong decisions in what quite often is a very tight and limited time span. Chapter 8 describes the PANDORA Project which is a European FP7 funded project aiming to make use of emerging serious gaming concepts and technologies to develop an innovative and more effective training environment for the strategic decision makers (the Gold Commanders) so that they can cope more effectively with such difficult and challenging situations.

Chapter 9 takes a different view on education and training to explore how the use of serious games can function in the context of crime prevention. It describes the Choices and Voices project and systems. This is an interactive simulation encouraging young people to explore and discuss the underlying issues and adverse influences, which can lead to divisions and tensions in communities. In various scenarios the player faces a number of moral dilemmas in which their decisions define their own outcomes, as well as those of their friends and family. Although the game offers the same range of choices to start with, each player makes a different set of decisions that substantially alters the outcome of their game. The structured group discussions in response to the game further emphasise how real life decisions can have significant consequences.

Technology, society and law enforcement

Section 3 considers the broader issues of ICT use and its impacts on the activity of LEAs. Chapter 10 explores how LEAs might best draw on insights from the use of ICTs for knowledge management to strategically manage data, information, knowledge and the intelligence they hold. The chapter proposes a conceptual framework for use by LEAs when developing methodologies to best strategically manage intelligence in the context of crime and terrorism detection and prevention. The chapter provides a definition for strategic intelligence and views it as: "a process of creating value added Learning Processes (i.e. knowledge) so that knowledge becomes the strategic resource of a law enforcement agency with measurable and quantifiable value in successfully combating a crime or act of terrorism". The chapter develops a conceptual template for the construction of a methodology (CTCM) in this domain and considers its application in an example case.

Chapter 11 takes a different approach to considering the role of data, intelligence, information and knowledge in combatting crime. In this case the chapter examines the specific needs with regard to data exchange in the context of detecting and preventing human trafficking. Trafficking in persons is a complex and growing global problem that requires a comprehensive cross sector response. It occurs across and within national borders. It affects virtually every country either as a country of origin, transit or destination for victims. It involves the exploitation of people and the fundamental breach of their human rights. Every year, thousands of men, women and children fall into the control of traffickers, in their own countries and abroad. Trafficking in Human Beings, (THB) involves the exploitation of people through force, coercion, threat, fraud or deception and may include acts generally defined as human rights abuses. Trafficking takes many forms, trafficked persons are exploited into prostitution, forced labour and services, slavery-like practices, and their body organs may be removed and sold. Improving current data/intelligence systems and the ability to harmonise and use the data and exchange information is advantageous and would enable in-formed national action strategies and planning at both strategic and tactical level; improved monitoring and evaluation; targeted and informed awareness and prevention campaigns; enhanced training; targeted victim care and provision; identification of links between source and destination countries; improved and informed investigations and prosecutions.

Chapter 12 looks to crime that exists only because of the existence of ICT, namely cybercrime. Rather than focus on the technical fixes to this phenomenon the chapter explores the extent to which the social and individual responses to this phenomenon produce contexts in which individuals can fall victim to this type of crime. A significant percentage of the populace do not consider or understand "what and how" cybercrime is committed, nor how they might be a victim of it, and many fear they might unconsciously be part of it. Reducing the opportunities for cybercrime is not a simple task. It will require co-operation between many players, and fundamental changes in common attitudes and practices. When considering legal implications of the misuse of technologies, it is worth noting that crossing national borders results in a change in the laws that people are subject to. Some countries do not consider hacking and online identity theft as high priority crimes. Similarly, the technological divide leaves gaps in the laws in those countries that are less technologically advanced. The aim of this chapter is to examine the relationship between online behaviour and computer victimisation. Understanding the trends of cybercrime and the strategies employed by cyber criminals in order to commit cybercrime will help to identify the steps that needs be taken to prevent such criminal activities.

Chapter 13 once again takes another view on the relationship between LEAs and ICTs. The chapter constitutes a case study of South Yorkshire Police's handling of a protest outside the Sheffield City. The demonstration occurred in the wake of a number of high-profile official reports advocating a more permissive approach to protest policing. The chapter describes and analyses two particular aspects of SYP's 'Operation Obelisk': the use of social media (such as Twitter and Facebook) to keep the general public informed of on-going or impending police activities as part of a 'no surprises' approach; and the deployment of a Police

Liaison Team, part of whose responsibility was to complement CCTV surveillance by feeding information on the mood and activities of the crowd to a remote command cell. The study concludes that such technological innovations have a vital role to play in complementing – and moderating the negative impact of – more established methods of policing political protest.

Chapter 14 addresses a key issue facing any LEA engaging with this constantly change social technical context – namely training and continuing professional development for LEA staff. This not only relates to the growth in new technologies, methods and practices but also national, international and EU policy developments around both LEA activity and ICT. Some key examples are described in chapter 2. Such European police cooperation needs to be underpinned by mutual understanding between the numerous police organizations that operate across the Member States. However, the very diversity of these organisations is a major factor that hinders this process. The demands for trans-national police cooperation result in a requirement for new integrated police learning strategies to be developed and implemented. These learning strategies will impact on European police culture, on agencies learning strategies and on the resources to be allocated, as well as on the use of the new ICTs.

Themes and issues

A collection such as this – written by a mix of academics, technology users, policy specialists, and industrial researchers – will provide a wide ranging and multi-faceted view of the issues under debate. The majority of the chapters are focused on specific examples, cases or technologies. We believe that taken as a whole a number of themes emerge which we will return to in our final chapter, these are:

- The use, development and management of data, information, intelligence and knowledge
- The complexity of the social, cultural, political and legal landscape in which LEAs deploy new ICT solutions
- The manner in which new forms of ICT themselves change the social, cultural, political and legal landscape for users, citizens, LEAs and criminals alike
- The desire by users and LEAs to best strategically use and manage the data, information, knowledge and intelligence they have
- The complexity and range of data, information, knowledge and intelligence available to contemporary LEAs
- The centrality of interoperability and standards to the utilization of this data across national and organizational borders
- The importance of addressing the social, economic, political and legal issues as much as the technical ones

- That technical and ICT solutions have to be undertaken hand-in-hand with a strong understanding of the social, economic, political and legal context in which such solutions will operate

  We will return to these themes and issues in our concluding chapter.

Section 1: The Odyssey Project

Chapter 2: The Odyssey Project – Understanding and Implementing User Needs in the Context of Ballistic Crime Data Exchange

Simeon J. Yates, Chris Bates, Babak Akhgar, Lucasz Jopek, Richard Wilson, Sarah J. Mitchell and Samantha Killick

Abstract Gun crime – that is potential and actual illegal events in which firearms, ammunition and other ballistic items are involved – happens widely across the EU, though the levels and definitions of such events vary. Such variations come from the multiple methods, systems and legal frameworks in EU member States. The majority of law enforcement agencies (LEAs) believe that criminals actively use and move firearms across the EU. As a result criminals, guns and evidence travel across borders. Unfortunately comparable levels of data on gun crimes held by LEAs does not travel across borders, despite gun crime information being collected widely across the EU. Especially as not all the data is collected electronically and database formats, structures and data fields vary. In addition different ballistics imaging systems are used across the EU. The Odyssey Project was part-funded under the EU FP7 programme to explore the challenges of establishing a Pan-European ballistics and crime information intelligence network and to propose solutions, including a demonstrator prototype system. This chapter reviews the overall findings from the Odyssey Project and the key features of the prototype.

Introduction

This chapter describes the work undertaken to research and develop a prototype solution to the linking, presentation and analysis of cross-border gun crime data within the European Union. This domain is one where technical, policing, national and EU legal frameworks and the behaviours of police forces and criminals regularly change, sometimes dramatically within a short time span. The proposed solution described below has been developed to ensure the system can remain responsive, domain relevant and effective whilst adapting reasonably dynamically to these changes.

The objective of the Odyssey Project has been to develop a prototype intelligence platform for the secure sharing and manipulation of data about ballistic crimes. Ballistic crimes are those which involve the use of firearms and other weapons, ranging from smuggling and the supply of illegal firearms through to homicides (Akhgar, 2009). Although Odyssey focused on ballistics data, the concept and architecture are immediately applicable to other forensic data sets including DNA, fingerprints, mobile phone records, and explosives analysis. The techniques developed within the project for querying and manipulation could be applied to any domain which involves rich data and personal records.

The platform is built on top of a distributed architecture using message queues to link a range of back-end engines that provide the following series of components:

- Security
- Data sharing (data selection and upload, querying, storage of query plans)
- Non-relational data manipulation (semantic querying, data mining and relationship discovery)
- Support for query development (domain-specific query language, intensional support)
- An alerting component which executes queries automatically

The Odyssey Project is funded by the European Commission. The project partners are: Sheffield Hallam University (United Kingdom), Atos Origin (Spain), Forensic Pathways Ltd. (United Kingdom), EUROPOL (Netherlands), XLAB (Slovenia), Politecnico Di Milano (Italy), West Midlands Police (United Kingdom), Royal Military Academy (Belgium), An Garda Siochana (Republic of Ireland), SAS Software Ltd. (United Kingdom),Direzione Centrale Anticrimine - Servizio Polizia Scientifica (Italy) and North Yorkshire Police (United Kingdom). The Odyssey Project also interacted with key external bodies including European Network of Forensic Science Institutes (ENFSI), European Homicide Working Group and the manufacturers of the main ballistic imaging systems in use in Europe.

Within this chapter we provide an overview of the work of the Odyssey Project and indicate some of the key outputs. The Odyssey project had three main elements: an initial 'user requirements gathering' phase; an implementation phase; and a testing phase. The chapter begins with a review of the key findings from the user requirements research and some detail of the policing and legal frameworks within which the project had to operate. Next the chapter presents a brief overview of the implemented prototype system with a focus on the architecture and user interface. The chapter concludes with some comments on users, standards and future developments.

User requirements - key findings

The requirements gathering phase was led by LEAs who were full project partners and had experience of gathering data on and assessing user needs. Requirements gathering events led by these partners provided the basis for identifying a set of detailed 'lay person described' user needs. The project broadly followed the Rational Unified Process (RUP) framework developed by IBM. Following RUP, user needs were translated into specific software requirements after a number of iterations and validation processes. The broad outline of these requirements was:

- All data to be held and exchanged securely
- Security by design should be a core approach
- LEAs in Member States can quickly register incidents involving ballistic items
- Potential links between ballistic, incident and intelligence data incorporated into Odyssey can be identified automatically and relevant users from Member States informed of potential links with a URN of the related records
- Firearms examiners/forensic officers can quickly examine potential links across Member State Ballistic data
- Investigating officers (OICs and SIOs) can quickly search for related incidents across Member State borders
- Analysts can quickly aggregate and assess aggregated data across member states generating intelligence products for use in prevention and disruption activity or future strategic planning
- Firearms and gun crime investigation experts can communicate with each other directly across Member State borders in a secure way
- To improve the supplier landscape for Member States through potential competition by creating less dependence upon specific ballistic analysis technologies
- An operating environment that promotes interoperability through the use of open standards (formal or de facto) and systems (such as Firetyde, XML, PKI, JMS etc.) but which maintains a robust and secure architecture that is scalable

Though these core user requirements were identified early on in the project, the economic, technological and policing context within Europe changed dramatically over the life of the project. As a result building a system that was flexible enough to address such change became an additional key user requirement. In addition to this the remit of the project included demonstration of the benefits of data-sharing, even though current legal and policing contexts might limit the actual extent to which this can be done at present.

Broader context

In order to better address these sometimes conflicting requirements and goals the project engaged in a wider review of the context of ballistic crime data collection and management around Europe. This work involved visits to a range of EU LEA's and joint work with ENFSI on understanding better the technologies on offer for the matching of ballistic items. In addition to project partners 13 EU members and nearby states (Russia and Turkey) were visited to understand available technologies and user practices. Fifteen EU member states contributed ballistic items to the joint work between the Odyssey project and ENFSI.

From this a number of key findings emerged:

- Gun crime – that is potential and actual illegal events in which firearms, ammunition and other ballistic items are involved – happens widely across the EU, though the levels and definitions of such events vary
- Many police forces and LEAs believe that criminals actively use and move firearms across the EU
- Criminals, guns and evidence travel across borders, though the levels of such use and movement are debated
- Gun crime information is collected widely across the EU, but not all the data is collected electronically, database formats, structures and data fields vary widely
- Gun crime information sharing is not routine across all member states
- Physical ballistics evidence is collected widely across the EU, and is in nearly all cases processed by experts trained in the ballistic forensics
- Roles within LEAs for the management of ballistic evidence vary widely from specialist forensic science teams to police officers trained in ballistics
- Ballistics data sharing is not routine, and the exchange of physical evidence is expensive and time consuming
- Different ballistics imaging systems exist in the market across the EU and the number and type of installations are changing (see figure 2.1)
- The different ballistics imaging systems are predominantly used for the purpose of reducing the 'search space' when matching ballistic evidence
- Matches in ballistic evidence are declared and used as evidence on the basis of direct examination by the relevant expert(s) within LEAs – not by technologies
- Gun crime prevention and detection include activity ranging from direct policing through to policy actions – at all levels good reliable data are needed
- LEAs often use multiple systems themselves to manage crime data including specific systems for ballistic data and other business information systems (BIS) to manage other crime data and business processes (see figure 2.1)
- BIS and Ballistics Systems are used for intelligence (to support on-going investigations or policy) and not for the production of evidence
- Evidential data a very small subset of intelligence data

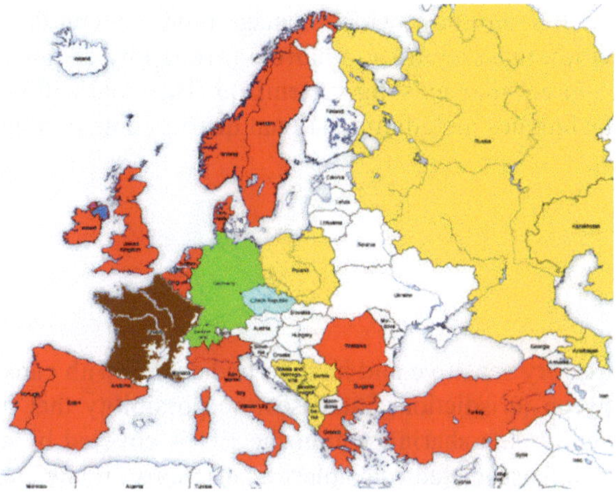

Fig. 2.1. Variety of ballistic identification systems in use in Europe

Policing context

A key aspect of the context in which the Odyssey prototype has been developed is that of existing police information systems. Internationally, there are a large number of bespoke systems including COPLINK, NABIS, HOLMES-2 and I-24/7. COPLINK is an information and knowledge management system aimed at capturing, accessing, analysing, visualising and sharing information between United States law enforcement agencies. COPLINK comprises of two components COPLINK Connect (CC) and COPLINK Detect. COPLINK Connect is designed to integrate disparate heterogeneous data sources, including legacy systems, to facilitate information sharing between police departments. COPLINK Detect tries to discover associations within police databases. It supports detectives and crime analysts in finding associations between people, vehicles, incidents and locations. The strength of an association is determined through the use of co-occurrence analysis and clustering. The system is able to search for meaningful terms in both structured (database tables) and unstructured (witness statements) data (Chen et al. 2003).

UK police forces have access to a number of independent database systems. These databases are used to record, monitor and manage offences in such areas as sex offences, gun crimes and major incident management. NABIS provides ballistic examination services, for twenty UK based police forces, through three hubs, which are based in London, Birmingham and Manchester (Sims 2010). I-24/7 has a European-wide dataset that, largely, retains information related to the individual (Interpol, 2007). A gap exists between the systems that collect, store and integrate data on ballistic crime within the EU and those which manage more general data about crimes and criminal activities. Odyssey tries to narrow this gap by combining data from a wider range of sources than existing systems do. This data will be interrogated using a variety of techniques including relational queries, data mining and semantically-based searches.

Legal context

Both personal and crime data are very sensitive and have to be handled with care. Moving any sensitive data between jurisdictions increases the possibility that it will be compromised. Consequently data sharing within the EU is covered by a range of legislation. These laws and associated rules place restrictions on law enforcement agencies as they do on individuals or on businesses. Some key foundational issues are detailed in the following sections.

The Swedish Initiative

This is a statement proposing a framework for the simplification of the exchange of information and intelligence between law enforcement authorities. It was adopted in December, 2006. Nygren (2008) points out that under this initiative the rules governing the cross-border exchange of criminal information and intelligence cannot be stricter than those applying to internal data exchange. In other words cross-border data exchange should be equally as open or as closed, and meet the same security standards as within-nation exchange.

Principal of availability

The principal of availability introduces a new form of cooperation in criminal matters within the EU. Law enforcement authorities in one Member State are empowered to grant access to their information to authorities in other Member States for the purpose of prevention, detection and investigation of criminal offences. Europa (2008) states:

> "The principle subjects the exchange of law enforcement information to uniform conditions across the Union. If a law enforcement officer or Europol needs information to perform its lawful tasks, it may obtain this information, and the Member State that controls this information, is obliged to make it available for the stated purpose".

Sharing personal information or information which could be used to identify an individual has always been difficult. Under the principle of availability

> "the exchange of personal data within the framework of police and judicial cooperation in criminal matters, notably under the principle of availability of information as laid down in the Hague Programme, should be supported by clear rules enhancing mutual trust between

the competent authorities and ensuring that the relevant information is protected in a way that excludes any discrimination in respect of such cooperation between the Member States while fully respecting fundamental rights of individuals".

Systems such as Odyssey should be built to both encourage the use of personal data where appropriate and to ensure its security at all times.

Prüm decision

A sub set of the EU Member States (Germany, Spain, France, Luxembourg, the Netherlands, Austria and Belgium) signed the "Prüm Treaty" in the German town of Prüm on 27 May 2005 (Prüm 2010). The European Commission supported the German initiative to transform this treaty into an instrument binding on all EU Member States and the Council adopted the Prüm Decision and its implementing provisions on 23 June 2008. The Prüm Decision is described by the EU DG Home affairs as providing for:

"The automated exchange of DNA, fingerprints, and vehicle registration data, as well other forms of police cooperation, between the 27 Member States".

Standards

The goal of the Odyssey project was to produce a prototype system that would facilitate the sharing and matching of ballistic crime data across EU member states. The above findings provide the organizational and legal context in which such a system needs to operate. From this we can identify three key barriers to effective data exchange within the EU with regard to crime data:

1. There is a lack of accepted standards either formal (e.g. set by ISO or CEN) or de facto due to established practice. This includes standards for: the methods, performance and data output of ballistic matching technologies; the storage and sharing of data; and for the declaring matches between ballistics objects either through software, technology or formal process.
2. There is a lack of interoperability between ballistic matching systems and police BIS
3. Lack of very routine data sharing caused by limitations of the technologies (their lack of interoperability), legal frameworks, security requirements and fears and lack of knowledge or data on the value added from such exchange

Implementation of the prototype

The detection of pan-national ballistic crime breaks down into a number of complex problems. The first is the realisation that such crime is happening and, for the individual investigator, that their crime might be related to ones which happened across the border. The second problem is to discover the related data. Where crimes occur in different jurisdictions there may be no way in which data about them can be shared readily or easily. Only by sharing data can investigators become aware that two incidents are similar or that they may form part of a larger pattern. The final problem is to share the actual ballistic data: meta-data about bullets or guns, images taken from comparison microscopes or automated imaging systems. The Odyssey platform demonstrates that all of these problems can be addressed using a suitably complex and distributed data management application

Architecture

The prototype uses both local nodes and a central hub with asynchronous communication between them across a message queue. Individual components of the prototype are wrapped in Web Services so that the platform can combine the flexibility and scalability of a modern Service-Oriented Architecture with the robustness and power of a centralised system.

A number of factors impacted upon the architecture including: the need to manipulate data which is distributed across member states; the importance of securing both data and access to it; the use of different back-ends to manipulate data; the data is likely to be both incomplete and noisy; and this is a distributed system with all of the problems which are typically found in such systems.

Data and processing have to be distributed across locations. The platform's mixture of back-ends would benefit from a single centralised data store containing records of all incidents of gun-crime from across the EU. Such a store would simplify the tracking of weapons or patterns of usage; but as noted above, the use and sharing of crime data is subject to many restrictions, some defined at European level, others set by national Governments. These regulations tend to emphasise the protection of the individual's right to privacy and generally mean that any data which might identify an individual cannot, as a matter of routine, be shared between member states. In developing software and systems for law enforcement this is usually taken to mean that data are always held locally but that individual records may be shared for specific purpose. This presents a difficulty for Odyssey which uses data mining to discover patterns within crime data. To be compliant with European regulations the platform can centralise ballistic data (guns, bullets, etc.) and some data about incidents but nothing which might be used to identify victims, witnesses or perpetrators.

Security is an important requirement for any system used by law enforcement agencies. The data which Odyssey stores and manipulates is sensitive because it often relates to on-going criminal investigations. The architecture has to balance the competing need to keep data secure and the need to share data with colleagues who, since this is a pan-European system, may work in different jurisdictions. Odyssey has a fairly standard security scheme in which users must authenticate on to the platform with an ID and a password before being given access to data and processing based on their role and location. Messages moved across the queue are encrypted using a public key infrastructure whilst the queue itself runs over a VPN. For more on the security solutions developed by the project see chapter 2 of this volume.

The platform has three different data processing modules. There is a standard relational database which holds bulk data and handles queries in which target records are known or can be easily identified. There is a data mining system which is used to discover patterns within the data. Such a pattern may be a set of records which appear to be related to a particular record of interest but which do not have direct connections in the relational data, or changes to the data as when a new type of weapon enters the market and is seen to move across Europe. Finally, we have an Intensional Querying module which through understanding the data helps investigators formulate better queries (Giacomo, 1996).

There are no standards defining the data which are gathered during investigations. Each country uses its own approach – individual organisations within the same country may even gather different data. Often the data is incomplete because officers do not have the time or expertise to enter it correctly into a computer system. Data is also incomplete because investigations are live processes. As an investigation proceeds more data is gathered and new relationships are created and existing ones modified or removed. The platform has to handle these changes and make them explicit to investigators.

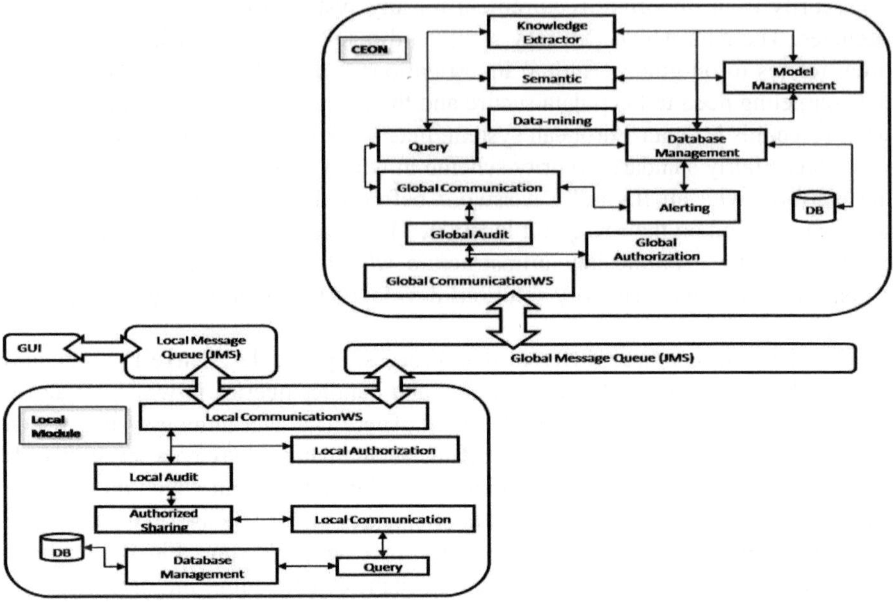

Fig. 2.2. Architecture of the Odyssey Prototype System

The prototype has had to be designed to handle some of the more common problems of distributed systems. Processing queries can take a long time, especially when they rely on mining of large data sets. The central system has to be able to handle multiple concurrent queries which may be resident on the server for long periods. Clients cannot remain connected to the server whilst their long-running queries execute. The architecture has to be built so that clients receive responses to their earlier queries when users authenticate onto the system. This can be achieved in many ways, on the Odyssey platform it is done through the use of an asynchronous message queue.

The Odyssey platform is built from three separate modules: a local node, a Central Odyssey Node (CEON) that has richer functionality and a message queue.

Local nodes

The local node is the primary repository within the platform. The local node has a PostgreSQL relational database which holds data about ballistic items and crimes within a particular jurisdiction. The database is accessed through a local message queue and an endpoint which parses incoming requests and translates them into SQL commands which are then applied to PostgreSQL.

The local node routes "agency to CEON" and "agency to agency" communication. Using the Odyssey platform authorities are able to share secure messages including queries and their results. But its function is also an encryption of all messages, decryption and verification of all incoming messages, auditing of communication, access to local database through the IDatabaseComponent interface, interfacing with GUI components through ICommunicationComponent interface, interfacing with JMS broker, and authorizing data to be sent to CEON.

Each police force or other authority runs its own local node. When the platform is fully operational there are many local nodes running but all are independent of each other. The Odyssey desktop client gives users access to their local node but not to any of the other nodes in the system thus avoiding problems of trans-jurisdictional access to data. A node can be any size. Some may hold data for an entire nation whilst others might contain just the data for a particular area.

Using only the local node has few benefits over using existing Police information systems since any results are based on data which are likely to be in those other systems. The power of Odyssey comes from combining local and central results.

CEON

CEON is at the heart of the platform. CEON has exactly the same queue endpoint as the local node and a PostgreSQL database which has exactly the same structure as the local one. CEON also has connections to an Intensional querying system and to a data-mining application, SAS 9.2. The platform has an experimental Semantic Web engine which tries to provide a richer querying interface through domain-derived taxonomic structures.

Relational database

The main data store in the platform is a relational database developed using PostgreSQL 8.4. The database structure reflects the types of structure used in systems such as COPLINK, NABIS and by some of the databases used at EUROPOL. Most of its tables hold metadata with relatively few required to store the details of incidents and investigations. Figure 2.3 shows a fragment of the structure. The database structure is replicated at each local node. Each Local authority includes only its own data in its local node. Any data which it wishes to share with other authorities is uploaded to CEON where the same database structure appertains.

Manipulating the data

The user requirements identified in the initial work of the project clearly indicated a need to move beyond simply database matching. The research and development work within the implementation phase of the project explored four distinct approaches to the manipulation of data within the system:

- Traditional database matching
- Intensional querying
- Data mining
- Semantic querying

The traditional methods were based in standard relational database searching and matching techniques. The other three methods represented attempts to solve the problems of making large and complex data easily accessible to the variety of identified potential users – from investigating officers, through forensic specialists to data analysts and policy advisors. As both an added security layer, audit tool and a method to unify search processes and their representation a 'domain-specific language' (DSL) was developed for the Odyssey system. The following sections describe the design of the three more novel methods of searching the data.

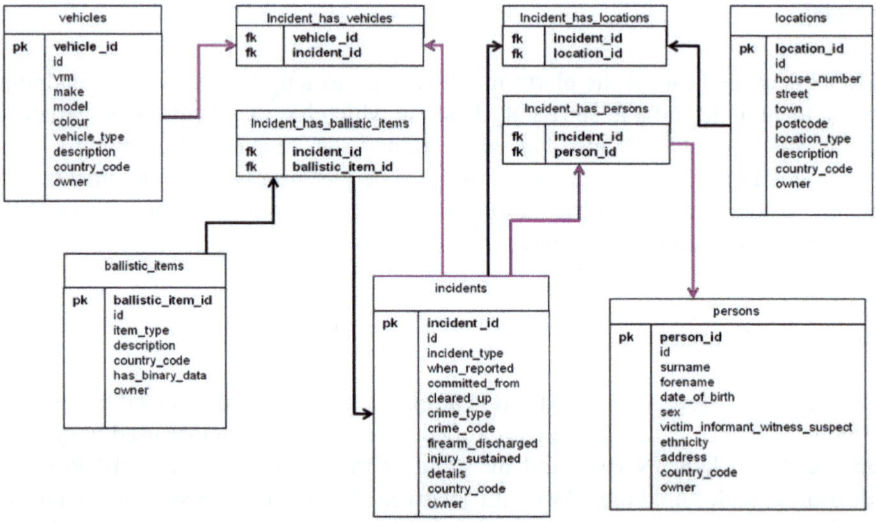

Fig. 2.3. Elements of the relational database structure

Intensional querying

The application of data mining techniques to extract useful knowledge from datasets has been researched over a number of years (Nath 2006). Implementations have been tried in a number of Police information systems, notably COPLINK (Chen et al. 2004). By mining frequent patterns from repositories, it is possible to provide the investigators with partial, and often statistically-supported, results.

However, such results can never be guaranteed to be completely accurate and may send investigations in the wrong direction by suggesting the wrong line of enquiry.

The Odyssey platform uses the uncertainty of data mining to give investigators implicit knowledge from the repositories and to use that knowledge to formulation more effective queries (Strohmaier et al, 2009). When a user faces a large and complex dataset for the first time they will not know its features. Frequency patterns provide a way to understand what is contained in the dataset. Summarizing the vast integrated dataset shared by different EU Police Organizations can increase the quality of results, accessing the most promising results for a given query. To this end the Intensional Querying module has been developed. We envisaged two possibilities for the use of approximate knowledge:

- The user directly queries the association rule base.
- The user queries the Odyssey repositories, but also receives an approximate answer.

In both cases the user will be provided with some useful general knowledge related to the mode of investigation. In the following trivial query, expressed in Odyssey's querying DSL:

```
WHAT ABOUT Incident Person WHERE country_of_crime = 'UK' AND
gender='m' WITH CONFIDENCE 0.9
```

The statement will trigger the intensional knowledge system to return any information about the listed elements given the defined conditions. Thus every association rule containing:

- (at least) attributes from the relations translated from the keywords in the WHAT ABOUT list (for example Incident, Person)
- in which elements satisfy the conditions (for example country_of_crime = 'UK' AND gender = 'm')
- having confidence more or equal than the stated value (for example 0.9)

The results are sent back to the intensional system for further processing such as ordering. The completed result set is returned to the client where it acts as a prompt, or set of prompts, to the user to help them either refine or widen their search criteria.

Data mining

The CEON component includes a full SAS data-mining system which is used to manage data uploads through its excellent GUI tools and to mine the repository looking for patterns and hidden structures. The data-mining and knowledge extraction modules need to pre-process the database data in order to extract information for its later use. In particular, SAS data-mining solution requires for a de-normalised version of the data (Wilson et al, 2010). Processes to load any data which has changed into SAS and add it to the de-normalised structure are triggered periodically to keep it up-to-date. Mining queries may then be re-executed. The reason that Odyssey has a central database is so that it can mine data. The benefit of centralising and sharing is that much richer results can be obtained. When a data mining query discovers data it actually returns only record IDs. The middleware sends these IDs to the CEON instance of PostgreSQL where they are used in SQL SELECT statements to retrieve complete records. These records are returned to the user who initiated the query.

Semantic querying

The final component which is available to users is a Semantic engine. One of the first acts of the Odyssey project was to define the taxonomy of ballistic items and ballistic crimes. Inputs to, and outputs from, the platform must be structured according to this taxonomy.

Organisations using local nodes are able to share data by uploading it into CEON. Typically they will upload a subset of their local database composed of records which they have permission to share. Most of the data held in Odyssey can be shared without encountering problems of privacy or confidentiality. For example, the details of a used cartridge case are not likely to be confidential. Data about crimes and possible crimes are more sensitive since from these it might be possible to identify people. Where data is sensitive in this way the platform lets authorities share those columns which will not conflict with data management legislation.

The kinds of queries which investigators ask are conceptually rich and include a lot of uncertainty (De Bruin et al. 2006). In Odyssey these queries are handled using a semantic engine which runs at CEON. Queries are converted into SPARQL and applied to the data through a Jena engine. Both the semantic engine and SAS are used to automate and simplify the process of discovering similar data to that which is being investigated. This gives detectives the opportunity to find hidden relationships within trans-national datasets which they would otherwise never find.

The semantic engine lets users build queries which are dependent on their role. A crime analyst may want to ask different questions to those which a detective asks - they may be more strategic or intelligence-led, whilst the detective is focussed on operational matters. Such roles are not static. The same user may sometimes require intelligence data and at other times require operational information. Vallet et al, (2007) note that

> "Users may have stable and recurrent overall preferences, not all of their interests are relevant all the time. Instead, usually only a subset is active at a given situation, and the rest can be considered as noise preferences"

The platform has to take into account the changing context within which a user queries the system. For a broader view complex context in which such semantic solutions need to operate see chapter 10 of this volume.

Both semantic technology and data mining are aimed at efficient retrieval of desired information. These technologies work on the raw data with the goal of retrieving useful information as an end result which can provide the baseline knowledge needed for Intelligence Management (see chapter 10). But each of these technologies pursues the same goal using different approaches. Semantic modelling techniques focus on representing the raw data using formal structures. Information retrieval from the formalized structure becomes very efficient by as they enable intelligent reasoning and inferencing. On the other hand, data mining techniques rely on the use of efficient algorithms to retrieve useful knowledge from the data as shown in the figure 2.4.

Fig. 2.4. Semantic search versus data mining

As a result semantic technology pushes the level of complexity high on the efficient representation of data whereas data mining techniques impose high complexity on the efficiency of the extraction algorithms. So, a balance can be maintained between the two extremes and it is possible to get the best of both technologies. In context of Odyssey given the previously identified user requirements and ever changing context of criminal investigation processes, it was essential to combine both data mining and semantic approaches.

Query language

Users of the Odyssey system will be experts in the gathering and analysis of complex, incomplete data. Detectives and crime analysts or other civilian support staff are experts in the understanding of crimes through the use of rich data such as statements or observations (Smith & Tilley, 2005). This intellectually-complex work requires a clear cognitive focus and well-honed skills. The Odyssey platform is a very complex piece of software. Users cannot be expected to know that their queries are being applied to different back-ends or what data structures are used within the system. Indeed their use of the platform should, wherever possible, be natural so that the system supports and enhances their usual working practices.

A domain-specific language (DSL) is an artificial computer language which is used to describe solutions to constrained problems. A DSL provides a natural and effective interface between a complex system and its users, (Fowler & Parsons, 2010) which can be more expressive than operations constructed purely through a GUI. DSLs express complexity at a particular abstraction tailored to both current and future needs (Yu, 2008). A DSL lets non-technical people understand the overall design of a platform and interact with it, using an understandable notation that reflects their particular perspective (Bonino et al. 2004).

The DSL that was created is called the Odyssey Semantic Language (OSL). It supports the modelling of active crime investigations by operational detectives and facilitates the linking of generic crime features to ballistic data. Its innovative features are associating data retrieval techniques with data-mining results and encapsulating multiple services. Moreover, the language facilitates modelling of investigation processes and is an integral part in the platform's security.

Defining the DSL

OSL is a formal language specified by a context-free grammar. The OSL grammar was structured to make use of tokens taken from the English language in such way that the resulting constructions, that is, those sentences considered valid by the grammar, resemble the natural language of investigators so as to facilitate their construction and interpretation, (Jopek et al, 2010).

The grammar is defined in the Extended Backus-Naur Form within the ANTLR framework, a language recognition tool that simplifies the construction of a parser and lexical analyser pair from the grammar definition, as well as allowing for additional embedded code - in this case in Java. This simplifies the creation of a translation into the languages needed for the subsystem modules which are mainly SQL.

The language has relatively few keywords. Most keywords actually occur inside meaningful phrases as shown below:

GET CHARACTERISTICS returns a taxonomic structure: GET CHARACTERISTICS Person returns all the fields that describe a person (gender, ethnicity, age, etc.)

IS IT TRUE THAT returns "Yes" if the condition is true otherwise "No". For instance IS IT TRUE THAT Vehicle HAS PROPERTY VehicleMake WITH VALUE 'Saab'

SHOW STATISTICS gives simple statistical information such as average value, standard deviance and variance about records matching certain criteria. For example SHOW STATISTICS ON PersonEthnicity WITH VALUE 'white'.

SHOW SIMILARITIES BETWEEN: SHOW SIMILARITIES BETWEEN Person WITH VALUE 1 AND 13.

SHOW QUERY / SHOW ALL declare a simple retrieval from database. The difference between them is that SHOW QUERY creates normal joins between tables whereas SHOW ALL does a full outer join between tables.

WHAT ABOUT executes an intensional query: WHAT ABOUT Person Vehicle WHERE VehicleMake = 'Ford'

SHOW SIMILAR returns all records that are share the value of at least the given number of columns with the given instance: SHOW SIMILAR Person WITH VALUE 1 HAVING 4 EQUAL COLUMNS

CONFIDENCE: the value specified affects the number of results returned to the user. The higher the confidence the smaller the returned result set. For example WHAT ABOUT Person WHERE ethnicity = 'white' WITH CONFIDENCE 0.5.

The example below presents a query expressed in Odyssey Semantic Language (OSL) that retrieves firearms with a twenty-two calibre:

QUERY firearm WHERE calibre HAS VALUE 0.22

Typically requests into the system begin with QUERY. This term was chosen because there are so many possible terms (SEARCH, GET, FIND) that we needed one which was neutral and meaningful. OSL is used to upload data, share it and modify it which is why all operations need to begin with a keyword which identifies the operation (QUERY, UPLOAD, MODIFY, ALLOW).

In the example, firearm is used to identify the database table that is going to be searched. Users are never told that this is a table. They interact with a set of objects which come from their domain, from detective work. These include firearm, cartridge-case, bullet and incident. All queries are assumed to return a set of records which are presented to users as domain-level objects rather than as records, although that set may be empty or may contain just a single item.

Queries are retrieved from the message queues by a layer of middleware that parses the OSL and converts it into one of SQL, SPARQL, SAS's ProcSQL or into an intensional query. The choice of backend language depends upon the nature of the query. Queries for the PostgreSQL database begin with the keyword query, those for the SAS data mining system with SIMILAR and those for intensional with WHAT ABOUT.

The conversion from OSL into a query language gives heavily optimised queries with the minimum effort from users. The following example shows how a simple statement becomes a query across three tables with a series of optimised joins.

```
QUERY ballistic incident WHERE weapon_manufacturer HAS VALUE
Sig Sauer AND victim_gender HAS VALUE female

SELECT * FROM odyssey.ballistic_incident

LEFT JOIN ballistic_incident_has_recovered_firearm ON
(ballistic_incident_has_recovered_firearm.recovered_firearm_oid
= ballistic_incident.oid)
LEFT JOIN ballistic_incident_has_recovered_firearm ON
(ballistic_incident_has_recovered_firearm.recovered_firearm_oid
= recovered_firearm.oid)
LEFT JOIN ballistic_incident_has_case ON
(ballistic_incident_has_case.ballistic_incident_case_oid =
ballistic_incident.oid)
LEFT JOIN ballistic_incident_has_case ON
(ballistic_incident_has_case.ballistic_incident_case_oid =
case.oid)

WHERE case.gender_of_victim = "female"
AND recovered_firearm.manufacturer = "Sig Sauer";
```

Alerting

A key element of the user requirements was an alerting component. The alerting component monitors a set of queries defined by the user. These might include an alert should any newly input evidence become linked to on-going investigations. For example should a vehicle, person or ballistic item be introduced to the database (local or CEON) which links relationally to a current item of interest. Alternatively should the results of any other stored query defined in the Odyssey DSL change due to changes in data within the local or CEON repositories an alert can be raised. The alert will go to those LEA end users who instantiated the query or indicated an interest in the item. The alert provides them with the details of the query whose results have changed. As a minimum the alert provides details of the URNs relevant to the items and the member states to which they belong. This provides a minimum data exchange in order for LEA officers to determine if further data exchange is needed, or if a new line of enquiry has been identified.

User interface – hiding the DSL

Users have been at the core of the Odyssey project, but which users? In undertaking the broader work on user needs, user context, user practices and available technologies the project identified a wide range of potential and actual users of ballistic identification systems and crime BIS. As noted above these users range from investigating officers, through forensic specialists to data analysts and policy advisors. In many cases user expertise will be in policing, forensic science and only in a few cases information system use, database querying or data analysis. In our research we did note the extensive use of graphical representations of the relationships between data items. This may have been for use by specific groups of experts or for communication between staff with differing roles. Often actual or potential links between crimes, events, items of evidence, people and locations were presented in networked graphs. This may be supported by specific tools, such as those provided by i2 (which merged in 2009 with the software provider of COPLINK), or may be 'drawn by hand' in standard vector graphic tools. Such network diagrams have become a standard form of visualization within this law enforcement domain. The Odyssey project therefore sought to use this form of representation within the interface to the underlying data, and as a visual method for execution of operations and queries within the system.

The Odyssey platform returns results as sets of linked objects. These are displayed in a desktop application. The user is able to see graphs of objects and, by manipulating their properties, can build new queries easily and quickly. Query plans can be saved so that the query can be re-executed later. These plans are simple OSL statements which can be shared between users, for example on email.

The GUI does not present a differentiation between queries intended for the semantic, relational or mining back-ends. Queries are executed across all of the querying systems unless the user edits the OSL to prevent this. Results from all of the back-end systems are integrated into a single graph.

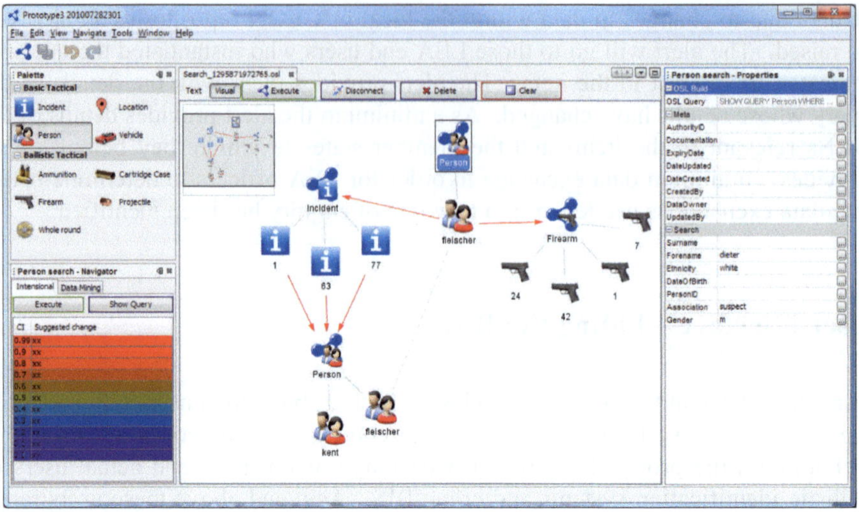

Fig. 2.5. The GUI applying the networked graph representation

Figure 2.5 shows how the graphical user interface of the Odyssey platform facilitates search and browsing across the entire crime and ballistic dataset. It takes the full advantage of inductive and deductive approaches so that the end-user can inductively find relevant information and deductively identify values while browsing and narrowing down the possibilities based on the information presented. The interface enables building advanced queries while hiding the complexity of the underlying data structures from the user.

The output of the intensional module is shown on the left of figure 2.5. Different colours are used to indicate the strength of association which the module has discovered. The user may choose to modify their query using the changes which are suggested here. This is done simply by selecting a suggestion - the GUI automatically re-writes the query for the user.

Presenting result graphs and using them to build new queries is an established GUI technique. The Odyssey project validated the approach through extensive testing with users. The project's validation process included a demonstration of the applications and services developed in the prototype. Users were also given opportunities to interact with the prototype. This allowed the Consortium to review the high level objective of the Odyssey platform, whilst evaluating the Stakeholders continued expectations and needs. In line with the adapted research method the lesson learned during the validation process was elaborated into new set of requirements for the third validation cycle.

Conclusion: users and standards

The Odyssey prototype has demonstrated the potential advantages for end users of a pan-European ballistic crime system. To transform this into a fully operation system deployed within a key EU body (for example EUROPOL) with support from the full range of EU LEAs would require a number of key next steps – most of which are not technology challenges. These can be grouped under: users; standards and policy.

Users

The user studies within the Odyssey project have identified three key *roles* but multiple *jobs* with different goals within the various member state LEAs with regard to ballistic crime detection and prevention. The three roles broadly defined are:

- Investigation
- Ballistics and forensics
- Analysis

Each role has differing goals and hence relationships to crime data. Investigators are primarily concerned with the operational and tactical use of data. They are looking for hints, tips, leads and intelligence which may lead to best routes of enquiry. They are not looking for evidential quality links in data, nor are they often looking to broad overviews of ballistic crime. Forensic officers are more concerned with evidential quality data and establishing firm links between items, especially when looking to support prosecution of offenders. Analysts are looking to the broad strategy overviews of data which support policy and policy based actions. These are of course broad-brush representations of the observed user practice and roles which may not map on to specific jobs within specific LEAs. In a small number of notable cases, especially in the LEAs of smaller member states, all three roles may be undertaken within the job of one or a set of post holder, who may also be serving police officers. In other cases each role has become specialised within the organisation. The Odyssey system has sought to provide solutions to these various potential end users. A full implementation would require further work to ensure the system provided full functionality to for each role and flexibility to integrate into different LEAs organizational structures.

Standards

With regard to standards considerable work remains to be done in defining these and implementing them through policy actions within the domain of ballistic crime data within the EU:

- There are no accepted Open standards for data capture, processing and representation in original and meta-data forms
- There are no accepted Open standards for comparison, audit, and regulation of system usability, performance and reliability

These points hold for both ballistic imaging and matching systems and for ballistic crime BIS. There remains the potential for a de facto standard to come into force via the market dominance of one product or range of products, or through a merging of common practice within larger member states or LEAs. At the time of writing the opposite processes appear to be taking place. The market for ballistic imaging and matching systems is growing and there is evidence of fragmentation in operational practices within larger member states The XML schemas used within the Odyssey platform could provide an initial template for such a standard within the domain of ballistic crime. Having said this data standards for ballistic imaging systems and standards for processes of data acquisition have yet to be established. The current market for such systems does not support the development of open standards and may require policy intervention. Further outputs from the joint work between the Odyssey project and ENFSI may provide some grounding for such standards.

Policy

As noted above there is a very strong policy framework in the EU for high quality data exchange between member state LEAs – as defined by the Swedish Initiative, the principal of availability and the Prüm decision. The implementation of this policy will require extensive and further investment in relevant research and development projects (of which Odyssey represents one such project) as well as infrastructure developments within, between and among member state LEAs. From the user and contextual research undertaken by the Odyssey project a key policy development has to be that of identifying, defining and establishing key standards for data exchange.

Next steps

As an information system the Odyssey platform demonstrates the possibilities for EU member states in combatting gun crime through a pan-European approach to sharing data. The system incorporates the use of advanced data mining techniques enriched with semantic technologies. It extracts information from various data sources and indicates how the information will be used next. Moreover, it creates an ontology-driven knowledge repository that enables the analysis of information in a more abstract way, which gives an advantage of being able to illustrate global tendencies or crime patterns. Odyssey platform uses a novel approach for incorporating dynamic user requirements into system realisation (i.e. OSL). The repository is used to operate and investigate real cases using logic reasoning and knowledge interference. Additionally, the platform is able to generate unified graphical results and clearly demonstrate the outcomes of complex analysis. Finally, the platform operates on a very specific domain, which enables the concentration of explicit problems, constantly evaluating outcomes, and suggesting the most promising solution.

The fully implemented version of the platform has the potential to fill a major gap in cross-national investigation and security systems. National police forces would be able to increase their investigation potential by accessing the refined data and graphically represented data patterns. Moreover, the Odyssey platform is structured as a framework which could be easily replicated for other forensic data sets as well as applied to different domains, thus re-defining the standards of information exploitation for large data sets. The latter provides a major millstone for truly integrated and pan-European law enforcement knowledge management Systems.

References

Interpol, 2007. Connecting Police: I-24/7. Available at: http://www.interpol.int/Public/ICPO/FactSheets/GI03.pdf. [Accessed February 3rd, 2011]

Europa, 2002. Proposal for a Framework Decision on exchange of information under the principle of availability. Available at: http://europa.eu/rapid/pressReleasesAction.do?reference=MEMO/05/367&format=HTML&aged=0&language=EN&guiLanguage=en [Accessed January 25, 2011].

Prüm, 2010. Prüm Decision. Available at: http://ec.europa.eu/home-affairs/policies/police/police_prum_en.htm [Accessed January 25, 2011].

NABIS, 2009. National Ballistics Intelligence Service. Available at: http://nabis.police.uk/database.asp [Accessed January 25, 2011].

Akhgar, B et al., 2009. A Pan European Platform for Combating Organized Crime and Terrorism (Odyssey Platform). In Centeris Conference on Enterprise Information Systems. Ofir, Portugal.

Akrivas, G, Wallace, M, Andreou, G, Stamou, G, Kollias, S, Context-Sensitive Semantic Query Expansion, in Proceedings of IEEE International Conference on Artificial Intelligence Systems (ICAIS'02. pp 109. 2002 .

Bonino, D, Corno, F and Farinetti, L, 2004. Domain specific searches using conceptual spectra. In 16th IEEE International Conference on Tools with Artificial Intelligence. ICTAI 2004, pp. 680-687.

Bundeskriminalant, 2004. Firearm Type Determination. Available at: https://www.forensic-firearms.bund.de [Accessed January 25, 2011].

Chen, H. et al., 2004. Crime data mining: A general framework and some examples. IEEE Computer, 37(4), pp.50-56.

Chen, H. et al., 2003. COPLINK: managing law enforcement data and knowledge. Communications of the ACM, 46, pp.28–34. Available at: http://doi.acm.org/10.1145/602421.602441.

De Bruin, J. S. et al., 2006. Data mining approaches to criminal career analysis. In Proceedings of the Sixth International Conference on Data Mining. Sixth International Conference on Data Mining. pp. 171-177.

Fowler, M and Parsons, R., 2010. Domain-specific Languages, Addison Wesley.

Giacomo, G, 1996. Intensional query answering by partial evaluation. Journal of Intelligent Information Systems, 7:4, pp 205-233. Published by Springer Netherlands, Nov. 1996.

Jopek, L., Wilson, R., and Bates, C, 2010. An application of a domain specific language facilitating abstraction and secure access to a crime. In Proceedings of IARIA 2010. pp 29-33, Lisbon, Portugal, October 2010.

Mernik, M., Heering, J. & Sloane, A.M., 2005. When and how to develop domain-specific languages. ACM Comput. Surv., 37, pp.316–344. Available at: http://doi.acm.org/10.1145/1118890.1118892.

Nath, S. V., 2006. Crime pattern detection using data mining. In Proceedings of the 2006 IEEE/WIC/ACM International Conference on Web Intelligence and Intelligent Agent Technology. International Conference on Web Intelligence and Intelligent Agent Technology. pp. 41-44

Nygren, F, 2008. The Swedish Initiative. http://www.daten.european-police.eu/2008/nygren.pdf [Accessed January 25, 2011].

Sims, C, 2010. National Ballistics Intelligence Service Update Report. Available at: http://www.west-midlands-pa.gov.uk/documents/committees/public/2010/12_PerfandOps_22April2010_National_Ballistics_Report.pdf.

Smith, M. and Tilley, N. 2005. Crime Science: New Approaches to Preventing and Detecting Crime, Portland, USA: Willan Publishing.

Strohmaier, M., Kröll, M. & Körner, C., 2009. Intentional query suggestion: making user goals more explicit during search. In Proceedings of the 2009 workshop on Web Search Click Data. WSCD '09. New York, NY, USA: ACM, pp. 68–74. Available at: http://doi.acm.org/10.1145/1507509.1507520.

Vallet, D, Castells, P, Fernández, M, Mylonas, P, and Avrithis, Y, 2007. Personalized Content Retrieval in Context Using Ontological Knowledge. IEEE Transactions On Circuits And Systems For Video Technology, 17:3. MARCH 2007.

Wilson, R., Jopek, L., and Bates, C, 2010. Sharing Ballistics Data across the European Union. In Proceedings of IARIA 2010. pp 8-13, Lisbon, Portugal, October 2010.

Yates, S., et al., 2009. Semantic Interoperability between Ballistic Systems through the Application of Ontology. In IADIS WWW/ Internet Conference. pp. 153-157.

Yu, L., 2008. Prototyping, Domain Specific Language, and Testing. Engineering Letters.

Chapter 3: Secure Architecture

Rodrigo Diaz Rodriguez

Abstract Defining robust security architectures is vital for protecting IT infrastructures from cyber-attacks. This is especially true when the IT infrastructure is going to be used by investigators and law enforcement agencies to combat crime across EU. A compromise between the level of security and the level of acceptable risk must be found. As a first step it is mandatory to perfectly understand the security requirements applicable to our infrastructure, the security services needed and how these security services should be distributed over the logical layers of the system. This chapter describes the analysis and the methodology followed in the Odyssey project (see chapter 2) to define a security-layered architecture able to support a secure Pan-European ballistics and crime information intelligence network designed to help tackle organized crime and terrorism.

Introduction

Protecting IT infrastructures from cyber-attacks is one of the main challenges when developing and deploying IT applications and services in the Internet era. The importance of security in systems aiming to help investigators within law enforcement agencies is extreme. The loss of sensitive or critical information could seriously compromise on-going investigations and potentially advantage criminal activity. In this environment, a secure architecture that addresses the security requirements and the risks of the particular scenario and which specifies what security controls are to be applied and where they are mandatory. Security controls include such things as: confidentiality; integrity; availability; accountability; and assurance. This security architecture should be defined together with the system architecture in order to build a system "secure by design." This approach ensures that security considerations make up a significant part of infrastructure architecture.

Security is all about compromise. A balance should be achieved between the level of security, the level of acceptable risk, the level of inconvenience and the cost associated with the implementation of the security policies. By increasing the level of security, the costs associated with its implementation and the inconveniences to the users also increase, whereas the level of risk that the organization needs to sustain decrease. In some cases, the security solutions adopted address a very specific vulnerability with a minimal impact in the larger picture of the secure information system. Organisations implement these solutions without knowing if all security requirements have been met or what the impact of these solutions is in the overall system.

The focus of the following sections is to identify the various layers that exist in large distributed systems, such as the one proposed by the Odyssey project[1] and to lay the groundwork for defining security requirements for each layer allowing for a mapping of the security implications that each layer has on other layers. This will result in the design of a layered security architecture that could assist in mapping out all required or successfully implemented security requirements at various levels of information systems.

Security requirements

Gun crime is one of the biggest threats facing society today and helps organised criminals and terrorists stoke fear in our communities. Enabling cooperation across the EU is vital to efficiently combat this global threat. Nowadays, there is both political and operational commitment to share data and there is no shortage of ballistics and crime information data across the EU. However, there is currently no technical means to do this. Odyssey is a part funded project by the 7th European Framework Programme that has conducted the necessary research and development to fill this gap and provide a Platform to demonstrate the effect and potential of an EU wide Platform using technical forensic data and crime information. The Project has developed a demonstrator of a secure interoperable situation awareness platform for the automated management, processing, sharing, analysis and use of ballistics data and crime information to combat organised crime and terrorism also to increase the safety and security of all EU citizens.

The security requirements of a pan-European system, such as the one introduced above, must take into account the legal landscape, especially as it relates to the capture, aggregation, analysis and dissemination of information. This landscape includes, but is not limited to, the restrictions placed on Member States by European Data Protection and Human Rights law.

The user community (law enforcement agencies) involved in the Odyssey project required that the Odyssey system should be developed in line with existing legislation that affects the aggregation and sharing of information between Member States. This legislation includes but is not limited to that contained within the Data Protection Act (DPA), the Freedom of Information Act (FOIA) and the European Convention on Human Rights (ECHR). Other legislation local to Member

[1] ODYSSEY (Strategic Pan-European Ballistics Intelligence Platform for Combating Organised Crime and Terrorism) - http://www.odyssey-project.eu/

States, such as the Computer Misuse Act within the U.K. should be considered for relevance but should not be allowed to act as a barrier to the aims and objectives of the Odyssey project.

This leads to one major requirement that impacted the system architecture. Users required partitioning the Odyssey system in such a way as to enable Member States to "turn off", withdraw and delete their data from Odyssey as and when required without significant impact upon other Member State data held within the system. From user's discussions, it is clear that each Member State data should be carefully partitioned within the system to facilitate effective local control of the data. Moreover, Member States must have complete control over the nature and extent of information they release to the database and must be able to choose whether data they have added to the system may be shared by default with other Member States.

The figure 3.1 below shows a conceptualised view of the prototype Odyssey system with each Member State's data carefully partitioned within the system to facilitate effective local control of the data by local Member State administrators of the Odyssey system. This view makes no assumptions as to whether the data is centralised or federated or a combination of both, it merely seeks to reinforce the user community's desire to retain direct control of their data at all times whilst it is shared across Member States within the Odyssey system.

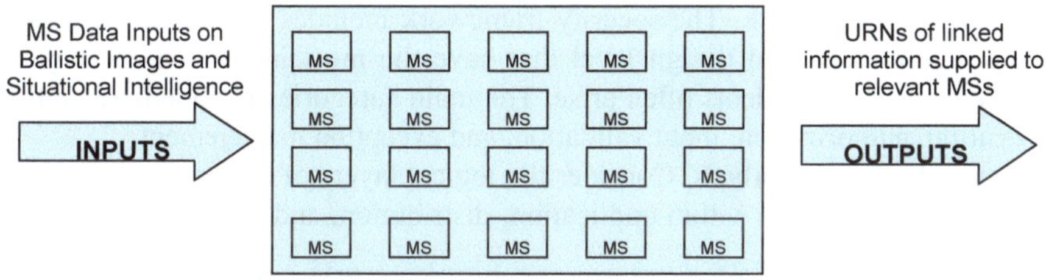

Fig. 3.1. Odyssey Member States data partitioning.

The information contained within the Odyssey system will be managed and protected by the competent central authority, and investigative links will be reported to Member States through relevant unique reference numbers (URNs). This will allow Member States to communicate with one another about the link and make their own data sharing arrangements, thereby retaining overall control of the actual information sharing process.

In addition to this requirement to partition Member States data, the Odyssey system must include security services to protect the access, storage and transmission of/to this data. These security services can be mainly categorized and summarized as follows:

- Member State data and any meta-data derived from it as well as all other data captured and stored within the Odyssey platform must be retained securely so as to prevent inadvertent or malicious access that may lead to compromise of investigations or the ability of Member States to prevent and detect gun crime.

- Security controls appropriate to each Member State's requirements should control the flow of access to and from their data within the database. As a consequence, Odyssey system must include appropriate Role Based Access Controls to manage levels of access designated to the varying types of end users, administrators and developers etc. Additionally, the identification of users should be done via a secure electronic process with a minimum of two factor authentication.
- Data transmission to, from and within the Odyssey system must be subject to appropriate security standards with regard to the level of sensitivity of the data being transmitted.

Methodology

There are three major aspects to be considered in defining a security architecture (see figure 3.2):

1. **Deployment and infrastructure**. At this level, the constraints imposed by the underlying infrastructure-layer security and the operational practices in use should be considered.
2. **Security framework**. The security framework includes considerations at both the architectural and design level that have the most impact on security and where security incidents often arise. The main categories included are: authentication, authorization, input validation, and exception management.
3. **Layer-by-layer analysis**. Consider the logical layers of the system, and define the security choices within application, distribution, and data access logic layers.

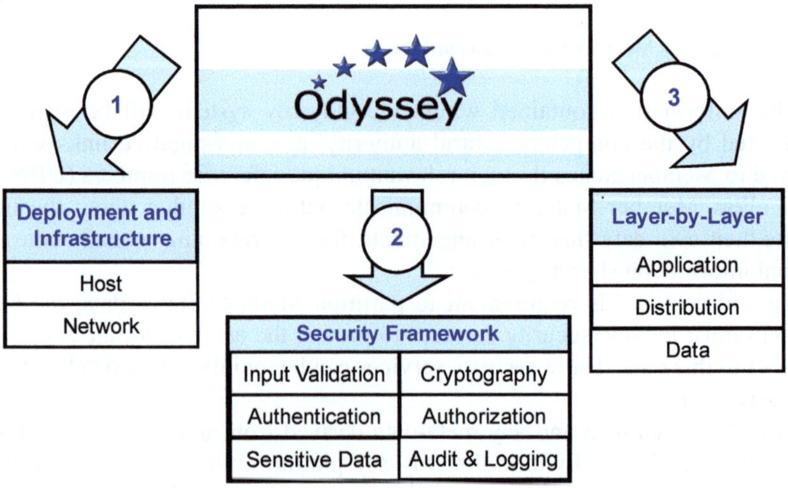

Fig. 3.2. Security Architecture Methodology.

In the following sections will describe the work done in Odyssey project for defining the security framework and the layer-by-layer analysis carried out to identify in which layer should be implemented the security controls.

Deployment and infrastructure

The cyber-security of the IT infrastructure is vital for the success of such complex distributed system, particularly when the system deals with information susceptible to be tampered by organized crime or terrorists groups. The deployment and protection of the IT infrastructure was outside the scope of the Odyssey project. Odyssey focused on the development of the system itself, not in its operation. However, there are other European research projects, such as MASSIF[2] project, focused on the protection of service systems, platforms and infrastructures from threats therefore increasing their trustworthiness.

The MASSIF is a collaborative project co-funded under the European Commission's FP7 ICT Work Programme[3] that aims to provide a new generation SIEM (Security Information & Event Management) framework for service infrastructures supporting intelligent, scalable, and multi-level/multi-domain security event processing and predictive security monitoring.

Nowadays, SIEM solutions have become the backbone of the all Service Security systems. They collect data on events from different security elements, such as sensors, firewalls, routers or servers, analyse the data, and provide a suitable response to threats and attacks based on predefined Security rules and policies. Despite the existence of highly regarded commercial products, their technical capabilities show a number of constraints in terms of scalability, resilience and interoperability.

MASSIF project aims at achieving a significant advance in the area of SIEMs by integrating and relating events from different system layers and various domains into one more comprehensive view of security-aware processes and by increasing the scalability of the underlying event processing technology. The main challenge that MASSIF will face is to bring its enhancements and extensions into the business layer with a minimum impact on the end-user operation.

---

[2] MASSIF (Management of Security information and events in Service Infrastructures) – http://www.massif-project.eu

[3] European Commission's FP7 ICT Work Programme - http://cordis.europa.eu/fp7/ict/home_en.html

Security framework

This section describes the security services and controls applicable to the system proposed by Odyssey project. These services could be seen also as a categorization of the vulnerabilities that could have impact in our system.

Authentication

Authentication refers to the process of verifying the identity of a user, typically through credentials, such as a user name and password. Authentication answers the question: "Are you who you say you are?" The main vulnerabilities in this area are: using weak passwords, storing clear text credentials in configuration files, passing clear text credentials over the network, permitting over-privileged accounts, permitting prolonged session lifetime and mixing personalization with authentication.

Special attention should be paid to database servers. Most of them provide some form of authentication although authenticating to the database can have some pitfalls sometimes resulting from the use of highly privileged accounts, such as administrator accounts used by development teams. This means that the processes executed by developers not only have access to their own application's data but also to all other data stored on the same server including database server configuration information and settings. In fact, a number of database related security issues such as SQL injection are merely bugs that exploit high privileged environments. In general when operating with a database server, it is strictly recommended to use a low privilege account, with separate connection strings and accounts for database reads and writes, and as far as possible using operating system based authentication so as to avoid storing credentials in the code or in configuration files. Additionally, it is recommended to use well-known and tested authentication protocols such as Kerberos. Similarly, relying on the operating system based authentication mechanisms is also considered best practice. However, many IT applications are demanding even more stringent authentication mechanisms, at least for the administrative users. Over the last few years, multi-factor authentication has become immensely popular. These schemes have attempting to combine multiple unique facets such as:

- Something you know (a password or a PIN).
- Something you have (a token or a smart card).
- Something you are (a biometric quality).
- Somewhere you are (geographic coordinates).

Perhaps the most popular example nowadays is the smart card which uses strong asymmetric key cryptography and the concept of a PKI to enable authentication within an organization. Other examples include your ATM card, RSA SecurIDs and USB security tokens.

Authorization

Authorization refers to the process of establishing and enforcing a user's rights and privileges to access specified resources. After a user (or entity) is authenticated, authorization determines what that user can do on the system. The main threads or attacks in this area are: elevation of privileges, disclosure of confidential data, data tampering, luring attacks and token stealing.

In the context of authorization, one of the most universal best practices is the "three-by-three" rule of thumb. This means checking three attributes – the principle attempting perform the operation, the resource the operation is being performed on and the operation itself – thrice – when the user interface is generated, in the user interface logic on the client side itself and finally right before executing on the operation. The two first checks are not only recommended from a security point of view, but also to avoid unnecessary server round trips when legitimate users make innocent mistakes. Nevertheless, server side authorization controls should never be replaced for client side checks.

Authorization mechanisms should be considered as early as possible in the system development lifecycle, normally once all the potential user groups and objects have been identified. Dealing with this issue at early stages of the development helps us on the creation of standards for all the developers as well as figures in the test plans created by the software quality assurance teams. Moreover, it also prevents assumptions by developers that go along the lines of "I thought he/she did the authorization check".

Cryptography

Cryptography refers to how the system enforces confidentiality and integrity. Confidentiality refers to limiting information access and disclosure to the set of authorized users, and preventing access by or disclosure to unauthorized ones. Regarding confidentiality, most common threads or attacks are: stealing sensitive data, theft of encryption keys and man in the middle attack. Integrity refers to the trustworthiness of information resources. It includes the concept of "data integrity" – namely, that data have not been changed inappropriately, whether by accident or deliberately malign activity. It also includes "origin" or "source integrity" – that is, that the data actually came from the person or entity you think it did, rather than an imposter. About integrity, the typical attack is data tampering.

Input and data validation

Input validation refers to how the system filters, scrubs, or rejects input before additional processing. It can be seen as a particular case of integrity where the challenge is to guarantee that the person or entity in question entered the right information, but it is not limited to the user inputs, also other sources such as databases and file shares should be validated. These types of vulnerabilities are more critical in web applications where non-validated inputs could be used to generate the HTML output stream or SQL queries (SQL injection).

Sensitive data

Sensitive data refers to a wide range of information and can include: your racial or ethnic origin, your political opinions, religious or other beliefs of a similar nature, membership of trade unions, physical or mental health or condition, sexual life and/or the commission of any offence or criminal records. This type of data must be protected either in memory, over the network, or in persistent stores.

Auditing and logging

Auditing and logging refers to how security-related events are recorded, monitored, and audited. Sooner or later, every network experiences accidental or deliberate disruptions, from system failures (either hardware or software), human errors or attacks. Most common threads/attacks in this area are: repudiation, denial of services or disclosure of confidential information. Keeping detailed logs of the system could help to troubleshoot system failures. If troubleshooting demonstrates that a network problem was deliberately caused, audit information is critical for tracking down the perpetrator.

Layer-by-layer analysis

With the aim of analysing certain security aspects in the Odyssey system, it has been divided in three main layers: the application layer, the distribution layer and the data layer. The application layer will provide for an external view of the system. It will address user and user group roles, policies as well as any inter-organizational issues. The distribution layer will address communication-based security. The data layer addresses secure data storage.

The security architecture will examine the aspects of authentication and identification, authorisation, confidentiality, integrity and non-repudiation at each individual layer and will try to answer the question: which layers are responsible for providing the specific security service for a particular Odyssey entity?

	Authentication & Identification	Authorization	Confidentiality	Integrity	Non-repudiation
Data			√	√	
Distribution	√	√	√	√	
Application	√	√			√

Fig. 3.3. Mapping between layers and security services.

Data layer

At this level the protection of the data storage will be addressed. Data itself does not need to perform access control. The authentication, identification and authorisation services are therefore not relevant services required for data, usually they are most often associated with users or user groups. The identification, authentication and authorisation of data will not be considered. However, let us assume that an obvious technology for the data layer would be a database management system (DBMS). In this case, the DBMS should include the required authentication and access control mechanisms to fulfil the security requirements.

The confidentiality of data should be addressed in the data layer. It should be clear how the storage and distribution aspects need to be sensitive to confidentiality requirements. This is often, but not exclusively, achieved through cryptography. In the context of Odyssey, all information will be stored in the central repository anonymised, but in the case of managing data considered as confidential, the storage of encrypted information should be considered. But, confidentiality does not only consider the protection of the data itself, also the protection of all resources that can compromise the confidentiality. Log files are examples of how data can leave a trail, compromising the confidentiality of the whole system. Safeguarding log files is therefore essential to confidentiality.

The integrity definition implies the prevention of unauthorised modification. Firstly, we should identify which layers prevent the unauthorised modification of data. The data layer can provide data integrity by preventing any data corruption. But, preventing data corruption is a more difficult task and often depends on the correct functioning of the hardware.

As discussed above, the data layer does not perform access control and can therefore not be considered for the identification, authentication and authorisation services. Consequently, the safe storage of data cannot prevent unauthorized modification of communication or task related information. The question remains whether ownership of data has any ramifications on confidentiality or non-repudiation requirements of the communication.

Finally, non-repudiation of data will be considered. For instance, preventing any situation where the validity of data is questioned. Non-repudiation is a security service that is not directly related to the data layer, since at this level it is difficult to have the complete knowledge to provide this type of service. But, the auditing and monitoring of the operations at this level could be used to implement this type of functionality.

Distribution layer

Generally speaking a communication or transmission can be initiated without performing the authentication of the parties involved. An example would be a web server that accepts incoming connections regardless of who initiates the connection. However, in the scope of Odyssey we consider that it is very important to authenticate both, sender and receiver, before initiate a communication.

The distribution layer needs to ensure also the confidentiality of the communication. An example of a security-enhancing technology at the distribution layer is IP Security (IPSec). IPSec is a set of protocols developed by the Internet Engineering Task Force (IETF) to support a secure exchange of packets. IPSec claims to address authentication, confidentiality and integrity at the OSI (Open Systems Interconnect) network layer. In Odyssey, a VPN (Virtual Private Network) has been used to guarantee the confidentiality of the data transmitted between the central repository network and the local authority network. But, VPN does not guarantee the end-to-end confidentiality, for this reason when transmitting data considered as confidential, the transmission of encrypted information should be considered.

The distribution layer has to ensure that for each transmission, the sent and received data are identical. Additionally, distribution layer could implement integrity by means of detecting and possibly correcting data corruption. Parity checking and cyclic redundancy checks are technologies used in error detection. Hamming codes are able to perform error correction provided that only minimal corruption has occurred.

Application layer

The security services more relevant to the application layer are the ones in change of the identification, authentication and authorization of the users/entities.

The application layer plays no role in ensuring confidentiality or integrity. Mostly, an application can request or provide information but cannot assure its confidentiality or integrity. However, some mechanisms should be included in the Odyssey system at application level to ensure the validation of the user inputs.

The proposed solution

One of the most important requirements highlighted by the user community in the Odyssey project was the need of an interoperable system based on open standards. As a consequence of this premise, Odyssey project has adopted a Service Oriented Architecture (SOA) based on Web Services (WS). WS are implemented in most cases using HTTP as transport protocol but, in Odyssey project, to enhance the reliability and scalability of the system, while making up for the weaknesses introduced by HTTP, we have chosen the transport protocol JMS (Java Message Service). Consequently, we decided to use a SOAP (Simple Object Access Protocol) over JMS approach for connecting components internally over the Odyssey network. However, a HTTP transport for connecting outside components (over Internet) could be still considered if required.

Two different approaches can be followed to protect WS architectures, apply security at transport and/or at message level. Transport layer security represents an approach where the underlying operating system or application servers are used to handle security features. Whereas, message layer security represents an approach where all the information related to security is encapsulated in the message. In Odyssey we have selected this second approach since it offers several advantages, but the most important one is the increase of flexibility. Parts of the message, instead of the entire message, can be signed or encrypted. This means that intermediaries can view the parts of the message that are intended for them. This feature adds the support for auditing, where intermediaries can add their own headers to the message and sign them for the purpose of audit logging. Nevertheless, a VPN has been set up in Odyssey protecting also the messages at network level.

Traditional security technologies are not sufficient for Web services security because of the need to secure data and components on a more granular scale. Because Web services use message-based technologies for complex transactions across multiple domains, traditional security processes fall short. A Web service message can traverse several intermediaries before it reaches its final destination. Therefore, the need for sophisticated message-level security becomes a high priority and is not addressed by existing security technologies. In addition to the traditional threats (message alteration, confidentiality, man-in-the-middle, identity spoofing…), Web services are exposed to some specific security threats summarized below:

- Content-borne threats: Threats against XML payload elements.
- Schema Poisoning: This involves manipulating the WS schema to alter the data processed by an application.
- XML Parameter Tampering: Injection of illegitimate scripts or content into XML parameters.
- Coercive Parsing: Injection of illegitimate content into the actual XML payload.
- XML Routing Detours: Redirecting data addressed by an XML path.

As a consequence, to deal with the threats described above, we have selected WS Security standards (WS-Security or WSS) that describe enhancements to protect SOAP messages through XML digital signature, confidentiality through XML encryption, and credential propagation through security tokens. WS-Security mechanisms can be used to accommodate a wide variety of security models and encryption technologies whereas it can be used in conjunction with other Web service protocols to address a wide variety of application security requirements.

To make the security process as independent as possible to the application layers, we have developed a security layer (see figure 3.4) that includes in/out interceptors. These security interceptors are responsible for processing the incoming and outgoing messages and hiding the security issues to the application layer.

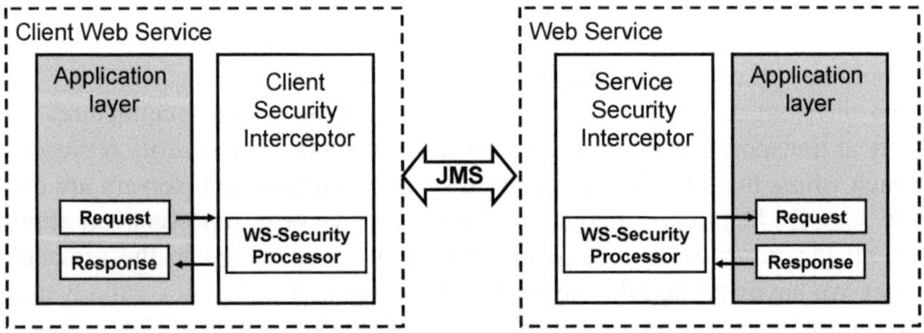

Fig. 3.4. Security interceptors

Whenever a Web service client requests that a message be sent, the SOAP message is "intercepted" by the security handler. The interceptor adds the authentication, signature, and encryption WS-Security elements to the SOAP message, and then forwards the message to the receiving Web service. Each receiving Web service also has interceptors that can decrypt, verify signatures, and authenticate the incoming message. The service interceptor captures the message and decrypts, verifies, and authenticates the message. When sending a response message, the service interceptor in the Web service adds a WS-Security header with integrity and confidentiality. The client interceptor interprets the header and delivers it to the client application.

The main intent of the service interceptor is to establish a security context of execution for SOAP operations, nevertheless, the security handlers will perform all the required security validations (such as checking whether the timestamp is expired, checking of the key status, verifying signatures, etc.). In order to perform all these validations, the processing model must go through all the elements in the SOAP security header.

As introduced in the requirements section, the user community remarked that identification of Odyssey users should be via a secure electronic process with a minimum of two-factor authentication. Consequently, one of the factors could be "something you know" (e.g., password or PIN), and the second one "something you have" (e.g. smartcard or token).

With this premise in mind, we have designed and implemented a multi-factor authentication mechanism based on the ownership of a key storage where the users will be asked first to have a valid Odyssey key storage, secondly the password to open this key storage and finally, the password to access to the private key that will be used to decrypt and sign messages. This scheme makes mobility of users much easier, since could be included in a USB memory "simulating" and USB token or smart card.

The implementation of the Odyssey authentication mechanism has been built on the Java Authentication and Authorization Service (JAAS). JAAS is a Java security framework for user-centric security to augment the Java code-based security in a pluggable fashion. This permits Java applications to remain independent from underlying authentication technologies. New or updated technologies can be plugged in without requiring modifications to the application itself. An implementation for a particular authentication technology to be used is determined at runtime. This feature is particularly interesting in Odyssey since we can establish different authentication mechanism for each component, taking into account its security requirements.

For controlling the access to the data, a Role Based Access Controls (RBAC) mechanism has been incorporated in the Security Module allowing components or the GUI to check the user privileges before authorizing a user operation.

Conclusions

This chapter has presented the applicability of information security concepts for the protection of the Information Technology (IT) systems supporting law enforcement operations or investigations. Within ODYSSEY, a security infrastructure has been developed to protect the sharing of ballistic information in criminal investigations. The MASSIF project is producing a system for managing the security of the infrastructure itself, further improving the reliability of the security measures in such IT systems for law enforcement systems and critical infrastructures.

Chapter 4: Interoperability - A Requirement for Tackling Gun Crime

Gary Herrington

Abstract This chapter looks at the impact of gun crime on communities and the ease with which such crime can cross physical and other boundaries, making it a signal crime that must be addressed through effective collaboration between Law Enforcement Agencies across EU Member States. It further considers barriers that exist between the disparate disciplines of investigation, intelligence and scientific examination of evidence and potential changes to law that may be required to facilitate a true EU wide interoperable gun crime system.

Gun crime statistics

Gun Crime poses a significant and recognized threat to all Law Enforcement Agencies (LEAs) across the European Union and yet it only constitutes a very small percentage of actual crime committed. Provisional Government figures for 2009[4] in England and Wales showed that:

- 8,063 firearms offences were committed, accounting for just 0.2% of all crime across England and Wales.
  Of these offences:
- Handguns were the most commonly used firearms, with the weapon accounting for over one-half of non-air weapon firearm offences recorded.
- Shotguns were used in 8% and rifles in 1% of these offences

The statistics go on to show that the overall figure for gun-crime only rises to 0.3% of all crime if air-weapons are also taken into account. Despite these relatively low numbers of offences, the public perception of gun crime is that it remains far more prevalent than these figures prove. This perception is often driven by the effect of media and local hype that surrounds such offences as will be demonstrated later in this chapter. The degree of misunderstanding of the true nature of gun crime by the public also leads this type of crime to being a major issue for politicians at all levels across society. Further, this can and does disproportion-

[4] The Home Office Standard Note, SN/SG/1940, on Firearms Crime Statistics published June 2010

ately affect the investment required to alleviate these fears. However, the potential cost, even in monetary terms alone, to society must not be underestimated. This too will be demonstrated here with figures from the UK Government that estimate the cost of just two high profile gun crime families residing in the Birmingham area of England.

Public perception of gun crime

Many members of the public, and even some law enforcement officers and other associated staff, still see gun crime as predominantly a gang on gang or criminal on criminal issue. This perception often impairs the recording of events involving firearms and lowers the apparent desire to tackle the issues at source. Such perception can be extremely damaging to the objectives of governments and LEA's alike resulting in a reduced flow of key information and intelligence that can make the task of investigators and intelligence analysts far harder.

Whilst this perception is often true within communities and at the front-line of law enforcement, it is rarely true within strategic layers of policing and government. This is particularly so in the UK, where the effects of gun crime on communities and other innocent members of the public have been recognized alongside the economic costs to a society of failing to act proactively to reduce this type of violence. It's clear that gun crime has a disproportionately negative affect on the public's perception of crime and their neighbourhoods and communities. This sets gun crime out as a signal event that is ignored by all law enforcement and other relevant public bodies at their peril. Signal events are key indicators of the health, or otherwise, of a community and the investments in time and resources to deal with them effectively, whilst significant, are necessary to prevent escalation to far more serious issues and much greater cost in future.

Media effects of gun crime

Gun crime attracts the press and generates publicity on a scale that is often rarely seen otherwise, as the case of Charlene Ellis and Letisha Shakespeare clearly demonstrates. These two young women were shot and killed leaving a New Year Party in Birmingham on 2 January 2003. Such events can and do trigger 'moral panics' in the media, becoming the focal point for extensive media coverage of a specific social or cultural issues – in this case gun crime.

A quick trawl of media and other websites reveals a plethora of material available to examine in the smallest detail almost every key incident that has occurred where firearms were believed, rightly or wrongly, to have been involved[5]. The Internet has also facilitated the wider dissemination of information from action, support and protest groups that have grown up around gun crime. These groups are able to take advantage of the capability afforded them by the web to lobby officials and create the necessary impetus behind their cause to demand recognition at higher levels of government than previously possible.

Social media also has a similar affect and this, in some ways, has again first been recognized by criminals. After a recent shooting in London, members of a criminal gang set up their own social media sites to warn off members of the local community who may have been considering contributing evidence, information and intelligence to the authorities to support investigation of the incident. It is essential that all LEAs recognize these forms of media and the potential they afford both criminals and LEAs alike across the globe.

The power of social media has never been more apparent than it has been in various Arab countries over recent times and it is extremely clear that it can equally be harnessed as a significant power for positive or criminal intent. LEAs must not miss such an opportunity or the initiative is likely to shift to or remain with those whose would use is for criminal purposes. The Internet and all its capability is a threat to and an opportunity for LEA's and must not remain the domain of small numbers of isolated specialists or the true potential to use this technology to tackle gun crime will never be realized.

Using the Internet to facilitate effective communication between LEA's and the experts vested in the disparate disciplines of gun crime prevention and detection requires not only the harnessing of the technology but also a means for bringing together the differing cultures and vocabularies of all partners involved. Such exploitation of the Internet and modern technologies offers the chance for true interoperability, the harmonization of systems and processes, not only between LEA's across the EU but also across continents as the travel of gun crime is clearly not restricted to the EU alone.

Case studies

The following case studies and description of the National Ballistics Intelligence Service in the UK are presented to demonstrate how these issues have impacted on local communities and the UK Government and the potential for improvement, and even cost saving, if the appropriate investment in resource and technology is made.

---

[5] See: Guardian online at: http://www.guardian.co.uk/uk/2005/mar/18/ukguns.ukcrime

Case study 1 - The shooting of Charlene Ellis & Letisha Shakespeare

In the UK, the shooting of Charlene Ellis and Letisha Shakespeare, a single incident where innocent victims were caught in the crossfire of warring gangs, had more negative impact on public perceptions than a significant number of other such incidents that had happened over a good number of years previously.

Charlene Ellis and Letisha Shakespeare were shot and killed leaving a New Year Party in Birmingham on 2 January 2003. They were innocent bystanders caught up in the crossfire between the Johnson Crew and the Burger Boys, two notorious and violent criminal gangs based in the Birmingham area. The Johnson Crew and Burger Boys had been in violent dispute over their territories for many years that resulted, it is believed, in the death of a key member of the Burger Boys gang in December 2002. The victim's brother, believing the Johnson Crew to be behind the killing, planned his revenge. He recruited a number of people to assist in exacting that revenge, including the half-brother of Charlene Ellis.

Several items were obtained to assist with the revenge attack, including a red Ford Mondeo bought from Northampton. On the evening of the fatal party, the Burger Boys and their recruits drove up outside the salon where the party was taking place and "sprayed" the partygoers using a Mac10 sub-machine gun. This was an indiscriminate shooting because, although the intended target may have been present, the weapon, known colloquially as "spray and pray" because of its recoil, was almost impossible to aim with any accuracy. Clearly the criminals discharging such a weapon in public had little or no regard for anyone else caught up in the situation.

The national publicity that surrounded this incident and the on-going trial over the following years resulted in a perception that was formed not only of gun crime generally, but of the local area involved as well as Birmingham as a whole. This negative perception was identified as a serious risk to local regeneration and potentially even the economic development of the whole region. It has been estimated by the UK Government that the two dynastic families, whose notorious gangs were responsible for these shootings, have cost the public purse over £37m[6] in detecting and punishing their crimes over a period of 40 years. When the wider costs, including medical treatment etc., of dealing with the fallout of the gun related activity of these gangs are taken into account, this figure rises to a staggering £187m over 40 years.

This case also resulted in significant changes to the way trials were conducted and the processes that were permitted for the giving of evidence in British Courts. These changes permitted the giving of evidence by anonymous witnesses whose lives would otherwise have been put in significant danger and who might other-

---

[6] MailOnline at: http://www.dailymail.co.uk/news/article-1296682/37MILLION-Huge-taxpayer-crimes-just-TWO-families.html

wise have felt unable to give the testimony that ultimately resulted in the successful prosecutions. However these changes did not occur easily within UK law and resulted in the loss of a high-profile murder trial at the Old Bailey in June 2008. The cost of that lost case alone was identified at £6m to the UK taxpayer and it was estimated that dozens of other cases were at risk of failing or being successfully appealed if UK law were not changed.

As a consequence of this, emergency legislation in the form of The Criminal Evidence (Witness Anonymity) Bill was rushed through both the Houses of Parliament and The House of Lords during July 2008[7]. Without these changes to national legislation, it is likely that gun crime investigations and prosecutions would've continued to fail at early stages as witnesses felt unable to come forward.

This is a prime example of how changing the law that surrounds both this and other types of crime can truly help in catching and convicting criminals. Such changes can also aid substantially in deterring criminals in future but they also highlight the need for the issues surrounding gun crime as a whole to rise for consideration and action by the highest authorities. Within the EU, the opportunity for travel across borders is a significant advantage to criminals wishing to commit gun crime directly or to facilitate it through others. In many cases, existing legislation, such as that relating to data protection, human rights and computer misuse, can be seen as a barrier to the sharing of information, evidence and intelligence that has the power to prevent and detect this crime, saving countless lives and serious injuries and substantially reducing the costs of such crime in the process.

Analysis

The above case demonstrates the impact that a single event can have on a community but also highlights the substantial cost of gun crime and its associated criminality to the whole of society. It also demonstrates the need for the changing of laws where these are found to assist the criminals in protecting them from detection or prosecution. This event, along with a series of others that bore similarities were the reason for a review of gun crime being commissioned by the Association Of Chief Police Officers (ACPO). This review led, in turn to the establishment of the National Ballistics Intelligence Service within the UK.

Key Risks

What are the key risks not only for the public but also for the LEAs attempting to protect the public from gun crime? It is true to say that many members of the pub-

[7] See MailOnline: http://www.dailymail.co.uk/news/article-1029045/Jack-Straw-plans-emergency-law-dozens-murder-trials-face-axe-anonymity-ruling.html

lic tend to assume that LEAs already have the capability to share information, at will, across all borders and that they know everything there is to know about this sort of criminality. Obviously, this is not the case and, unfortunately, many too many criminals understand this only too well.

There are many examples of criminals using their knowledge of the frailties of LEAs and other government agencies to ensure they can continue to commit gun crime with much reduced likelihood of detection. This especially includes the now far simpler act of traversing borders within the EU. Obviously this reduces the deterrent effect of LEAs within Member States and increases the likelihood of further gun crime in future.

However, it's often not just geographic borders or contradictory legislation that separate information from those who would best make use of it. The differing disciplines of investigation, intelligence and forensic science can often create divisions within an LEA or even within an investigative team. Bringing these disciplines together in a way that ensured the whole was greater than the sum of the parts was a key objective of the National Ballistics Intelligence Service in the UK and has resulted in a step change in the way that gun crime is investigated and prevented.

National Ballistics Intelligence Service (NABIS)

In 2007, a project to construct the National Ballistics Intelligence Service was commissioned within the UK on behalf of the England & Wales Association of Chief Police Officers (ACPO). The project was led from within the ACPO Criminal Use of Firearms Group after it was recognised that the existing framework for tackling gun crime had a number of built in barriers to improved performance.

The barriers to performance existed at both operational and strategic levels and required addressing across all criminal justice partners involved in tackling this type of crime. The key barriers identified were delays that were built into the process for obtaining evidence relating to potentially linked firearms incidents across the country, the inability of the police service to effectively share evidence and intelligence that had been gathered within previous investigations and the reactive nature of gun crime investigations that resulted from the processes imposed as a consequence of these issues.

A decision was taken to build the new ballistics service, bringing together the disparate processes and providing a new database that could be updated and researched by all relevant partners. This involved working closely with all police forces and, in particular, those few that covered geographic areas that contributed most to the number of offences recorded across the country. However it was also necessary for the relationship between the police service and its forensic providers to be re-examined in detail. This examination resulted in the conscious decision to bring some forensic examination services back under the direct control of the police service. Whilst this placed some strain on the relationship with the service, as its forensic partners, this was managed proactively by engaging relevant members of each partner supplier to help them understand the need for change and the service that they would be asked to provide in future.

NABIS is delivered through four key centres, NABIS Hubs, based within strategic areas for gun crime, and a database delivered nationally alongside the UK Police National Computer. The NABIS Hubs are augmented by the NABIS Operations Centre and National Intelligence Cell based in Birmingham. This coverage provides a truly UK wide service. The NABIS Operations Centre coordinates activity between forces and disparate investigative teams as well as across countries where relevant issues are identified. They also provide administrative functions for the NABIS Database.

The NABIS Intelligence Cell provide backup to operational and investigative teams but also generate strategic reports from the database and other sources that analyse the effectiveness of NABIS activity as well as identifying up and coming gun crime issues that affect forces in the UK. These issues include the supply chain for weapons as well as other movement of firearms and organised gangs across geographic borders.

In the initial stages of constructing the NABIS service, the three key stakeholder groups of senior investigators, forensic scientists, including those from suppliers of forensic services, and intelligence analysts were brought together to gather their requirements against a newly identified core strategy. This new strategy is aimed at reducing the time taken for key information to be made available to investigators involved in recent incidents and the development of an approach to preventing future crime that focused on the knowledge that can be deduced and inferred from existing evidence and intelligence.

The disparity between purpose, language and culture of the three groups was highlighted during the requirements capture process but these sessions also offered the ideal opportunity to tackle those differences head on and find resolutions that would drive up the effectiveness of policing gun crime. The key objective of the scientists, for example and understandably, was to provide evidence to investigators of the links between recovered ammunition cartridges and/or weapons. The process required to produce evidential quality information from these items was detailed and relatively lengthy. Whilst the process could be accelerated in serious or high-profile cases, there was a considerable feeling among the investigators that earlier provision of this information could lead to improved opportunities for identification and conviction of offenders as well as reducing the likelihood of further offences by implementing interventions preventing retribution between gangs and other such retaliatory attacks.

Further review of these processes identified that the scientists were often able to give an opinion as to whether there were relevant links at an early stage of the evidential process, however they had previously been reluctant to voice these opinions for fear of doubt being cast on the scientific processes at a later stage or operational and investigative staff acting inappropriately on the information provided. The investigators and intelligence analysts, however, identified themselves as experts in evaluating uncertainty surrounding information and that the advantages of reduced timescales for the development of intelligence, investigative strategy and tactics far outweighed the potential disadvantages that had been perceived by the scientists.

As the requirements came together, further opportunities were identified for the development of strategic information to guide and direct future crime prevention activity nationally and internationally. These opportunities included traditional management information as well as a change in focus from what was known (i.e. the recovered ammunition and weapons) to that which could be inferred (i.e. that there were other weapons, as yet unrecovered, that were available to criminals to continue committing gun crime). This switch of focus to identifying and tackling "inferred weapons" directly has greatly improved the effectiveness of gun crime investigation across the UK and has led to improved investigations, proactive operations and intelligence activity as far afield as the United States of America. The following two case studies demonstrate this change and the potential positive impact of such a cultural change on the way gun crimes are tackled by all LEA's.

Case Study 2 - The role of armourers in gun crime[8]

Fig. 4.1.: Recovered Firearms from Operation Newhaven[9]

---

[8] Details provided by NABIS Operations Centre. Also see Liverpool Echo at: http:// www. liverpoolecho.co.uk/liverpool-news/local-news/2011/04/20/liverpool-gun-gang-get-57-years-jail-after-uzi-and-glocks-seized-100252-28551038/

[9] Image supplied by NABIS Operations Centre

In late 2009 scientists from NABIS northern forensic hub in Manchester received cartridges from 3 separate crimes, in 3 different police force areas, with a distinctive 'left rifling' pattern that had not been seen before. This indicated that there might be a new 'firearms factory' or source of firearms supplying firearms for criminal use.

Based upon this information NABIS hosted a meeting between senior investigators from the 3 forces concerned and an intelligence sharing protocol was agreed. Operation NEWHAVEN was commenced to investigate the availability of firearms and ammunition in one of the force areas and concluded in early 2010 when officers recovered a sub machine gun and 3 self-loading pistols from one of the main subjects of the investigation. As part of the operation a warehouse forming part of an engineering company was identified, 4 offenders were arrested and the premises were searched. A large quantity of firearms, associated paraphernalia and component parts were recovered during the search.

It became apparent that firearms were being reactivated within the premises using pre 1995 deactivated firearms as a base product for the process. In addition numerous 'Sten' guns were recovered in various stages of manufacture; it appeared that these guns were being manufactured from scratch within the premises.

An ammunition press and 200 rounds of ammunition were also recovered suggesting ammunition was also being produced at the premises. The ballistic material from the premises was submitted to the NABIS Northern Hub where the 2,000 rounds of ammunition were examined. As a result NABIS identified this gun 'factory' had produced at least forty-five reactivated or converted firearms. Potentially almost all of these items were sub machine guns. Four offenders have been convicted in relation to this operation and received a total sentence of 57 years imprisonment.

Analysis

This case study shows clearly the part that criminal armourers play in the supply and protection of firearms for serious and organised criminal gangs across the country. Without the supply chain being maintained, the availability of firearms and, in particular, the harder to obtain multiple discharge weapons, would be significantly reduced with the opportunity for death and serious injury ameliorated too. This case also demonstrates the ability of criminals to traverse the self-imposed boundaries of traditional policing, especially with the discovery of a link between one of the armourers involved and criminal activity taking place in the USA. The following case study shows this link clearly.

Case Study 3 - The use of travel as an aid to gun crime[10]

Following the recovery of the three self-loading pistols from one of the main subjects of Operation Newhaven enquiries were made to try and trace the source of these weapons from the point of manufacture through the supply chain to the individual concerned. It was established that the 3 Glock pistols had been purchased by an individual in North Carolina, USA, using a credit card in his own name. In order to fully exploit the intelligence opportunities arising from this discovery, ownership of the investigation was passed to a Regional Task Force covering a number of police force areas. This presented an opportunity for enhanced levels of intelligence sharing across police forces during the operation. One of the first things that the Task Force did was to establish operational interaction with the Bureau of Alcohol, Tobacco, Firearms and Explosives (ATF) in the USA.

Enquires made by the ATF established that the suspect had travelled to the UK on numerous occasions in 2010. It is apparent that during these trips to the UK the suspect was carrying firearms in his stowed baggage. The suspect was placed under daily surveillance in the USA, during which he was seen to purchase 16 x 9mm Glock pistols. In the summer of 2010 he was tracked to a North Carolina airport where he checked in four bags, he did not declare any firearms inside his luggage. The luggage was intercepted and found to contain sixteen firearms and thirty-two magazines. The suspect was arrested and detained in custody in the US.

During the surveillance the suspect was seen to dump thirty-three Glock Security Boxes supplied with the firearms, ATF Agents collected these. Along with the boxes and other associated items were a number of fired cartridge cases. Eighteen of these cartridge cases were flown to the UK where they were added to NABIS' Integrated Ballistics Identification System (IBIS). In autumn 2010 one of these casings was matched by NABIS to a shooting incident in Greater Manchester where an individual was subject to a non-fatal drive by shooting. In a subsequent search relating to this incident, four further firearms where found at an address in the force area. One of these firearms was a Glock 26 pistol that was purchased in the USA and is subject to another on-going investigation. The other three firearms were unrelated; however NABIS analysis shows that two of the firearms are connected to eight firearms discharges in the North West going back to 2000.

Analysis

Examination of this case study shows not only the ease with which some criminals are able to obtain firearms and ammunition in foreign countries before returning to

---

[10] Details provided by NABIS Operations Centre

their own or another country to supply them, but also the readiness of such people to do so in full view of the authorities. As is often the case, it was the intelligence surrounding this individual that offered a context that facilitated his arrest and prevented a myriad of weaponry from being available to commit gun crime.

EU opportunities

The success of NABIS in the UK has prompted consultation within the EU into ways in which the lessons learned in the UK could be could be combined with experiences with the region and propagated to all Member States, thus raising the bar for the tackling of gun crime across the whole of the EU. It became very clear during this wider consultation, with experts from each of the disparate law enforcement disciplines, that the sharing of ballistic, crime and intelligence information and the ability to analyse it effectively remained a key blocker to improving the fight against gun crime across EU borders.

The legal frameworks that exist within individual Member States and the variation in approach and culture between them further complicate this situation. The disparate technologies that are used by LEAs and other scientific establishments to record crime, intelligence and ballistic classification and imagery information add to this confusion rather than reduce it. The requirements that were articulated as a result of this consultation thus had a substantial emphasis on the need for open standards that are essential to breaking down barriers such as those identified in order to assist the effective fight against gun crime. It would be foolish to attempt to address any of the cross-border issues without taking into consideration the need for levels of security that are commensurate with the crimes being tackled.

Information security

Obviously, where threat to life and, in some cases, many lives is involved, the information and intelligence that surrounds these people and events must be protected sufficiently to substantially reduce the likelihood of compromise that may raise the risk of further harm rather than lower it. All of this must be done in a way that is seen to protect the public whilst building in “privacy by design” and "proportionality" within system and process. Within the UK the NABIS Database has been accredited as CONFIDENTIAL under the Government Protective Marking Scheme (GPMS). This designation has a significant impact upon the storage, use and dissemination of information that impacts squarely on cost and timeliness if not managed effectively. Without all of these factors being fully appreciated and adopted within any proposed EU wide solution, confidence would remain low and leave that solution lying unused on the proverbial shelf, where it can little afford to be.

Cost

Whilst considering other potential blockers to systems and processes, it is important to address the potential cost of a system designed and built to address all of these issues, especially at a time of austerity for all Member States of the EU. It's a fact that all LEAs are seeing budgets cut and staff reduced. Efforts are being made to maintain front-line services but the definition of these can often be difficult. Whilst it is not expected that anyone would not see gun crime as a front-line issue, there may be doubt about some of the services that are believed by LEA's to be essential to supporting it. It's also essential, therefore, that any development to tackle these issues takes into account the affordability of any potential solution for all LEAs across the EU and that every opportunity to automate processes and outcomes be taken to minimise the impact of reducing resources imposed on those LEA's.

Future of managing gun crime information

Technology and informatics has advanced greatly over recent years and is likely to continue to do so for the foreseeable future. The understanding among practitioners, scientists and academics of the chaotic nature of gun crime has improved substantially and will go on doing so with improved methods of information capture and analysis. The sciences of Emergence and Complexity offer the opportunity to determine key links and signals from a wealth of data and information available to modern investigators and strategists alike. Automating these processes will enable front-line resources to be tasked efficiently to tackle this most serious of crime types.

Future solutions

It is into the landscape described in the above paragraphs that any new system and/or technology, such as that proposed by the Odyssey Project would be introduced. This is a complex and fast moving landscape that will demand the best of academics, technologists, strategists, business experts and politicians alike if systems and processes are to be made truly interoperable and capable of functioning effectively across the EU to tackle gun crime.

Chapter 5: How Complexity Theory is Changing the Role of Analysis in Law Enforcement and National Security

Richard Leary and Jenny Thomas

Abstract The Science of Complexity is primarily concerned with the examination and understanding of the workings of complex adaptive systems and we argue that crime and terrorism are examples of complex adaptive systems. In this chapter we explore the implications of this for the detection and prevention of organised crime and the role information technology has to play in this. In order to exploit mass collections of Counter Terrorist, Organised Crime and Human Trafficking data we need intelligent methods of exploiting the ability to compare or combine any item of data with any other item of data as well as to routinely undertake various types of inferential and statistical analytical calculations and combinatorial experiments (correlations) upon the data. We must also be aware of the fact that we can never gain total knowledge of the present state, measurement always falls short of certain accuracy and, it simply is not possible to recover "everything" about a given state of affairs. Systems evolve, change and evolve again simply as a result of the interaction of those constituent parts over time and as a result of their individual rule sets. By examining evidence about past and present events we can begin to draw a range of both linear and non-linear inferences about future events.

Introduction

This chapter is concerned with how technology, informatics and complexity theory can change the role of analysis in law enforcement and national security. It examines how a relatively new approach in science can be used to help us understand systems of all kinds including criminal and terrorist networks. These too are 'systems' as will be explained.

We exist in a world of astounding complexity. Whether in large or small organisations our daily routines are dominated by a complex array of information systems, structures and relationships. The organisations, structures and systems in which we operate fluctuate between states of stability and states of chaotic instability. Dealing with this diversity presents policing with varied problems to solve. Gaining an understanding of the characteristics of complexity presents us with opportunity's to harness it and use it to our advantage in strategic planning and tactical policy making.

The Science of Complexity is primarily concerned with the examination and understanding of the workings of complex adaptive systems and we argue that crime and terrorism are examples of complex adaptive systems. Criminal and terrorist activity is committed by criminals many of whom know each other, they interact with each other in many ways as well as go on to plan and commit crimes together. We believe that criminal activity and terrorism are in fact systems made up of diverse variables that can be gathered, measured, compared and contrasted in an effort to understand the cause, effects and relations between them. Complexity Theory offers many useful lessons to help us understand how systems work, how they behave and how best to interact with them if we need to control them, measure them, exploit them or change them. Complexity Theory can be used to help us understand many types of system be they mechanical, human, digital, animal, real or virtual. A number of important factors differentiate complex systems from other systems.

A complex adaptive system cannot be explained by breaking it down into its component parts because the interaction between the parts needs to be considered as a whole. As a result of these interactions complex systems exhibit emergent behaviour. As we move forward in an ever more connected and complex world governed by 'information' we must be ready to understand and grasp the fact that systems are more than the sum of their parts. The whole is much larger as a result of the emergent properties created by complex interactions between the parts.

What really creates complexity in any system is the fact that any one constituent part of the system may have its own set of rules that governs the way it operates. These rules may be very simple but the combined effect of even a small number of variables can be massive. Rules can come to us in many forms. Legal rules, policies, attitudes, outlooks and many more are all examples of the sorts of rules that govern the way a system works. Any response to a complex system must be able respond to basic and complex changes in the governing rules of any one or all of the constituent parts of the system.

The relationships between the component parts of a complex system result in non-linear relationships which in turn result in the "turbulence" in the system that creates complexity. Any small interaction can result in new interactions which in turn can produce massive outputs. The behaviour of any system that exhibits emergent properties is very difficult to predict.

One of the resulting characteristics of complex adaptive systems is their extreme sensitivity initial conditions. That is, the conditions that exist at any point in times can have massive impact on what follows. In the future we need to become acutely aware that even the most insignificant variable in a system can produce complexity and turbulence. Every part of the system is a 'part of the overall system' with the potential to have massive impacts and emergent behaviour.

In the future we need to be able to deal with emergence by recognising it, managing it and in effect using it where we can to our advantage. Optimisation techniques are needed to 'map' change and re-adjust the system to a state that suits are purpose. It is our experience that complexity theory can help us to build better information systems based on an understanding of the way in which systems behave under certain conditions. Complex adaptive systems is a new field of science studying how parts of a system give rise to the collective behaviours of the system, and importantly, how the system interacts with its environment. Social systems including crime networks, gangs, terrorist cells and the like are in our view complex adaptive system. We should think about these systems as possessing 'non-periodic flow' just as many other complex physical as well as biological systems do.

Complexity Theory has been massively informed by modern technology. The impact of information science in recent years has been as profound as the impact of mechanisation in the industrial age that began 200 years ago. The 21st Century is proving to be the age of the 'industrialisation of information' on a global scale along with all the changes it brings, the problems that arise and the potential solutions that result.

Our world is undergoing massive change. Much of this has been brought on by the proliferation of information as well as the technology that acts as an enabler for the free-flow of information globally in highly complex ways. It is important to think about these information flows because many of them are created or are descriptions or adaptations of human activity. We use them to organise, socialise, work and for many other processes. We are concerned with the exploitation of 'information' as well as the technology which enables this because it has implications for both the management creation of complexity. The Information Age offers many opportunities for access to information and for many purposes. This has affected the way people live, work, socialise and organise their lives and business affairs. People and organisations can now communicate instantaneously across the globe, access information on a massive scale, influence each other in social networks, set up businesses entirely on the internet, create content and share information as well as learn better ways to do things at a speed truly unimaginable fifty years ago.

Three facts characterise the Information Age. The first is the speed at which information can be transmitted globally, the second is the relative ease of access to information and the third is the impact this is having on the world and our lives. In terms of speed we can now send, receive and broadcast messages right across the globe in fractions of a second. Wide-scale speedy access to information and the ability to communicate effectively across continents means that communities are self-organising and adapting much quicker than the formal structures and hierarchical management structures we have been used to. What results from this is a set of diverse systems of information flows that are not centrally managed or controlled and can adapt to emerging conditions. As a result, we see the self-organisation and adaptation of large communities simply by their possessing the ability to share information outside the control of the current an old centralised state about issues that concerned them. The organisation of society is now becoming more defused and influenced by small but important events anywhere on the planet. This in itself raises challenges but perhaps the most surprising fact is that these systems emerge not from a centralised control mechanism. They simply emerge from de-centralised functions and the interaction of the varied constituent parts of the system over time.

Our traditional political and economic systems tend to be largely centralised and governed by functions that we know and understand. In other words there are clear rules that when applied to given conditions they in turn give rise to certain results. We can control and to some extent predict ranges of results. However, the changes we have seen in speedy access and transfer of information has resulted in a new dynamic set of paradigms that not only create complexity they are complex in themselves.

Whilst this has an impact on the way crime is committed it also has implications for the way in which crime can be investigated. This chapter is concerned therefore with the way in which policing and national security is increasingly affected by a world with an increasing tendency to create complexity , how it needs to grasp the dilemmas this presents and how properly understood, complexity can present some very valuable metaphors for strategists and policy makers. The science of complexity has many practical applications for policing and if other disciplines are initiating new and novel applications based upon it to solve problems they face, why not policing?

The impact of science, technology and socio-political change has resulted in a new environment for policing. Sir Edward Crew (formerly Chief Constable of West Midlands Police) said "change is the only constant and complexity is the only apt description of the environment in which we operate." But how can we respond to this, how can we operate in this complex environment and what are the challenges ahead? The systems this chapter discusses are those organisational systems that are complex in the sense that there are a high number of independent variables interacting with each other in a great number of ways. A fine balancing act results between a state of stability and a state of instability.

In policing, we already have some notable examples; The National DNA Database and the Automated Number Plate Recognition System are systems with large and complex data sets constantly changing with new scenarios and new information over time. There is massive potential here for new connections and combinations to be discovered between events, people, locations and time. These links and connections can be used to generate new understanding about the environment in which the systems operate thereby enhancing our ability to control it. The complexity that exists in even these modest sized systems is infinite and requires special tools to manage and use it.

The police environment and the criminal systems and social orders they must protect and serve are made up of complex variables. When these are combined and we examine the potential for complexity we are faced with some big numbers to deal with.

The potential for complex combinations can be illustrated by a simple example; if we assume that there were only 10 variables operating within this complex system there would be 1013 different ways of combining and assembling them into patterns. If there were 25 variables (for example, simple categories like people, events, locations,) there would be 33,554,406 ways of combining and assembling them into interesting combinations. If there were just 50 variables involved the number would be immense and over 1.126 x 10 to the power of 15. Now think about the number of calls, incidents, crimes, arrests, the police deal with over time. It is a complex system of interactions requiring more than a linear approach.

Even if we wanted to we could not possibly explore all possible interactions and even if we did in the case of just 25 variables each combination of which taking just 1 minute to deal with would take up 69,905 person days or 268 person years to deal with. Not only would this take an immense amount of time it would prove to be enormously non-productive. Exploring over 33.5 million actions in order to find one of interest to you would not be a productive use of time.

The whole is worth more than the sum of the parts

Interoperability and data sharing of intelligence information in the way advocated in this chapter presents major strategic and tactical benefits. For example, each and every item of information has an inherent ability to combine in many different ways with other items of information in the same or related data collection. We can thus discover a great deal simply by trying and testing many different combinations in parallel using technical non-personal information. This is simply a process of strategically using computers to undertake automated search and retrieval of known important associations in datasets. For example, Forensic Pathways has developed a methodology for the routine stream processing and cross correlation of many datasets simultaneously for suspect identities. When relevant 'outliers' or 'matches' are discovered they are 'flagged' by the computer to a user as a 'Red Alert'.

A combination of data in this way is the fusion of two or more attributes of data that may correlate or tell a story important to solving a problem. The user decides the relevance of the processing domain and datasets and the computer sets about its 'situation awareness processing'. The data is a 'gold-mine' of information about activity important to sustainable security and the decision and threat assessment function.

In order to exploit mass collections of Counter Terrorist, Organised Crime and Human Trafficking data we need intelligent methods of exploiting the ability to compare or combine any item of data with any other item of data as well as undertake various types of inferential and statistical analytical calculations and combinatorial experiments (correlations) routinely upon the data. Furthermore, we need a method to help us reduce the massive possible numbers of combinations down to numbers we are capable of dealing with and making sense of. This is a process we call 'Data Churning'.

Policing and complexity

Why should policing be concerned with complexity? A simple answer to this is that it can provide us with a deeper level of understanding of the environment in which policing operates. Casti (1994) describes two scientists talking about complexity and reports their conversation. The first states "Complexity is what you don't understand" and the second scientist respond "You don't understand complexity". The exchange serves to highlight two very important issues surrounding complexity. First, complexity can help us to understand behaviour or states within a system and second, that complexity depends upon how you look for it. Casti explains that:

> "In short, meaning [complexity] is bound up with the whole process of communication and doesn't reside in just one or another aspect of it. As a result, the complexity of a political structure, a national economy or an immune system cannot be regarded as simply a property of that system taken in isolation. Rather, whatever complexity such systems have is a joint property of the system and it's interaction with another system, most often an observer and/or controller." (Casti, 1994, p.269)

It is fairly easy therefore to see how an intelligence analyst, an investigator or a strategic decision maker in policing interacts with the system to draw on relevant information of interest, thereby enabling a conclusion to be drawn, or, to set about asking another question and eventually sending the results back into the system. This iterative two-way input, output and feedback process can be seen in operation when the results of strategies are operationalized. Changes in the environment can be seen like incidences of crime, the lack of availability of illicit substances following a protracted drugs initiative or an increase in visible policing activity in a neighbourhood.

What are the implications for police work?

If the rules that control the system or network are linear, the range of outcomes is directly relational to the inputs. By establishing what the inputs are it may be possible to predict the outcomes presenting the police policy maker with an ideal tool. However, as in most scenarios where highly variable groups of people and highly variable descriptions and categories and records of events are concerned, as in crime, then the system may display features of non-linearity. A decision to arrest or investigate a network of crime or criminals is an input in itself and will have some degree of effect on the structure of the network.

A practical example here is a police intelligence system. There are highly variable categories of information and highly contentious levels of quality in the accuracy of information; some information will always be subject to questions about its credibility. This is not a feature of a lack of professionalism; it is a feature of the type of environment the police operate in. Witnesses and those supplying information are susceptible to the vagaries of the senses and sometimes their ethical standpoint or motives may be otherwise than those they state to the police. Even physical and forensic evidence must be quality checked; it never arrives with its credibility credentials stamped on it, they have to be assessed, measured and declared by a human expert.

Imagine that the intelligence system has identified that currently a network of confidence fraudsters has been preying on vulnerable elderly persons in a particular geographical area. Let's also assume that we have what we assess to be very good descriptions of 10 suspects from witnesses who saw 10 of the crimes take place. In addition we have obtained two DNA profiles from fingerprints left at two of the scenes. We believe from our experience of dealing with these types of crimes before that this method has been connected with travelling family groups who centre their operations around a leader or a 'key player' within their extended family. The key player travels the area to identify vulnerable elderly victims.

The family groups are widely dispersed with most persons related in some way to other members of the group. Identifying the 'key player' will inevitably raise smaller potential networks of related persons to treat as suspects. However, the current state within the intelligence system suggests two likely 'key players.' However, we do not possess DNA profiles from either to use as elimination samples. The potential involvement of these two suspects suggests family group members to treat as suspects in the extended network.

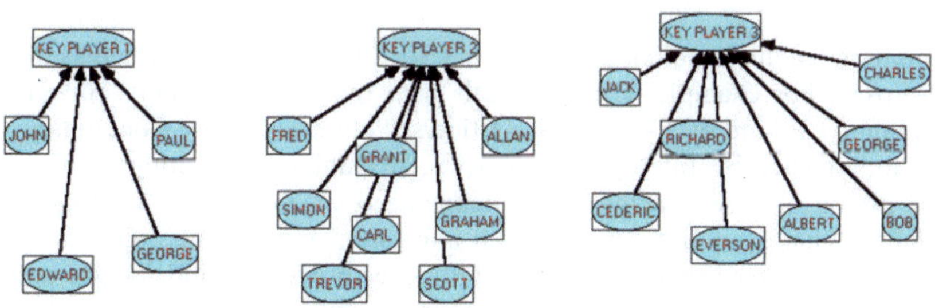

Fig. 5.1. Selecting the key player

The ability to select the right "Key Player" in the right network will be crucial in identifying the offender from the range of "possible" suspects. Imagine that we receive information from a questionable but not entirely unreliable source as to the identity of the 'key player.' Although this is just one detail of information within a mass of other information about other criminal suspects, this small fluctuation may have massive effects upon the efficiency of the system to predict likely suspects. In this case the new information about the likely player directs our attention to an entirely different extended family network. Remember, only small fluctuations can have massive effects.

One retort here could be "well what is the point of employing or engaging complex systems and techniques if the outcomes are unreliable?" The answer is simple: if we are able to identify when we have unpredictability we can avoid the consequences of it – the consequences being an inability to control and master the system or network. The ability to predict the apparently unpredictable state is a very useful tool – to know when we know and to know when we don't or, put another way, when we are in danger of losing the potential to gain knowledge or just simply losing control of that ability.

Another use for complex systems is that they are very good at extending our knowledge from the known to the unknown; we move from a state when we know what the system holds and we can predict on the basis of it to a state when we attempt to fill in the gaps in our knowledge and discover what we don't know but perhaps need or ought to know.

Unfortunately, no linear system exists which is so comprehensive it can deal with and predict all the events we are likely to need in the future quite simply because the world is a complex place not linear. However, given static and deterministic values linear systems play an important role. Neither complex nor linear systems provide the answer and neither should be treated as exclusive. Neither alone can create a utopian system – we need both.

Using complexity to deliver solutions - thinking in silos

A common feature in policing now is what Sir Edward Crew described as thinking in "silos." For example, crime is dealt with by Detectives and Crime Policy, Community Affairs by Community Officers, Public Safety by Community Officers, Intelligence by Intelligence Analysts. In addition, operating above this is some notion or assertion that all policing needs is to have an intelligence led model and that everything else will fall into place. What is missing is a rigorous and clear understanding of what that intelligence model should look like and why that model should exist. Furthermore, what are the fundamental principles upon which it operates and measures to assess effectiveness?

Each of these "silos" impacts and interacts on the other and so treating them in isolation limits our ability to respond effectively and comprehensively. The intelligence model, which logically should be the glue that holds the policing model together, is a poorly understood tool in our tool box. This area is where the silo exists in its greatest form – Information and knowledge is endemic in all human interactions and cannot be left to a standalone system which is not "hot- wired" to the other silos.

One of the greatest examples of the "intelligence silo" is the scenario in which the police officer responsible for a sector seeks intelligence about a problem from an intelligence cell only to be confronted with the question of why they want access to it. This question "what is your need to know" is a reductionist view. Whilst this may be perfectly proper for security reasons it does nothing for the officer attempting to come to terms with the complex and diverse array of associations between different elements affecting the maintenance of stability and order on his or her sector.

Networks - what can we do with complex crime networks?

Crime networks are simply interrelated groups of people associated and connected by virtue of their activity and communications links. They may be offending together, planning crimes together or disposing of stolen property after the event. A stark feature always seems to be some level of synchronised activity. Research is indicating now that these groups are not always hierarchical as is so often assumed. They are often chaotic and have distinct self-organising properties about them. Take out one of the links and new a one will appear. Re shape the network by disrupting the elements and a new shape may appear sometimes very different to the one we set out to disrupt. It is becoming increasingly clear that these networks are more often than not "flat" rather than hierarchical and this presents us with a different problem to solve. In a hierarchy there is assumed to be some level of control from the top down and the structure is designed for predictable, specific purposes. This hierarchical view of criminal networks, see the illustration below, is based upon a linear view of the world. It ignores the inter-relatedness of the elements as well as the feedback loops operating within the network. If as we suspect, hierarchies are not as common a feature of crime networks as we once thought, we need to rethink our approach. We need to "complexify" our view of the world and realise that they are self-organising systems with no real top and no real bottom.

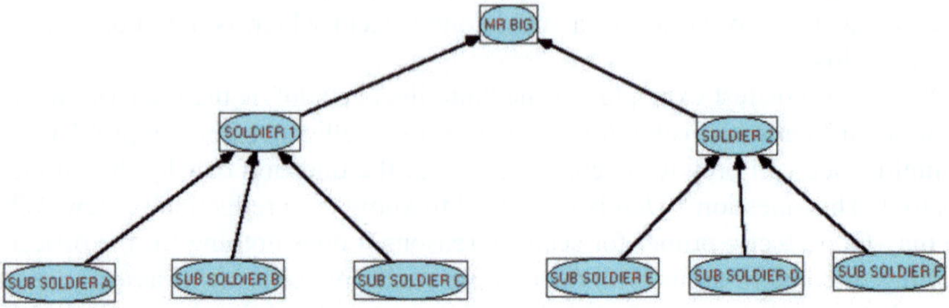

Fig. 5.2. A classical hierarchical view of a crime network

Research indicates that these are rare and not common as is often assumed in policing. Figure 5.2 is an illustration that the connectors or "Arcs" flow in a hierarchical way and there are no arcs flowing between distant elements. This may be a feature of some networks but it is suggested that this is rarer than we once thought. A crime network will more usually comprise a complex network something like this.

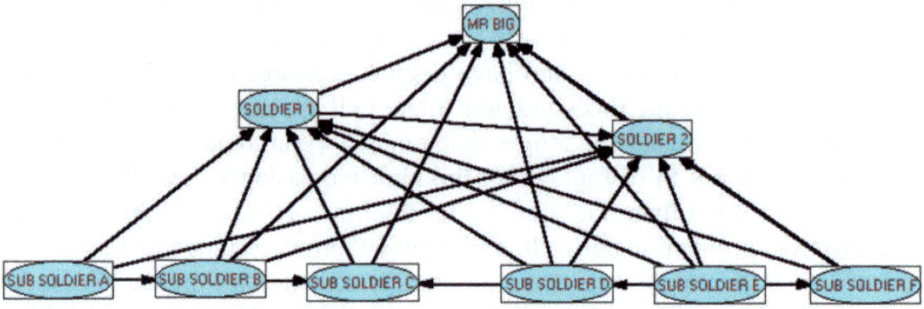

Fig. 5.3. A "flat" crime network

Figure 5.3 is a "flat" crime network. This is a common type of network. Links (arcs) between the nodes (people) do not appear in ordered layers flowing hierarchically top down and bottom up. There are parallel as well as vertical lines. The connections flow in complex unsystematic ways. Elements at the bottom of the network are often directly linked to those at the top. Different approaches will be needed in tackling hierarchies than complex networks. For example, when dealing with "informants" it will be crucial to establish whether they are operating from within a hierarchical network or a complex network. Information received from an informant who is at the bottom of a hierarchical network may be of limited value if the intention is to fragment the whole network because the informant will only have access to limited chains or pathways of intelligence. Conversely, information received from an informant who is positioned in a complex network may be able to access widespread and far-reaching pathways of intelligence due to the multi-faceted links between elements in the network. Another example of an important application is the deployment of covert technical aids. The efficiency of any covert sensing device for evidence and intelligence gathering will again be determined by its ability to "hook into" connections between elements of the network. Different results will be obtained depending upon where in the network the technical aid is deployed. Time spent analysing the network, the likely results of different deployment strategies and the overall aims of the operation will determine where that sensing device should be located. In the hierarchical network the decision may be somewhat simple, but in the complex network the opposite may be true.

A useful approach is to make policy based upon comparisons of the relative probabilities of the outcomes from different choice routes in order to maximise expected gains; these may be disruption, distortion or even the release of new information by fracturing particular parts of the structure. For example, "there have been 25 robberies in this area in the last 7 days therefore there will be 25 more identical cases in the next 7 days" may work on occasions, but we must be alive to its limits. What other factors affect this assessment, the geography, the actors available as victims, offenders and witnesses, the opportunity to commit crime all have their part to play and all make for a complex system. Some elements may wish to "trade" information in return for a reduced sentence with the authorities if confronted with overwhelming evidence of their involvement in the network of crime.

It is useful to be able to identify what fixed elements exist in a network because these are obvious targets for action. If they are fixed, they are deterministic and their effect on the outcome of the network is more likely than not to be likewise fixed. One way of achieving such a state of known "fixed elements" is to introduce a measure of time, a measure of space (geography) or a measure of fixed elements like people and known events. Time is concentrated on here because it is a good example of a constant. By using this we can determine what the temporarily fixed elements in the system are and within a given time span. Move outside that time frame and change will eventually occur.

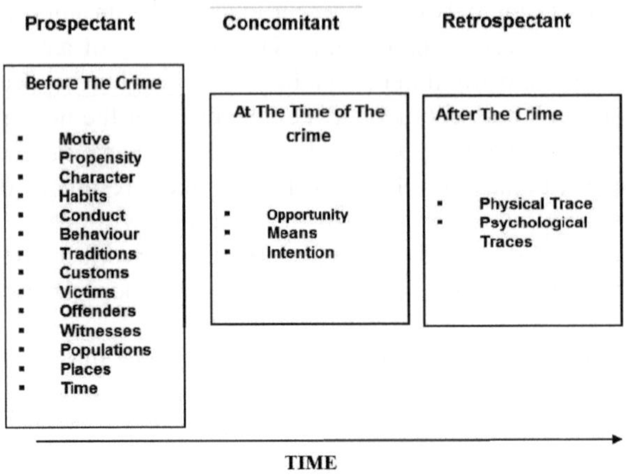

Fig. 5.4. Temporal Classification of Evidence

Figure 5.4 illustrates the way in which data can be classified into fixed elements over time. One of the authors of this chapter - Richard Leary – conceived and invented an approach to the management of intelligence and evidence that encompassed some of the ideas of complexity theory. Basically, Flints (Forensic Led Intelligence System) was designed to manage physical retrospective trace evidence relevant to inferences about opportunity and means of people (victims, offenders, witnesses, populations) places, events and time. Developments have enabled the system to manage prospectant and concomitant evidence relevant to inferences about people, places, times, motive, propensity, character, habits, conduct, behaviour, traditions, customs and time.

The benefits of Flints for the police service are to be found in the ability to combine different configurations of prospectant, concomitant and retrospective evidence in drawing inferences about links and connections between people, places, events and time. This allows the police analyst or investigator to access the rich array of connections, patterns and links which lay hidden beneath the layers of complex data. No one person can keep track of the possible combinations and layers of data as well as the possible connections and linkages that may result. However, computer based systems such as Flints, can assist in such necessary tasks.

An interesting issue facing any system that manages vast quantities of evolving data is the notion that each time a connection, link or new inference is produced by the system, say the potential connection of a robber or burglar to a series of crimes, is whether that output should be fed back into the system as an input. If this were to be done on a wide scale say by the inputting new inferences about newly discovered links and connections, then the system would begin to exhibit characteristics analogous to a self-organising complex system. That is, the vast number of variable and potential states of the system would be determined and conditioned over time by using the outputs of the system as inputs. An example of this would be to identify those people and crimes that should be targeted for DNA sampling. The people would be those persons who are strongly suspected of being prolific offenders and those crimes where DNA is likely to result in the identification of a person who had the opportunity to commit the crime. The automated electronic inputting of results of those DNA samples as well as matches discovered between them by the National DNA Database would create the cyclical conditions necessary for the outputs to be used as inputs. These conditions would create the basis of a self-organising complex system.

Time as a key variable

Time can be used as a key attractor to assist us in the classification of evidence or data about events when we are faced with a mixed mass of complex information. Wigmore used this method for the evaluation of evidence in single cases but it can be extended and transferred into volume cases as well. Simply classifying the evidence in terms of past, present and future time is a simple method we can use to assist us in trying to make sense and use of the evidence. Analysts should also be aware and encouraged to think about the way in which 'the present' shifts with each case. By examining evidence about past and present events we can begin to draw a range of both linear and non-linear inferences about future events. For example, if we are faced with a mass of information about a number of events of burglary crimes which we suspect may be linked we can assemble them into categories. What evidence do we have in our database about the motives or the methods used by offenders before they committed the crimes involved? Placing these species of evidence into categories like this may present us with opportunities to group similar facts together from which we may be able to draw inferences about similarities and links. What about evidence we might have expected to see, but do not, given certain patterns of events? Does that give rise to the premise that certain items or strands of evidence are missing or does it indicate that the evidence never existed? Did some person have a particular motive to commit the series of crimes, whereas others did not? Similarly, placing evidence about events that took place at the time of the crime can present us with powerful evidence to eliminate persons from suspicion and implicate others who cannot be eliminated. The presence of fingerprints, DNA, footwear or witness identification of the offender may present us with the means to show that a particular person had the opportunity and means to commit the crime. That may prove crucial in determining whom we can and cannot eliminate from suspicion. In addition, it presents us with the means to determine who may be committing certain types or patterns of crime we see emerging in our patterns of events which may extend into the future.

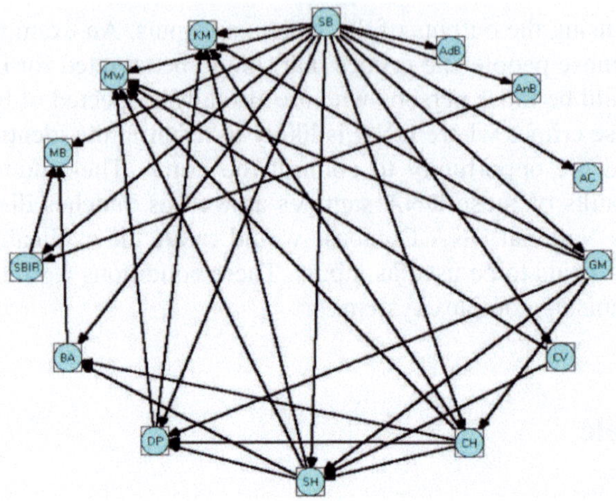

Fig. 5.5. Links between criminals on the basis of known intelligence

The network in figure 5.5 demonstrates links between criminals on the basis of known intelligence over a given time span. The links are made up from data about co accused persons – those criminals who have been arrested and charged alongside other criminals as co-accused. By analysing the potential links and the effects of removing those links, we can fragment the network and isolate certain elements from others. This could be by arresting them.

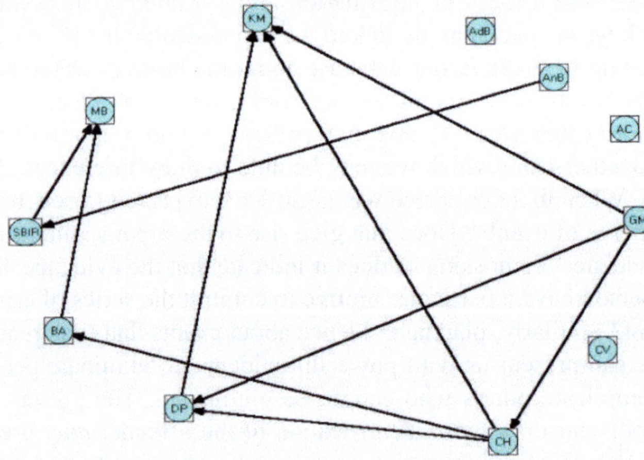

Fig. 5.6. In this case only three links removed resulted in this level of fragmentation.

The following illustration is a complex network of offenders linked by virtue of their previous co-offending habits and activities. In short, they have displayed a propensity for offending together.

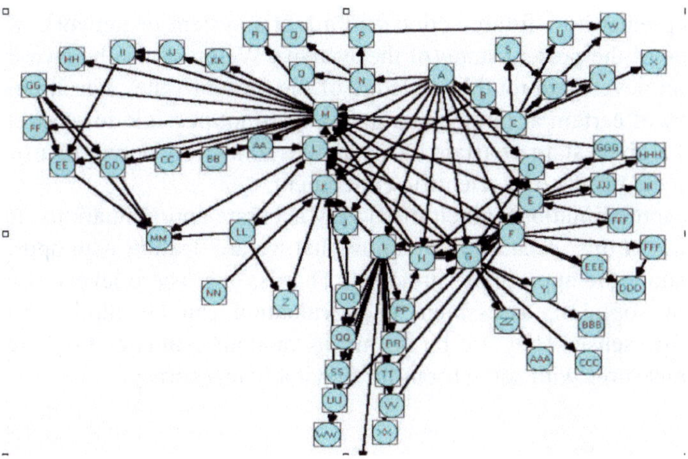

Fig. 5.7. A Complex Network of people Based on Co Offending Histories.

In this complex network we can identify the overall "whole" network and lots of "parts" or sub networks. If we decide that this network or parts of it, are a contributing factor or cause of instability within a geographical area we will be faced with the decision of deciding where our efforts should be concentrated. The decision about which elements to arrest will have inevitable consequences.

The following illustration shows the effect of removing only four elements key elements from the complex network; the network is beginning to fragment and certain elements are isolated. This may be the desired result and assist us in achieving our goals. What we must guard against is the way in which the isolated elements (called nodes in the illustration) may regroup or, how the remaining elements still connected will interact.

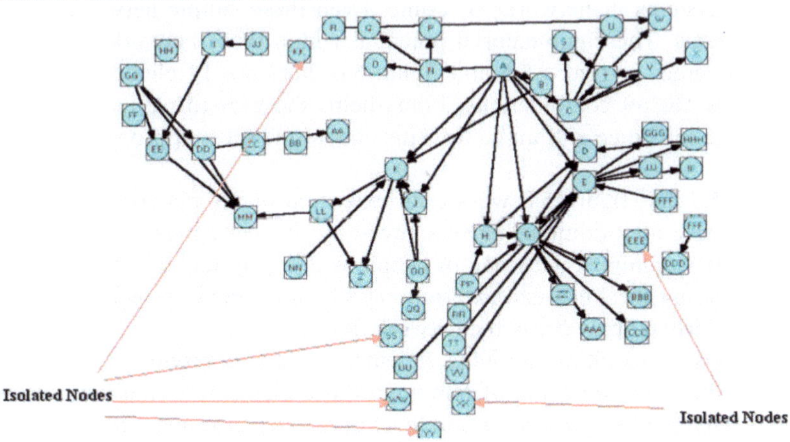

Fig. 5.8. Removing four nodes results in fragmentation – the network may adapt after those nodes are removed.

In order to predict how future action will affect a system or network we must gain knowledge of the present state (of the system). We must also be aware of the fact that we can never gain total knowledge of the present state, measurement always falls short of certain accuracy and, it simply is not possible to recover "everything" about a given state of affairs. This applies to a crime network, a financial market or even the results of a scientific experiment.

We deal in approximations, albeit often very accurate approximations. It is important to highlight this, because if we know that we are dealing with approximations we can adopt the appropriate mind set. That is, one where levels of estimation, judgement, opinion, assessment and evaluation can be applied but in a rational scientific sense. They are by no means random estimates they are fairly deterministic measures with some room for inevitable inaccuracy.

Prediction in complex police systems

Establishing present states, that is taking control of the systems we possess to find out what we currently know, allows us to find pathways and routes into the future and the making of predictions about we do not know but perhaps ought to know. Figure 5.5 illustrates a determined present state; we know those links exist because we have the evidence for them. Each element in the network had on previous occasions been arrested with other elements in the network. Having established that, we can set about predicting a future state of the network if we take particular types of action. In Figure 6 we see the resulting fragmentation of the network by the removal of certain elements.

In figure 5.5 and figure 5.6 we see some fairly simple examples of disrupting or fragmenting systems or networks of crime. Even these simple networks conceal complex patterns. The combinatorial potential within those networks in terms of prediction is large. In figure 5.5 and figure 5.6 there are 14 elements, in which case there are 16,369 combinations. Flints helps the user to navigate these networks, engage in choice and make decisions about the most appropriate action to take.

In figure 5.7 and figure 5.8 we see an extension of the network presented in figure 5.5. These are additional links sourced by the same means, FLINTS, and demonstrate how complex networks of people within a system can become. However, by analysing the links and determining which elements should be removed first, we can fairly quickly break the network down.

Figure 5.8 is the result of removing 7 elements and it represents a predictive assessment of the likely outcome of removing those elements. What we must also ask here is what the likely extent is and level of self-organisation will take place if we take that action. We might not want to force certain elements closer together by removing intermediate elements and furthermore, we might want to maintain a certain status quo whilst we engage in counter intelligence and insurgence activities.

If this was a shoplifting ring then our action might be less risky than if we were dealing with a drugs cartel across national boundaries. In any event, we know now that we have the ability to engage in predicting what the results of our activity or indeed inactivity might be. We can thus engage in informed choice – an important luxury for the decision maker. What we have engaged in here is modelling the current state of a network in order to find out the likely structure that would result if we interact with it. Present knowledge is transferred into future knowledge by assessing a range of possible outcomes or scientifically stated, a range of uncertainties. Remember, we need to assess the uncertainty of self-organisation after we act.

An interesting issue for discussion might be the impact that government performance indicators have on deployment policy and decisions staff in these kinds of scenario. If simplistic measures like the number of arrests, the number of detections, within given geographic areas over given time scales that might force decision makers to adopt arrest and detection options rather than solve overall problems. The study of complex systems reveals that simply going for the apparently most obvious solution, arresting those who may appear to be the most prolific offenders in the system, might not be the best course of action. It is not necessarily the same as adopting strategies to remove from the network the element most responsible for holding the structure together. Policing needs to understand that as Poincaré noted, what may appear on the surface to be apparently simple, might conceal a highly complex set of conditions and states beneath.

Conclusion

The need to seek out and identify critically important states within our systems is a key factor to our future. Our thinking must not be constrained by a willingness to accept a one strategy victory. Only a range of strategies will deliver the flexibility that the modern world needs and this requires a whole new set of metaphors and thinking. Police approaches, like many other disciplines and professions, have suffered from "silo" thinking. In police terms, this is a crime problem, that is a traffic problem, this a community affairs issue and so on. This serves only to restrict our capability to react to complexity and thwart chaos whenever it threatens.

Seeking to avoid unpredictable outcomes and maintaining control are the goals we will need to have. Simple linear or quantitative methods for assessing the state of affairs that pertains are useful but they have their limitations. If we can reduce the assessment to a simple count and assess the future on the basis of a direct relationship with the past then fine. However, the overriding message repeatedly experienced now is that our world, and hence the environment we operate in, is identifiable with complexity and complex systems. Simplicity and linearity are not underlying constants we can rely on and so we cannot accept the world as a fixed given. There may be phases that are fixed but complexity is quickly being identified as the overriding metaphor for our world. In such a complex environment we need flexible attributes and the ability to identify current states in order to predict the future states.

Flints is a system to help aid police decision making by being better able to cope with the complexity of the environment in which decisions are made. Because it has been designed to capture and monitor dynamic change within the system over time, Flints is itself a dynamic, complex system and the first such system to be used to aid policing in this way. The system engages in both linear and non-linear discovery and it employs both approaches in parallel allowing the user to gain speedily what is directly observable from the information then, just as importantly, observe what is indirectly observable from the information.

Rather than ignore the remnants of linear approaches, complexity and non-linearity, Flints acknowledges and harnesses them. This is important because what takes us by surprise is often the result of meeting face to face with something we had not contemplated; what we did not know. It is not unreasonable to suggest that we should engage the material of surprises.

Non-linear models produce surprises because the complex layers and associations of information within them conceal many of the hidden links. By accessing and tapping into these areas in which we can find surprises we gain new knowledge. Whilst linear systems do not present surprises, they are limited in the amount of new information or knowledge they can present. An important feature of the Flints system is the discovery of that which we do not know yet ought to know. If we can gain insights into information we need as well as information we have, we provide ourselves with many opportunities to further our goals. One goal may simply be learning what we know and another might be learning what we do not know.

References

Casti, J. (1994) Complexification. London: Abacus.

Section 2: Technologies for Strategic Intelligence Management

Chapter 6: Data Management Techniques for Criminal Investigations

Greg Mann

Abstract Good investigative practice should embody a consistent methodology. This methodology should emphasise accountability, standardized processes, and information sharing between investigations and agencies. It should also make use of appropriate tools to organise, manage, retrieve and analyse potentially large volumes of investigative data. However, an investigative methodology alone won't ensure that evidence is processed in a timely fashion. With greater amounts of data being available to investigators through public sources and data sharing initiatives, and improvements being made to data capture/entry facilities, bottlenecks may occur in the review of investigative data, potentially jeopardizing a successful outcome. Technologies such as text analysis, entity matching and resolution, and network analysis can be inserted into the investigative workflow to speed data processing, prioritise tasks, and facilitate search and analysis.

Introduction

The need to overcome the barriers that hinder data sharing between law enforcement agencies and to develop minimum standards for the management of intelligence and investigative functions received significant attention in the years following the 2001 New York attacks.

In the US, publications like the National Criminal Intelligence Sharing Plan[11] and the Fusion Center Guidelines[12] promoted a range of recommendations that focused on the leveraging of databases and systems to maximize information sharing, adopting common data representation and communication standards, and utilising a variety of intelligence products and technologies to help identify, prevent, investigate, and respond to terrorist and criminal activities.

---

[11] The National Criminal Intelligence Sharing Plan (2003) U.S. Department of Justice, http://www.fas.org/irp/agency/doj/ncisp.pdf

[12] Fusion Center Guidelines (2005), U.S. Department of Justice (DOJ) and the U.S. Department of Homeland Security. http://www.fas.org/irp/agency/ise/guidelines.pdf

While such plans and guidelines sought to increase the efficiency and scope of information and intelligence exchange, many of these functions (and their associated challenges) had been identified and implemented in the law enforcement domain for many years. Xanalys Ltd, a UK based software company, has been involved in the design, development and deployment of intelligence and investigative management solutions since the late 1980s. Its PowerCase Investigative Case Management system was developed to implement and support a standard process used by the UK Police Service for investigations into serial and serious crime. In this chapter, we will look at how technology has been used in PowerCase to build efficiencies into the investigative process, and to facilitate data sharing and intelligence capabilities.

The Bernardo Enquiry – Ontario Canada

In 1995, Paul Bernardo was convicted, declared a dangerous offender, and sentenced to an indefinite period of imprisonment for the sexual assault of up to eighteen women, and murder of three women between 1987 to 1992 in Ontario, Canada.

The Honourable Mr. Justice Archie G. Campbell was subsequently commissioned to conduct a judicial inquiry to review and report on the roles of the police and other agencies which ultimately led to charges being applied to Bernardo. Justice Campbell's final report[13] identified a number of systemic failures within the law enforcement and justice system. Amongst a set of twenty-seven recommendations, he called for greater cooperation and the sharing of data amongst different law enforcement agencies, and a "single uniform computerized case management system for the mandatory use in all serial predator investigations and all major sexual assault and homicide cases".

In response to this recommendation, the Solicitor General of Ontario adopted PowerCase, an Investigative Management system developed by Xanalys Ltd which possessed the following functionality identified by Justice Campbell:

- Recording, organisation, management, analysis and follow up of investigative data
- Ensuring all relevant information sources are applied to the investigation
- Encouraging and supporting the sharing of data across agencies
- Early recognition of linked incidents
- A "triggering" capability to alert users of commonalities in newly acquired data
- Standardised procedures and investigative methodology.

---

[13] Campbell, The Honourable Mr. Justice Archie G. 1996. "Bernardo Investigation Review". Report presented to the Solicitor General and Minister of Correctional Services, Province of Ontario, June 27, 1996.

The centralised PowerCase system was made available to all police services across the province in 2002[14] [4] and three years later, Ontario Provincial Legislation mandated the use of the new major case investigation and information sharing process, naming PowerCase as the technology that would be used to support the initiative. According to the legislation, investigators working on all major case investigations conducted within the Province of Ontario would be required to share information across jurisdictional boundaries.

While the concept of major or designated cases focuses on sexual crime and homicide, Ontario law enforcement agencies have also benefited from deploying PowerCase on organised crime and counter terrorism investigations. These can be extremely complex in nature and may extend over many months or years. Some of the characteristics of these case types include:

- A number of concurrent, related investigations
- A significant intelligence component focusing on special interest groups (including foreign organisations), hate crime/extremism, drugs, weapons & firearms, incorporation of open source intelligence
- Require frequent production of briefs, media releases, or information requests under Freedom Of Information legislation
- Regular identification of linked incidents
- Multi-tiered management/command post teams
- Large numbers of multimedia files to record and manage
- Telephone toll data analysis

PowerCase

Xanalys PowerCase supports a defined set of procedures that should operate in an "incident room" or "case office". These procedures were ascertained through a detailed requirements capture process and have been chiefly influenced by the Home Office Procedures in the UK. Although these procedures originate in the UK they are widely accepted in the law enforcement community as being representative of best practice. It is interesting to note that PowerCase as a product is as much a ready-made methodology as it is a software application.

To review and understand the technologies employed in this case management environment, it is useful to first understand some aspects of these procedures. The primary sources of information to the investigation are documents. These are usually unstructured text such as statements, intelligence reports, tips/messages, etc. but increasingly structured and semi-structured data is collected during an investigation – email, telephone call records, federated search results, etc. Documents are

---

[14] Tout, Sean and Healey Mark (2005) PowerCase as Electronic Evidence in the Courtroom: Waterloo Regional Police Service's Innovative Use of Case Management Software; The Canadian Journal of Police & Security Services Vol 3 Issue 2, Summer 2005

processed through a standardised workflow (which is also integrated with a Role based security model). Documents enter the system via a number of different paths:

- Documents can be typed or imported directly into the PowerCase environment
- "Off-line" document forms can be uploaded or pushed into the system via a web service
- Documents can be submitted through an integrated justice layer which pushes data into PowerCase via other applications (crime or intelligence systems).

Once documents enter the system they become part of the investigation management workflow:

1. Documents are registered on the system, alerting the investigative team of the availability of the new information, and also associating the document to the author – the automated referencing of documents back to its source is an important principal in PowerCase.
2. The details of the document (name, address, phone number, email), together with the text are entered into the system. This Indexing process is facilitated by a number of text analysis, data matching, and knowledge representation technologies which will be discussed below. Again, the system automatically links all derived data back to the source. This supports not only the obvious benefits of providing complete data provenance, but also an analytical function, making it possible to ask detailed questions such as "Who knew that X was associated with Y?" and be directed to each document that supports such an association.
3. The document is reviewed to determine whether any actions arise from the document content. When created, the new Action is automatically linked to the source document and the object(s) of the action (e.g. a person, place, vehicle, etc.).
4. Actions are allocated to members of the investigative team who then undertake that particular line of enquiry.
5. On completion, the results of the action are recorded in the system. Any new documents are registered and linked to the originating action, thus preserving the provenance of all information.

The entire process is quite a simple cycle: register a document, enter its details, index it, raise an action, the results of actions give rise to new documents – and so the cycle continues. It is clear that following such a process in too simplistic a fashion would give rise to an explosion of administrative activities that would divert the investigative team from its primary function. To ensure the teams goal is "intelligence gathering" rather than "blind data gathering", text analysis technologies, entity matching and resolution, and network analysis can be inserted into the investigative workflow to speed data processing, prioritise tasks, and facilitate search and analysis. In addition, the workflow should be flexible enough to allow the Case Manager to make decisions on what work needs to be carried out, and when.

Indexing

Indexing is defined as the process of extracting information from either the text of a document or associated structured details, and constructing an entity relationship model of this content. This process provides a richer representation of the state of the case knowledge that promotes analytical activities like social network analysis. PowerCase supports both manual and automated indexing.

Manual indexing is extremely labour intensive; so for this reason, an automated natural language processing facility called PowerIndexer is employed to automatically parse the main text component of documents, extracting entities and their attribute values. This automated entity extraction can be customized for particular domains via:

- Grammar: This is represented by a set of grammar rules that essentially define the structure of the phrases and sentences that are to be recognised.
- Lexicon: This is essentially a collection of word lists, which combined with the grammar rules determine what can be recognised.
- A Custom File: Elements of the Grammar and Lexicon can be enable/disabled through directives held in the custom file.

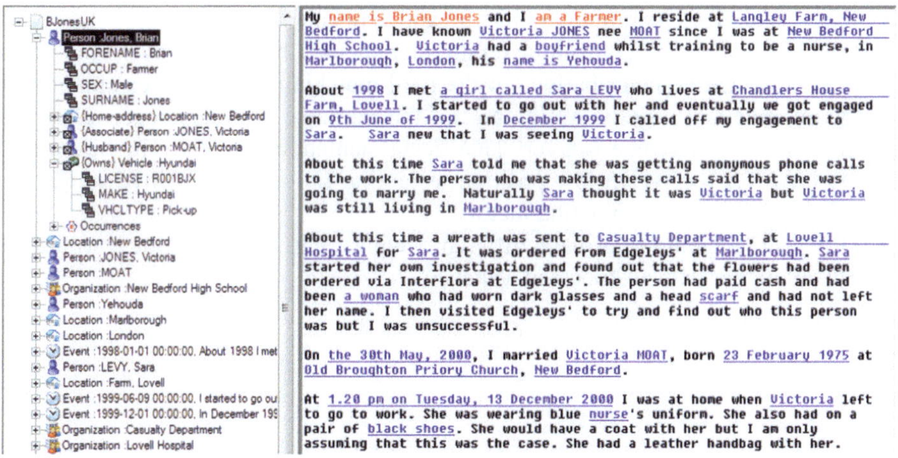

Fig. 6.1 Extracted data displayed in an Index Plan alongside the source text.

A feedback loop is also implemented to enable an element of learning in the system. As more records are added to the database, these are included in the PowerIndexing process on new documents, and in so doing improve the recognition accuracy. The output of the PowerIndexing process is presented to the user as an Index Plan (figure 6.1), a list of entities, attribute values, and cross references that define associations between entities.

Research

As entities and cross-references (i.e. links or associations) are added to the investigative database, an import aspect of this indexing process is the avoidance of duplicate records.

Research is a process of taking an object and its extracted attribute values and examining the database to see whether similar records already exist. While Research is designed to essentially be a one-click operation, it involves a number of distinct steps:

1. The attribute values of the Researched object are used to automatically populate a research query.
2. A database query is automatically generated and run against the database
3. A list of hits is scored, ranked and presented to the user, who can then either consolidate the new data into an existing entity or create an entirely new record (figure 6.2).

There are a range of research strategies that are used to calculate the ranking:

- Attributes may be grouped and matched together e.g. different Forenames are grouped for cross searching
- Attributes may be matched to varying degrees of accuracy using rules such as Exact, Soundex, Stemming, Synonym, and Truncated Match.
- Matching rules may confirm or refute the matching hypothesis by giving positive and negative contributions to the total matching score. For example both the positive and negative weighting for the Surname of a person are relatively high since the surname is a very significant element of a query. The Sex attribute however receives a low positive weighting but a high negative weighting since it is a strong eliminating factor.
- Different matching rules have different weights, e.g. an Exact Match would be ranked higher than a Truncated Match.

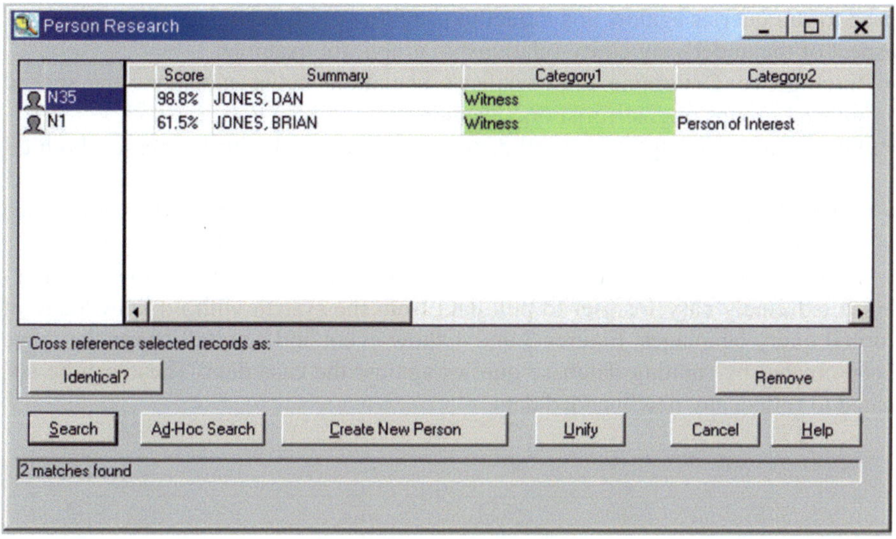

Fig. 6.2 Research results for the Nominal "Daniel Jones, Male"

All in all, Research is an extremely powerful facility that not only ensures a high level of data integrity (i.e. keeps duplicates to a minimum), but also highlights to the user potential matches and patterns within the incident.

Data representation – entity/relationship

The PowerCase data model is designed to allow the investigator to take unstructured textual information and by a process of indexing and analysis build a sophisticated network model of the actors and events representing the contents of those documents. At the same time the data model maintains a complete provenance chain so that an investigator can immediately track back to find the supporting evidence from which the model was built. This process of building richer representations of the data from source documents whilst keeping those source documents immediately accessible is key to the methodology required to successfully analyse a complex case.

Network analysis

With the entire investigative data set represented as an entity-relationship model, it can be exploited with query and visualisation tools. Xanalys Link Explorer is a network analysis tool that is integrated with the PowerCase system and can be used to run queries against this model to provide visualisation and analysis on any aspect of the underlying entity-relationship graph, for example:

- Intelligence: Determine and visualise associations between persons and special interest groups (e.g. terrorist organisations)
- Disclosure: Quickly identify all documents associated with Witnesses, both civilian and Officers
- Audit: Use the data-mining facility to interactively trace back the provenance of certain evidence, or reveal a timeline on user activity within the system.

Link Explorer supports the building of parameterised and ad-hoc queries, making it extremely easy for user to pull data from the system with no knowledge of formal query languages. Figures 3 and 4 show event and network charts that have been created by running database queries against the case data. These can be updated to reflect any newly added data.

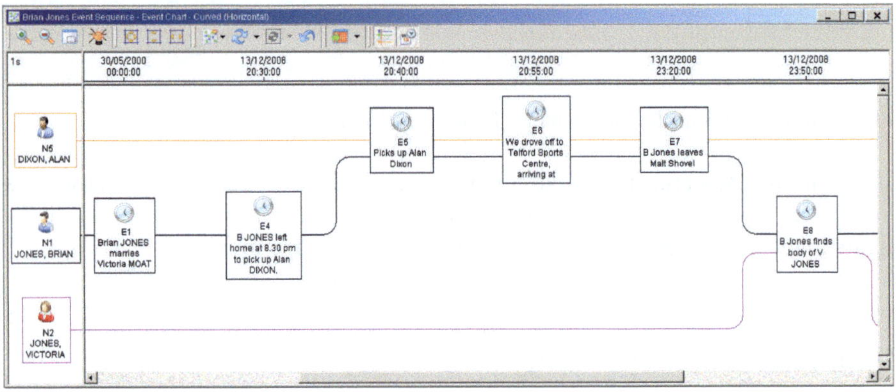

Fig. 6.3 Sequence of events chart

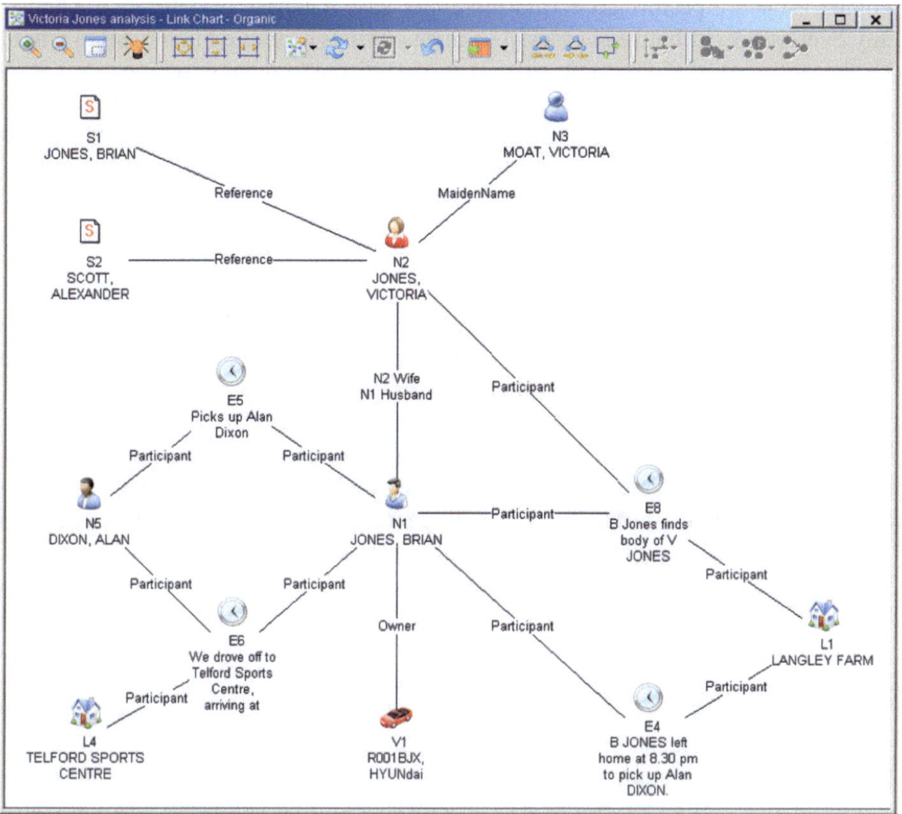

Fig. 6.4 Link chart displaying both source records (S1 and S2) and derived objects.

Triggering

A central finding of Justice Campbell's review was that serial predators often commit their crimes across a wide geographical area and that with limited sharing of data between agencies, individual investigations had limited ways of identifying linkages between incidents.

While the PowerCase architecture provides a central data store, individual agencies still control their case data and may not choose to expose case evidence to other agencies. Of course, agencies should maintain ultimate control over their data, but it is important that this does not result in the well-documented intelligence gaps created by data silos. To maximise the intelligence function across all cases, but still support data ownership and security requirements, the Ontario PowerCase installation implemented a Triggering facility whereby incremental comparisons are performed across the entire case database to determine whether any overlaps occur between cases. The most obvious example of an overlap would be the occurrence of the same suspect in two distinct (agency, region, etc.) incidents – but the solution can look for matches between any type of entity (e.g. vehicle, location, telephone, email address). Matches are flagged to the data owners who can then collaborate to conduct further analysis on the match.

Case linking

Once a linked series of cases are identified, it is important that these can be grouped and managed – a single picture of the criminal context may produce new evidence or lines of enquiry.

This scenario may occur when an agency intentionally creates a number of distinct teams to investigate a large and complex incident, and later decide that they need to unify their efforts, or when a Triggering notification alerts two agencies that they are working on the same or related incidents. In these types of scenarios, support is required to link two or more cases together as if they were one, whilst maintaining each independently as separate cases. This relationship is not necessarily symmetrical, as an agency may not want to share their sensitive data (e.g. informant details), with the owners of the other linked cases.

From an intelligence perspective, case linking provides a convergence of the underlying data graphs, providing a single picture or view of the cases. The system continues to maintain and manage each of the case graphs separately so that at any future time, if a case owner removes their case from the group, the associated data can be easily unhooked.

Current research

Pre-analytics

Not all information that is acquired by an investigative team requires detailed processing and analysis. For example, alongside the Intelligence Reports, Statements, Tips, etc., investigators will also wish to capture legal documents, investigation plans, expense details and other documents that while not evidentiary in nature, can provide crucial investigative audit and sequencing information. Users can elect to by-pass most of the document workflow discussed above to make the capture of this data as efficient as possible.

However, if a document potentially contains information that is crucial to the direction and outcome of the investigation, it is important that it is moved through the document workflow as quickly as possible. Obviously, a sudden influx of data may cause significant issues for the investigative team. In criminal investigations, a flood of tips received from the public or the results of a door-to-door canvass may produce thousands of documents over a short time period, resulting in boxes of documents sitting on the floor of the incident room, waiting to be input. This type of problem is likely to grow with the ever-increasing amounts of public data available via the Internet. With the efficiencies of data entry now available, the documents may now be sitting in a database rather than a paper format, but apart from free text search, the utility of this data is still low until processed – free text search is only useful if you know what you are looking for.

In a 2009 project funded by the UK's Technology Strategy Board, Xanalys and its partner, Sheffield Hallam University looked at how documents could undergo a stage of automated analysis when entering the Case Management environment.

The solution was composed of three core components:

1. Document analysis that extracted entities, attributes and relationships from the document set
2. A set of rules and techniques that determined the relevance of a document to the current state of the investigation. These included matches to existing known entities, (e.g. Persons marked as "suspects" or "persons of interest", identifying marks or clothing, M.O. , locations within a certain proximity) and matches across newly acquired data (i.e. we may not currently know of this person, but he/she has been mentioned by the public on more than one occasion)
3. A method of calculating a "score" based on the nature of the document content and the degree to which this content was connected to existing and new data.
4. Novel data visualisation techniques that provide users with rapid insight into the document content and its relationships to existing and newly acquired data.

Together, these techniques would deliver a ranked or prioritised list of new documentary evidence that would allow the investigative team to focus their resources on those documents which potentially containing the information of most relevance to the investigation. Figure 6.5 shows the visualisation technique used to provide a high-level overview of any particular document.

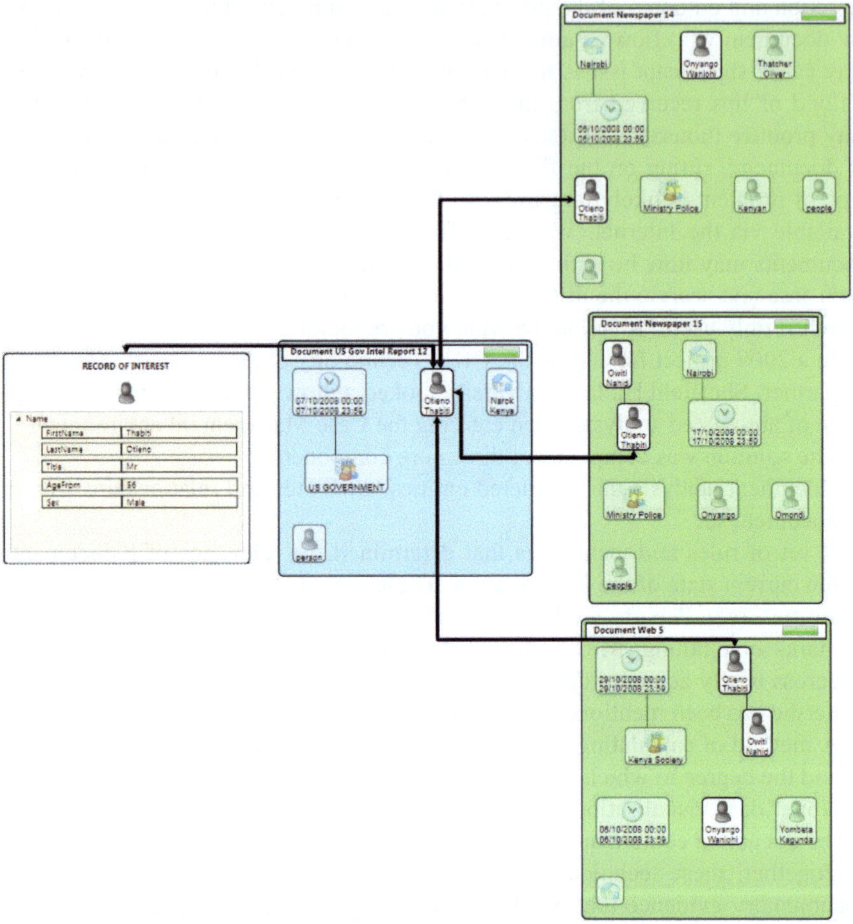

Fig. 6.5 Visualisation of document relationships.

The central blue rectangle represents the selected document – within it are the entities that have been automatically identified within the document. The green rectangles represent other newly acquired documents that are also yet to enter the formal document workflow. The white box represents an entity already within the incident database that has been marked as a "Person of Interest". Finally, the lines show matches between the different sources.

Looking at this visualisation, the user can quickly make decisions about the importance of the document and whether it requires closer review and analysis. Xanalys and SHU are currently looking at incorporating new technologies into this process that will broaden the extraction of data (e.g. concept and phrase tagging), speed up the identification of patterns (Formal Concept Analysis) and scale the solution to larger data sets. This pre-analytic stage fits in well with the existing

PowerCase interface, as users process outstanding Tasks (i.e. a stage in the workflow for any particular document) via a simple list interface. With the addition of a column holding the document "score", users could sort these lists and review and analyse those documents that may contribute most to promising new lines of enquiry.

Graph building

By representing all case data in an entity-relationship data model, users can perform a range of powerful analytical functions which allow them to investigate the deep relationships within their source data. Whilst this is a useful end in itself, experienced analysts know that it is important that they can build and test multiple hypotheses within the framework of their data, without irreversibly committing everyone to those interpretations.

Xanalys are developing a data model and framework to support graph building features such as add/delete/merge operations on graph nodes and links. These operations will not involve "hard" changes to the database (i.e. no original data in the graph is lost) and can be easily reversed. The data model extensions will support a "what-if" [5] style of analysis, providing analysts with an environment in which they can:

- Perform a virtual unification of two or more person entities that may actually represent the same Person
- Look at the effect on a network if a particular node or link is removed, i.e. disruptive analysis
- Insert a link between two entities to examine the impact on two sub-graphs, e.g. does the existence of such a link support observations in the real world?

Conclusion

An Investigative Case Management system should support an effective methodology across processes such as team management, the prioritisation and tracking of leads and lines of enquiry, the secure storage and management of documents and physical evidence, search and retrieval of data, and reporting/brief production.

However, an investigative methodology won't alone ensure a successful case outcome. With increasing amounts of data being collected during criminal cases, bottlenecks in data processing can pose a threat to the efficient use of human resources and lead to important information slipping through the gaps.[15]

[15] Heuer R.J. Jr & Pherson, R.H. (2010) Structured Analytic Techniques for Intelligence Analysis, CQ Press.

Technologies such as text analytics, entity matching and resolution, net-work analysis and data visualisation have been demonstrated to have a significant impact at different parts of the investigative workflow, helping users to understand and consolidate incoming data, generate intelligence that determines the future direction of the case, and create efficiencies through informed decision making regarding resource allocation.

Chapter 7: Fast 3D Recognition for Forensics and Counter-Terrorism Applications

Marcos A Rodrigues and Alan Robinson

Abstract The development of advanced techniques for fast 3D reconstruction and recognition of human faces in unconstrained scenarios can significantly help the fight against crime and terrorism. We describe a 3D solution developed within Sheffield Hallam University that satisfies a number of important requirements such as operating close to real-time, high accuracy in recognition rates and robust to local illumination. Experimental results in 3D face recognition are reported and two scenarios are provided that can be used to exploit the outcomes of this research for forensic analysis and for flagging potential threats in counter-terrorism.

Introduction

Some essential security requirements to societies across the world include the need to manage heterogeneous sources of data and perform advanced recognition and reasoning techniques in real-time to detect complex abnormal behaviour and potential security threats. At Sheffield Hallam University we have focused on 3D modelling and recognition techniques together with associated hardware development that can be applied in a real-time security scenario. The proposed concept of 3D CCTV is forward looking into technological needs for increased recognition rates. It lends itself to the integration of existing 2D databases and standard CCTV data with unique generation and manipulation of 3D footage. It has the potential to greatly improve the effectiveness of CCTV gathering, as it will make it possible to recover 3D information from video sequences in a novel and effective way.

We have been developing and patenting unique methods of acquiring 3D models using uncoded or lightly-coded structured light scanning – each model being recorded within one single video frame (40ms). The structured light principle is well known: project a pattern of light onto the target surface, and record the deformed pattern in a camera with a known spatial relationship to the projector. We have developed structured light systems for modelling faces and many other surfaces in industrial and medical applications [1—7].

The advantages of structured light scanning over stereo vision methods are numerous for instance: 1) the computationally intensive Correspondence Problem is avoided as only one image is used and the problem is then shifted towards the less computational intensive stripe indexing problem, 2) there is an explicit connected graph that makes surface reconstruction straightforward, 3) the density of the data can be controlled in the pattern design, and 4) smoothly undulating, featureless surfaces can be easily measured and this is not the case with stereo vision. The key disadvantage of structured light methods is that as the distance between projector, target and camera become greater, the light intensity reaching the camera becomes weaker. This means that it may be difficult to discriminate a dense light pattern, especially if a colour-coding scheme is used.

In order to realize non-intrusive 3D CCTV we developed techniques to project patterns of stripes in the NIR (near infrared) spectrum, which are invisible to the naked eye. The technique involves placing a NIR projector and two cameras in a known geometric relationship. One camera operates in the visible spectrum collecting standard CCTV footage, while the other camera operates in NIR providing means to recover the 3D structure of any desired frame or sequence of frames. Both visible and NIR spectrum cameras continuously save to disk. The difference between the two sets of data is that the visible spectrum camera contains normal texture of objects in the world, while the NIR camera images are illuminated by a NIR pattern of stripes as shown in figure 7.1.

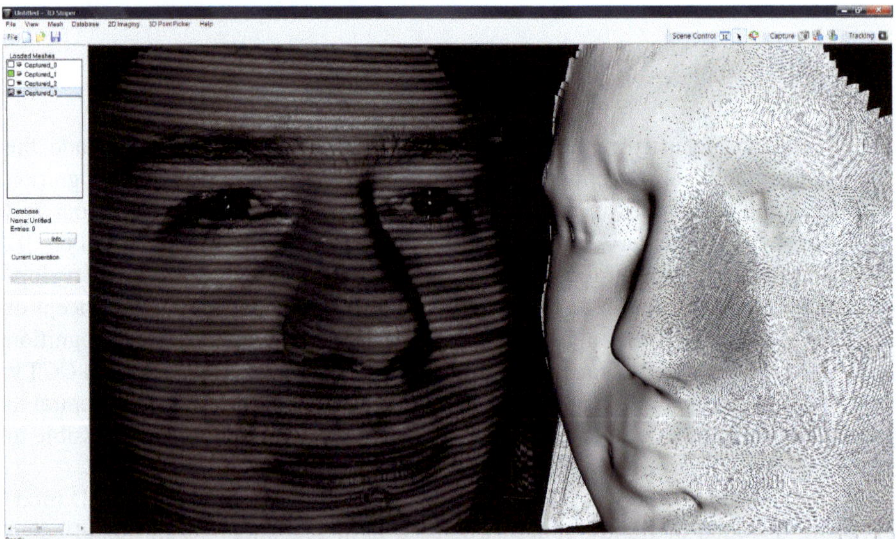

Fig. 7.1 Left, an example 3D model with NIR stripes on, right, wire mesh 3D model.

The way the 3D CCTV concept operates on human faces is highlighted as follows. A set of face detection and eye tracking routines have been implemented [7] which operate on the visible spectrum camera. As soon as a face is detected that satisfies predefined conditions (width and height larger than a minimum number of pixels) the projector stripes are switched on and an NIR image is taken. Both images are saved to disk, the NIR contains stripe information that allows 3D reconstruction in real time (i.e. within a video frame of 40ms) and the visible spectrum image contains texture information that can be overlaid onto the 3D model.

Steps in 3D face reconstruction and recognition

Concerning general research in 3D face recognition, the availability of 3D models and the format in which they are presented are not convenient for research aiming at fast recognition rates. While the Face Recognition Grand Challenge FRGC [8] has allowed the wider research community to test recognition algorithms from standard 2D and 3D databases, a severe limitation is that it was not designed to cater for real-time requirements. The FRGC database is standardized such that an application can load pre-formatted data for feature extraction and recognition. 3D data were reconstructed from human subjects taken from a frontal, but arbitrary view point and, given that these are large files containing the structure of the vertices in 3D, this rules out the possibility of testing algorithms in a real-time scenario. Therefore, while 3D data were profitably used to test recognition algorithms in the FRGC, the process does not represent a natural way in which 3D facial recognition systems are to be deployed. The 3D CCTV concept described here provides a contribution towards solving real-time issues in 3D face recognition.

There are prescribed steps that need to be performed in order to achieve fully automatic 3D face recognition based on vision systems:

- 2D tracking and filtering: face and eye tracking; image filtering; image correspondence (stereo) or projection pattern detection (structured light methods)
- 3D reconstruction and post-processing: generation of 3D point cloud and mesh triangulation; noise removal; 3D hole filling; mesh smoothing (optional); mesh subdivision (optional); pose normalization; feature extraction
- Enrolment and recognition: features are enrolled in a database for subsequent identification (one-to-many) or verification (one-to-one) recognition using appropriate algorithms

These steps are described in the following sections.

2D tracking and filtering

We use OpenCV face and eye tracking routines developed by Intel's Microcomputer Research Lab [9], which proved to be consistent and reliable provided that a number of constraints are specified. The general problem with such detection techniques is the number of false positives. For instance, on any image there could be various detected faces and some might not be real faces. The same problem happens with eye detection; the routines normally detect more eyes than there are in the scene. In order to solve this problem a number of constraints are defined: first, there should be only one face detected in the image and the face width must be larger than a certain threshold (300 pixels in our case); second, there should be only one left and only one right eye detected in the image, and these must be within the region of interest set by the face detection; third, the position of the face and eyes must not have moved more than a set threshold since last detection (10 pixels in our case) so to avoid inconsistent shots caused by rapid motion.

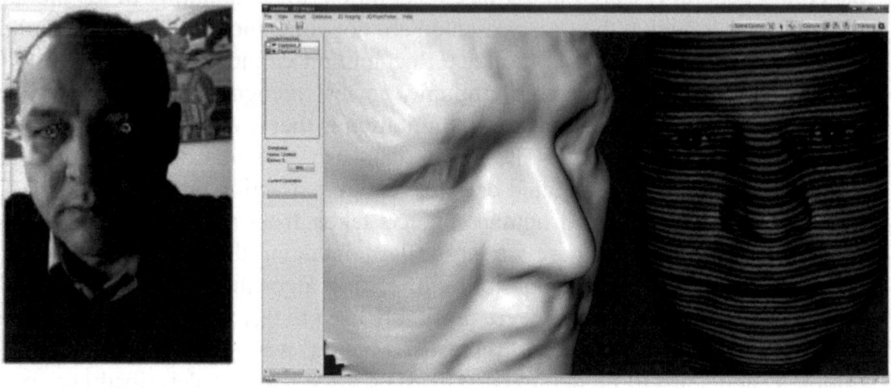

Fig. 7.2 Left, eye tracking in 2D using the visible spectrum camera. Right, a striped NIR image is taken and converted into 3D.

Figure 7.2 shows the visible spectrum camera continuously tracking and detecting (possibly multiple) faces and eyes, but only when the above conditions are satisfied a shot is taken. In this way, the system is apparently idle until someone places their face in front of the camera. When face and eyes are positively identified a near-infrared line pattern is projected onto the subject and a shot is taken and reconstructed in 3D as shown in the right of figure 7.2.

The next step in the process is to apply 2D image filters on the image that contains the stripe patterns namely a median filter followed by a weighted mean filter. This enables the detection of the stripe patterns in the image. Given that we know the geometry of the camera and projector, by knowing the stripe indices we can now fully reconstruct in 3D by trigonometry. While 3D models are shown in figures 7.1 and 7.2, details of the process have been published in [10].

3D reconstruction and post-processing

3D reconstruction is achieved by mapping the image space to system space (camera + projector) in a Cartesian coordinate system. We have developed a number of successful algorithms to deal with the mapping as described in [2, 10]. Once this mapping is achieved, a 3D point cloud is calculated and the output is triangulated using the connectivity of the vertices.

Once the surface shape has been modelled as a polygonal mesh, a number of 3D post-processing operations are required: hole filling, mesh subdivision, smoothing, and noise removal. There are several techniques that can be used to fill in gaps in the mesh such as the ones discussed in [11, 12, and 13]. From the techniques we considered, we tend to focus on three methods namely bilinear interpolation, Laplace, and polynomial interpolation. We found that the most efficient method for real-time operation is bilinear interpolation [14].

The next step is mesh subdivision that, depending on the recognition algorithm to be used may or may not be required. Our research indicates that mesh subdivision is strongly advisable. The reason is that we sample the mesh for recognition where the boundaries of the data are set based on vertex positions so increasing the density of the mesh will provide more accurate sample boundaries. We use a polynomial interpolation of degree 4 across the stripe patterns and this increases the mesh density while making features more discernible. This is demonstrated in figure 7.3, where in the subdivided mesh the region around the eyes and lips are better delineated.

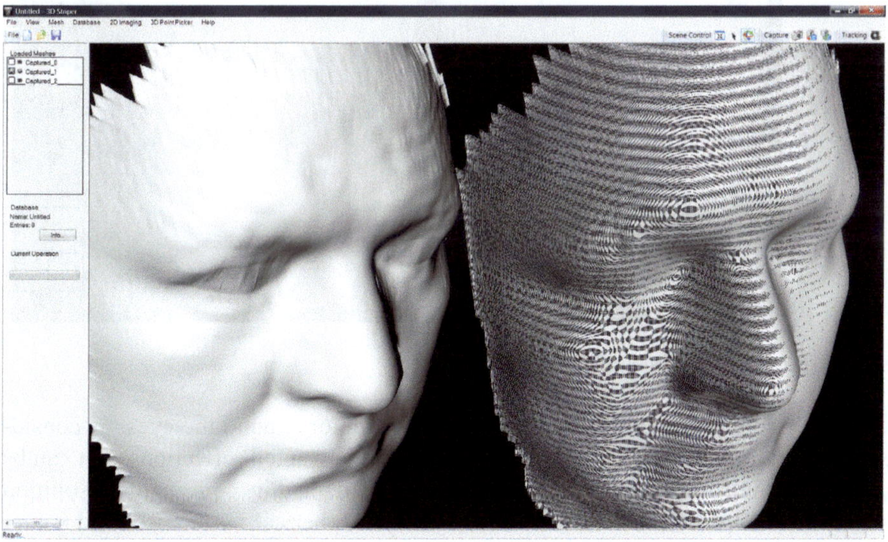

Fig. 7.3 Post-processing showing a sub-divided mesh (left) and non-subdivided (right)

We use two smoothing techniques namely moving average and Gaussian smoothing. Moving average is performed through cycling across and then along the stripes. The average of every three points is estimated and the middle point is replaced by the average. In this way the boundary vertices remain anchored. Gaussian smoothing is iteratively estimated by considering 8 neighbours for each vertex. A convolution mask of size 3x3 is applied and the centre vertex is perturbed depending on the values of its neighbours. The difference between each neighbour and the centre vertex is recorded and averaged as ΔV. A multiplier factor is provided (L) which determines how much of this average should be used to correct the value of the centre vertex; i.e., it defines the momentum of the error correction. We use L=0.9 and the number of iterations is set to maximum 35. In each iteration cycle i, the centre vertex V is corrected by Vi = Vi-1 + LΔV. The effects of smoothing are depicted in figure 7.4. It could be argued that smoothing has the effect to remove features from the model, such as the area around the lips is more pronounced in the non-smoothed model. However, non-smooth meshes can have severe spikes that impair recognition. From our experiments, we conclude that the best sequence for smoothing operations are Gaussian smoothing followed by a moving average.

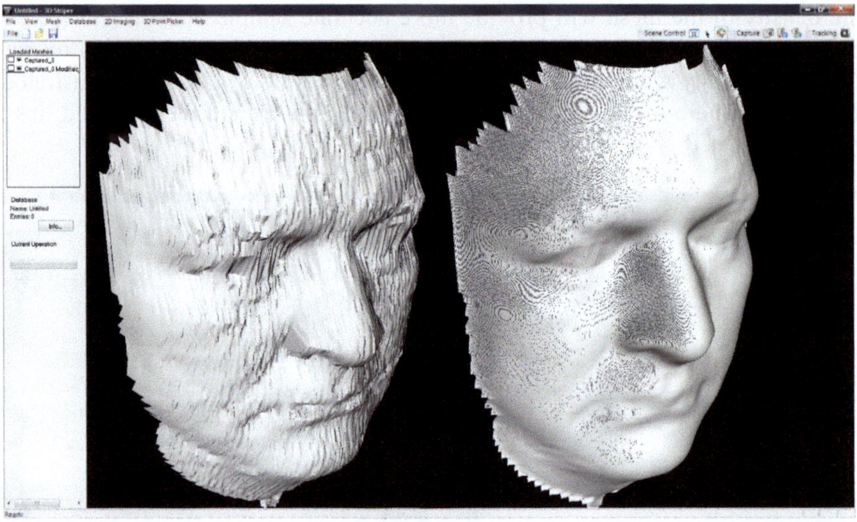

Fig. 7.4. The effects of smoothing.

Noise removal is mainly concerned with the region around the eyes, as considerable amount of noise exist due to eyelashes and unwanted reflections as it can be seen from the raw unsmoothed model on the left on Fig 4. A natural solution would be to replace the vertices in the eye by a spherical surface centred somewhere behind the face model. By experimentation, we chose the centre of the sphere at a position 40mm behind the face model in the same Z-axis as the centre of each eye. An elliptical mask is marked centred on each eye, and all vertices within the elliptical surface have their values replaced by their spherical counterparts. This however, resulted in unnatural looking models. A second solution, which is conceptually simpler, is to punch an elliptical hole centred at each eye and then fill in the holes with bilinear interpolation. This has proved to work well for the face models and it is the solution that is adopted here.

Pose normalization and sampling

All 3D models need to be brought to a standard pose to allow consistent recognition. We have chosen a standard pose depicted in figure 7.5 where the origin is placed at the tip of the nose. In this pose, the X-axis is aligned with the horizontal position of the eyes; the Y-axis forms a constant angle of $\pi/10$ with a point located on the front between the two eyes, and the Z-axis points away from the model such that all depths are negative.

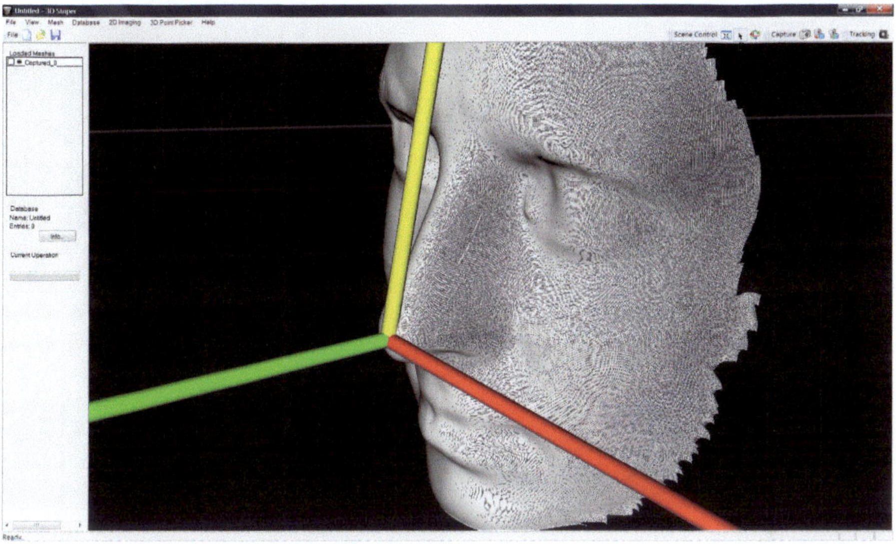

Fig. 7.5. The standard pose with the origin at the tip of the nose

The algorithm to achieve this standard pose is described as follows [1] (given that we know the position of the eyes (E1 and E2) in 3D:

1. Estimate the angle ß1 in the XY-plane between E1 and E2
2. Centred on E1 rotate the mesh around the Z-axis by angle ß1: Rot(z, ß1)
3. Estimate the angle ß2 in the YZ-plane between E1 and E2
4. Centred on E1 rotate the mesh around the Y-axis by angle ß2: Rot(y, ß2)
5. Find the intersection point on the mesh (above the eyes, on the front) of the arcs centred on E1 and E2 with radius 0.75 of the inter-ocular distance. Mark this point as F
6. Find the tip of the nose. This is defined as the highest point on the mesh below eye positions within a search threshold of one inter-ocular distance. Mark this point as T
7. Estimate the angle ß3 described by F, T, and the Y-axis
8. Centred on T, rotate the mesh around the X-axis by (π /10 — ß3): Rot(x, π /10 — ß3)

9. After this rotation, the highest point on the mesh defining T might have slightly changed. Repeat steps 6, 7 and 8 until (π /10 — ß3) is below a set threshold.

900 points are sampled for recognition defined within the boundaries of four planes: two horizontal planes (top and bottom) and two vertical planes (left and right) set the limits for sampling the 3D structure. All calculations are performed in 3D and the sampled points form the feature vector that uniquely characterizes a face and it is used for recognition. Figure 7.6 shows a face structure together with the sampled points.

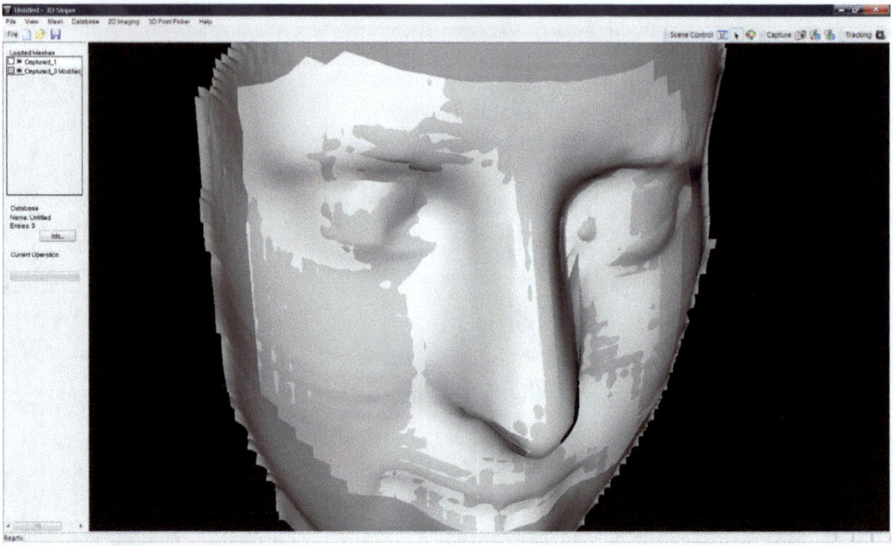

Fig. 7.6. Sampled data points from the face are marked lighter.

The delimiting planes for sampling (top, bottom, left, right) are defined as:

- ∏Top: parallel to XZ-plane at point (0, 1.3(E2 — E1), 0)
- ∏Bottom: parallel to XZ-plane at point (0, -0.66(E2 — E1), 0)
- ∏Left: parallel to YZ-plane at point (-(E2 — E1), 0, 0)
- ∏Right: parallel to YZ-plane at point ((E2 — E1), 0, 0)

Enrolment and recognition

3D recognition algorithms based on eigenvector decomposition [14] were tested on a 3D database where 300 models were used as follows. First 100 subjects were enrolled in the database. Then a second (unseen) model of each person was used for testing identification and set the threshold for verification allowing the lowest possible FAR (false acceptance rate). Figure 7.7 shows an example of output recognition: the image on the left is the unknown face and the image on the right is the closest in the database found by the algorithm. A distance measure of 32 is indicated, and these measures are used to estimate the correct threshold for minimum FAR.

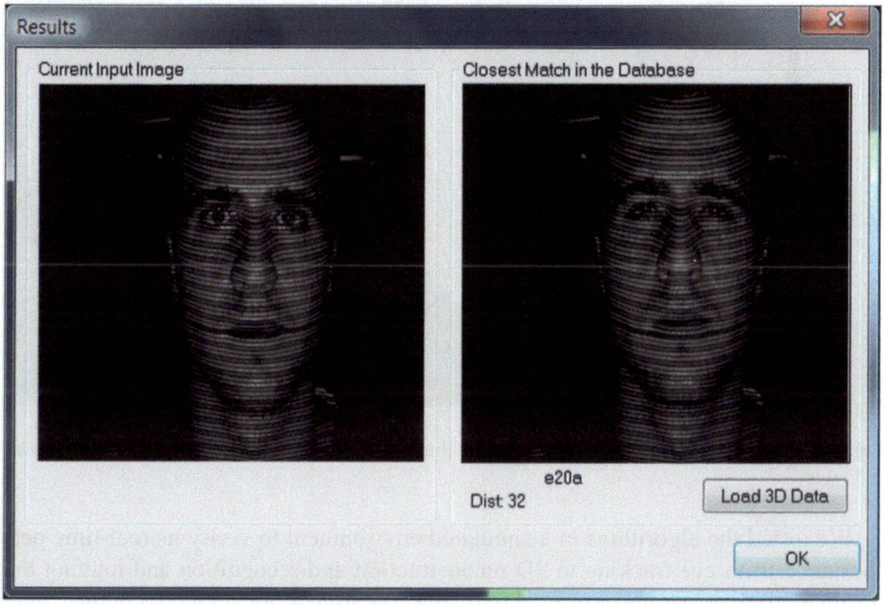

Fig. 7.7. Example of recognition showing the closest match and a distance measure

Figure 7.8 is the 3D counterpart to Figure 7.7: here the 3D models generated and used by the recognition algorithm are shown. The model on the right was used for enrolment and the model on the left is the unknown model.

The recognition results for the 100 unseen models was100%, that is, the algorithm always retrieved the correct identity for the closest match. Upon studying the distance measures obtained by the one-to-many identification it was noted that no distance was greater than 50. In order to set the correct threshold for minimum FAR, we then tested the database with models that were not enrolled in the database. It is expected that the closest match to these models (there is always a closest match) would have a distance larger than 50. In fact, this was verified and the system has proved to work with no FAR if the threshold was set to 50.

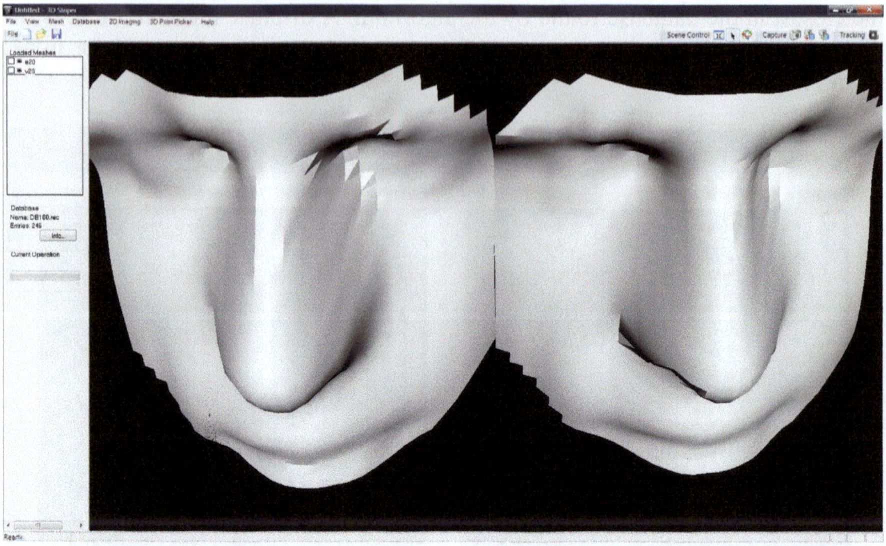

Fig. 7.8 The 3D models generated and used by the algorithm corresponding to the images shown in Figure 7.7.

We tested the algorithms in a simulated environment to verify its real-time performance from eye tracking to 3D reconstruction and recognition and logging the results with time stamps onto an HTML file. We used a Sony Vaio computer, Intel Core 2 Duo, 2.4GHz, 4GB memory. It has been shown that the methods presented here lend themselves to real-time operation as, from the moment the eye tracking algorithms lock on the eyes, it takes 1second 200millisencods to perform the following operations:

- Take a shot in 2D
- Run image filters (median and weighted mean filters)
- Detect the stripes in the image
- Convert the stripes into a 3D point cloud
- Triangulate the point cloud
- Perform hole filling on the mesh
- Determine the location of eyes in 3D
- Punch a hole in the eyes, fill with bilinear interpolation
- Find tip of the nose
- Normalize pose with origin at the tip of the nose
- Determine the sampling planes and sample the mesh
- Replace noisy points by reflection
- Search the database for the closest match
- Display results of recognition on screen
- Save to log file: time stamp, current image, closest match
- Continue eye tracking and repeat the sequence

Application scenarios for forensics and counter-terrorism

Having demonstrated the efficacy of the approach in terms of robust reconstruction and recognition and its real-time credentials, we turn our attention to possible applications to forensics and counter-terrorism – in addition to the most obvious application of identity verification for access control.

3D-2D identification from standard 2D facial databases

The idea in 3D-2D recognition is that accuracy can be improved over 2D-2D recognition by using a 3D subject against a standard 2D database. The comparison can take place either in 3D space, where the 2D data are reconstructed in 3D, or in 2D space, where 3D data are projected in 2D. This cross- dimensionality comparison is a classic computer vision problem, but advantage can be taken of the restricted nature of the application (human faces only). The 3D CCTV concept as proposed here allows 3D facial models to be reconstructed from saved footage: their position and orientation of the 3D facial models can then be automatically manipulated to match existing 2D photographs of suspects in a database at a higher accuracy than a 2D-2D comparison for challenging datasets in terms of pose and lighting. Incomplete facial models (say, a face seen from only one side) can be pose-normalized and, through mesh reflection, the unseen side of the face can be reconstructed together with the reflected texture.

3D-2D identification from standard 2D CCTV video sequences

The purpose is to compare standard 2D CCTV with 3D models acquired either from 3D CCTV as discussed above or 3D acquisitions from a person in custody. The method proposed here can enable substantial improvements in detection rate of CCTV footage. The Metropolitan Police in London states that the identification rate from CCTV is about 20% (personal communication). The 3D CCTV concept has the potential to substantially increase identification rates through the integration of 2D and 3D data. This can be achieved by projecting 2D video footage onto a plane in a 3D environment and by providing the means to manipulate 3D models over the projective plane. In this way for instance, 2D profiles can be compared to 3D model profiles.

The simulated pictures below illustrate the concept where Figure 7.9 shows a 2D CCTV standard footage to be compared with 3D models by fitting the 3D models by a profile view in 2D. Figures 7.10 and 7.11 elaborate on this concept by displaying a 2D image onto the projective plane. 3D facial models of suspects are overlaid on the same screen. Through a combination of rotation, translation, and zooming, a 3D profile can be fitted onto the 2D footage. In the example of figure 7.10, the model fits the person's profile. In figure 7.11, by using the "wrong" 3D model, coloured yellow (lighter), no amount of transformation can fit the profile. Such methods can be used off-line and can be used both for positive identification and for elimination purposes.

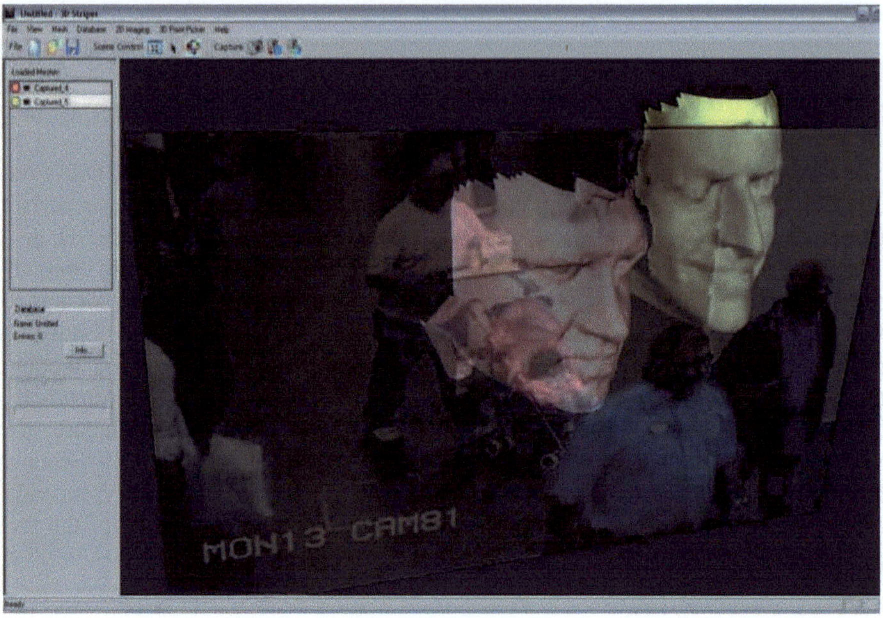

Fig. 7.9. Standard CCTV footage is projected on a 3D screen allowing the comparison of profiles

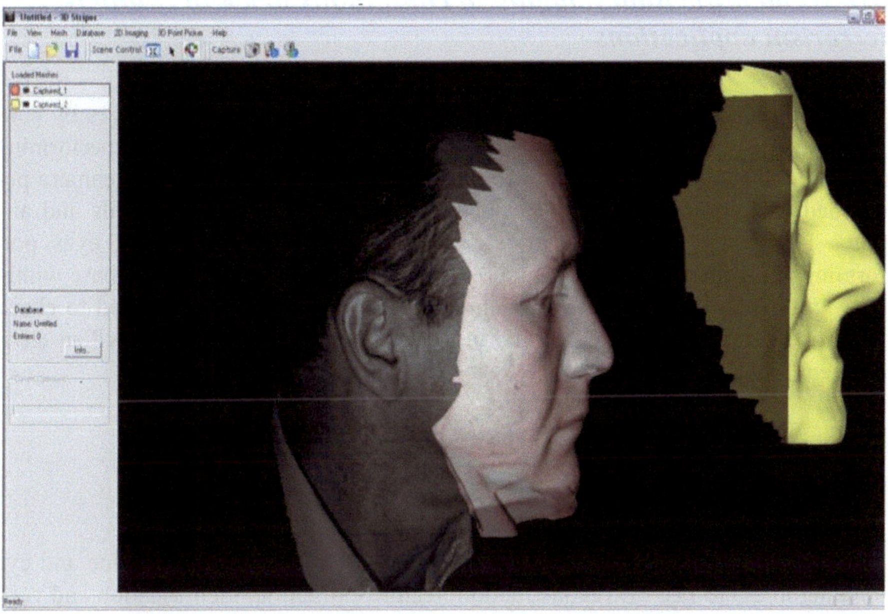

Fig. 7.10. The 3D model fits the 2D profile obtained from standard CCTTV

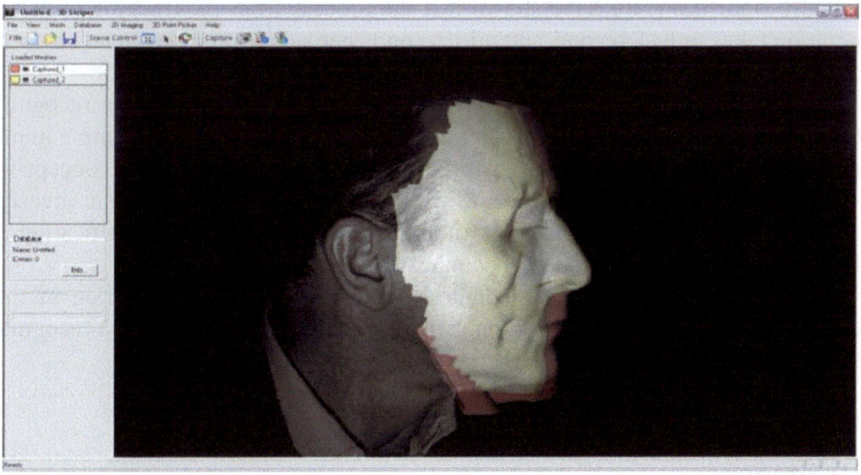

Fig. 7.11 No amount of transformation can fit a wrong 3D model (lighter) onto the 2D pro-file

3D-3D identification flagging in continuous mode in counter-terrorism applications

The main idea behind this application is to flag previously seen faces by continuously generating new models, enrolling into the database, and performing identification. A mobile robot platform can be used or a stationary 3D camera positioned at a strategic location in public places such as shopping malls and airports. The system is set into a fully automatic mode tracking faces and eyes, performing identification and enrolment. When a face is found in the database within a given threshold, the system will immediately flag this. It can be used to check the movements of suspected agents in a theatre of war or within a civilian environment in a shopping mall.

Conclusion

We have presented methods for real-time 3D face recognition from face and eye tracking in 2D to fast 3D reconstruction, feature extraction, identification and verification. Based on geometry alone, the reported recognition accuracy is a perfect 100% with zero FAR. We have used 300 distinct models in our experiments. Equally significant, we have shown that the process from 2D tracking to 3D recognition takes only 1 second 200 milliseconds per subject and thus, can be used in a real-time scenario given the speed and accuracy of the 3D recognition.

While the methods presented here have direct application in face recognition tasks for access control, we have discussed the possible application into a number of interesting domains such as integrating the proposed 3D CCTV concept with standard 2D CCTV in person identification scenarios such as forensic investigations. We also discussed the issue of operating in continuous identification and flagging mode for applications in counter-terrorism and intelligence.

Future work among others includes the design and implementation of mesh compression methods and algorithms enabling fast network-based 3D recognition systems.

References

[1] M.A. Rodrigues, A. Robinson, Real-Time 3D Face Recognition using Line Projection and Mesh Sampling. Eurographics Workshop on 3D Object Retrieval (2011) H. Laga, T. Schreck, A. Ferreira, A. Godil, and I. Pratikakis (Editors), pp 1—8.

[2] W. Brink, A. Robinson, M. Rodrigues, Indexing Uncoded Stripe Patterns in Structured Light Systems by Maximum Spanning Trees, BMVC 2008, Leeds, UK, 1-4 Sep 2008

[3] M.A. Rodrigues, A. Robinson, W. Brink, Fast 3D Reconstruction and Recognition, 8th WSEAS Int Conf on Signal Processing, Computational Geometry & Artificial Vision, Rhodes, 2008, p15-21.
[4] M.A. Rodrigues, A. Robinson, W. Brink, "Issues in Fast 3D Recon-struction from Video Sequences", Lecture Notes in Signal Science, Internet and Education, Proceedings of 7th WSEAS International Conference on MULTIMEDIA, INTERNET & VIDEO TECHNOLOGIES (MIV '07), Beijing, China, September 15-17, 2007, pp 213-218.
[5] M. Rodrigues, A. Robinson, L. Alboul, W. Brink,"3D Modelling and Recognition", WSEAS Transactions on Information Science and Applications, Issue 11, Vol 3, 2006, pp 2118-2122.
[6] A. Robinson, L. Alboul and M.A. Rodrigues,"Methods for Indexing Stripes in Uncoded Structured Light Scanning Systems", Journal of WSCG, 12(3), 2004, pp 371-378
[7] M.A. Rodrigues and Alan Robinson, Image Processing Method and Apparatus, European Patent Office, Patent GB2426618, 29 Nov 2006. Also published as WO2005076196 (A1), GB2410876 (A).
[8] FRGC, (2005). The Face Recognition Grand Challenge, http://www.frvt.org/FRGC/
[9] Bradski, G.R and V. Pisarevsky (2000). Intelapos' Computer Vision Library: applications in calibration, stereo segmentation, tracking, gesture, face and object recognition. Computer Vision and Pattern Recognition. Proceedings. IEEE Conference on Volume 2, 796 – 797.
[10] Robinson, A., L. Alboul, and M. Rodrigues (2004). Methods for indexing stripes in uncoded structured light scanning systems. Journal of WSCG, 12(3) 371–378, February 2004.
[11] Tekumalla, L.S., and E. Cohen (2004). A hole filling algorithm for triangular meshes. tech. rep. University of Utah, December 2004.
[12] Wang, J. and M. M. Oliveira (2003). A hole filling strategy for reconstruction of smooth surfaces in range images. XVI Brazilian Symposium on Computer Graphics and Image Processing, pages 11–18, October 2003.
[13] Wang, J. and M. M. Oliveira (2007). Filling holes on locally smooth surfaces reconstructed from point clouds. Image and Vision Computing, 25(1):103–113, January 2007.
[14] Rodrigues, M.A, and A.Robinson (2009). Novel Methods for Real-Time 3D Facial Recognition. ATINER 5th Int Conf on Computer Sc and Info Sys, Athens, Greece, 27-30 July 2009.
[15] Turk, M.A. and A. P. Pentland (1991). Face Recognition Uisng Eigenfaces. Journal of Cognitive Neuroscience 3 (1): 71–86.

Chapter 8: Simulations for Crisis Management – PANDORA's Box

Mohammad Dastbaz and Aamedeo Cesta

Abstract Natural and human created disasters are increasingly becoming a common feature of our lives. From the recent tsunami and its aftermath in Japan to Icelandic volcanic ashes, to terrorists instigated actions such as 9/11 and the 7th July bombings in London there is a clear need for better training of strategic decision makers as well as the operational forces who need to deal with very complex and almost always multi agency operations. Quite often the difference between an emergency and a disaster is one or two critically wrong decisions in what quite often is a very tight and limited time span. PANDORA is a 3.9 Million Euro European FP7 funded project that aims to make use of emerging serious gaming concepts and technologies to develop an innovative and more effective training environment for the strategic decision makers (the Gold Commanders) so that they can cope more effectively with such difficult and challenging situations.

Serious gaming and e-training

There is no doubt that over the last decade there has been significant developments in the serious gaming industry. The Games industry in the US alone took in about USD$9.5 billion in the 2007, and 11.7 billion in 2008 (Entertainment Software Association (ESA) annual report). Kotick (2008) told attendant investors that he thought the global video games industry would grow from $39 billion in 2008 to $55 billion in 2012. Zyda (2006) observed that as far as research and education is concerned there must be a more concentrated effort in developing research and educating the next generation of games developers.

The advent of the Web 2.0 and with it the development of collaborative on-line gaming environments with very complex provisions allowing players to work together to overcome challenges provides the basses for the use of these technologies in e-training.

A review of the EU R&D initiatives shows that over the last 10 years there has been some 46 funded projects related to games and simulation (either developing toolsets like "GAMESTOOL", GAMES@LARGE or DOTS which stands for Development of on-line telemetric software for the next generation of computer and video games) or exploring the use of computer games and gaming in the area of learning and training. Some of the interesting projects funded over the last five years include: IPERG (Integrated Project on Pervasive Gaming) run by the Swedish Institute of Computer Science, which aims to develop a new gaming experience for its players and: "to accelerate the transition of knowledge and experience crucial for developing pervasive games."

Other notable projects are:

- TIM (Tactile Interactive Multimedia Computer games for visually impaired children - TIM is intended to conceive computer games usable by young blind children in an autonomous way, without assistance of a sighted person.);
- IRSC (Improving remediation of spatial cognitive deficits in children) using table-top and computerized 'games'. The idea of the project is to develop a multi-componential remediation method of spatial functions including virtual reality (VR) and two-dimensional computer games, table-top games and supporting tasks.
- SIMWEB (Exploring innovativE eBusiness models using Agent SIMulation) which aimed at developing games that facilitate the task of eliciting information and knowledge from the different parties involved.

As far as the use of games in learning and training is concerned Atkin (2004) noted that: The academic literature relating to simulations and games demonstrates that they are powerful tools for facilitating scientific knowledge construction. This power comes from their ability to re-create reality, model complex systems, be visual and interactive, engage the user in the practise of science, and in construction and collaboration. Chan (2007) further notes that medical and security organizations are beginning to see the value of serious games for training. Games have the advantage of offering interactive and repetitive training scenarios. Some officials envision serious games becoming a primary training method for a wide variety of government training activities.

Ochalla (2007) writing about the rise of "Serious Games" quotes Suzanne Seggerman, co-founder and president of "Games for Change", the social change/social issues branch of the Washington, D.C.-based Serious Games Initiative as saying that: "I learned more about politics by playing Hidden Agenda than by reading 10 newspapers". So while the current research and development in the games industry has produced a very interesting set of tools and products there is a concentrated effort in extending the boundaries of games playing by "blurring" even further the fine line between reality and virtual reality.

Simulations for crisis management

In the era of virtual reality, the use of technology derived from gaming software for civil and military training has increaseed in a variety of application fields. Both COTS (Commercial Off The Shelf) products and custom products have been used for simulation-based training/crisis management. In part due to the extreme realism achievable from today's technology. These tools have been adopted for real training purposes by third-party entities such as commercial air vendors and/or government forces. State of the art in the area spans from integrated HW/SW simulation platforms (airplane, ships, submarine simulators), to visual aided situational awareness and tactical trainers (infantry troops combat manoeuvring, commanding skills planning and execution), and 3-D single-unit or squad-based first-person shooters (crew coordination and tactics).

Simulations are indeed one of the main approaches used to recreate crisis scenarios (the other being drills) and research has been widely presented in the literature, which deals with various aspects of crisis management such as disaster response, evacuation and planning. Some examples of such projects include:

- The RESCUE project (http://www.itr-rescue.org/) aims to explore technological innovations in order to deliver the right information to the right people at the right time during crisis response.
- The FiRSTE (http://firste.mst.edu/) project aims to develop a training simulation environment to allow first responders (those on the scene of a terrorist or natural disaster first) to train in numerous scenarios. Moreover, the project aims to identify how effectively virtual environments can be used for training first responders and to determine how trainees can be fully immersed in a virtual environment that realistically simulates an actual situation.
- The FireGRID project aims to develop simulation tools to predict the ways in which the fire spreads and relay the information to emergency services to assist their intervention.
- The SICMA project – Funded under the 7th EU Framework, (http://www.sicmaproject.eu/SicmaProjectSite2008/index.html) aims to improve Health Service crisis managers' decision-making capabilities by developing an integrated suite of modelling and analysis tools.

A very active field of research in simulating crisis management is based on the idea of software agents and multi-agent Systems (MAS), which are systems where agents cooperate towards the fulfilment of a common (system) goal. Although a detailed definition of software agents has not been agreed by the relevant research communities, it is widely accepted that a software agent is a software based programme that is capable of independent action and has the ability to demonstrate a number of properties such as autonomy, social ability, reactivity and pro-activeness (Wooldridge & Jennings, 1995). Some examples of this approach include;

- The Drillsim project (http://www.ics.uci.edu/~projects/drillsim/) is a multi-agent system (MAS) simulator focusing on response actions in a crisis scenario. The simulator is able to model different response activities and the information flow between different entities. Moreover, the simulator allows the integration of real life drills into the simulated response activity using an instrumented environment with sensing capabilities.

- The Robocup Rescue project (http://www.robocuprescue.org/) aims to promote research and development involving multi-agent team work coordination, physical robotic agents for search and rescue, information infrastructures, personal digital assistants, a standard simulator and decision support system, evaluation benchmarks for rescue strategies and robotic systems that are all integrated into a comprehensive system in the future.
- The ALADDIN project (http://www.aladdinproject.org/) has developed mechanisms, architectures, and techniques to deal with MAS and has applied its results to a disaster management application domain. The use of multi-agent based simulation using E-SIM has also been presented in the literature (Smith & Brokaw, 2008).
- The DEFACTO project (Marecki et al., 2009) has developed a MAS based system that is being used as a modelling and simulation tool to improve current training methods for disaster response.

There are numerous studies highlighting the effectiveness of useful and well-designed learning/training tools using game paradigms. The Federation of American Scientists (FAS) released a report in 2006 that identified skills that researchers found students could learn better from playing games than from conventional training. Those skills included the ability to make fast decisions in critical, high-stress situations. Chan (2007) also points out that Henry Kelly, president of FAS, claims that many of the most successful commercial games require organizational and management skills to win. He cited, for example, the popular online game "World of Warcraft," which had more than 7 million subscribers in 2006. People play the game in organized groups in which team members have specific roles and responsibilities.

Currently there are a number of "Serious Games" in development for training that stretches the state of the art of research for games beyond its current boundaries or more accurately "Beyond Simulation". Amongst these projects one can name: "JRATS MindRover", which is a is a three to four day long course that teaches procurement procedures to contractors competing for a hypothetical unmanned vehicle contract and "MassBalance" which is an online budget simulation game developed by "dragonfly" that allows citizens to cut monies, spend public funds and see the public effects of various budget allocations.

It is important to note that since the start of the new millennium immersive games have been considered to be going through a transitional state. Future games should build on current and emerging technologies to employ deeper simulation in order to achieve far greater levels of interaction and complexity, while simultaneously simplifying the learning curve for new players. Most game environments of the past have been based on crude abstractions of reality, limiting player expression and requiring users to learn a completely new vernacular in order to play. The games of the future will rely heavily on much more complex, high fidelity world representations that will allow for more emergent behaviour and unforeseen player interactions. Taken together, these next-generation design paradigms are not simply improvements over older models, but represent a fundamentally different approach to simulating real-world physics, handling artificial intelligence and interface usability (Smith, 2001).

So what do we mean by more complex and deeper levels of simulations in our new games approach. The literature highlights some interesting examples that we would like to explore further in our research. These examples are:

- The game "Thief" on the surface looks like a shoot 'em up game. However, the game design team at "Looking Glass" modelled sound propagation, lighting and AI awareness in a much more complex way, greatly expanding the possibility space of the first person perspective shooter. As far as the design of the game is concerned this means that this approach requires the player to receive a great deal more feedback.
- The game "Sims" (by Maxis) created a character "needs" model that, while appearing fairly simple, is far more complex in reality than anything used to represent the moods and needs of most game characters in other games. Most game units, of course, have no concept of anything much more than whether they can see an enemy. Even in all the games that rely heavily on the game industry's meat-and-potatoes of faux combat, units generally fight until they drop dead (instead of running away when badly wounded), fail to intelligently switch weapons (based on the situation or upon enemy defence), and lack any significant amount of tactical awareness with regard to their squad mates. In creating their character needs model, Maxis created a sandbox of possibility that was entertaining to explore, conceptually. It didn't feel like a game - in that there were no hard-and-fast victory conditions and little in the way of artificial conflict - but through its flexible system it allowed the player a lot more expression than most games (Smith, 2001). It is interesting to note that SIMs failed to make a significant impact as an on-line game and was overtaken by other more sophisticated virtual world – social games such as "Second Life" (for more details See David Gardener COO of EA's Worldwide Studios giving his key note at EIEF conference about the "Future of Games Design").

PANDORA's concept (advanced training environment for crisis scenarios)

Crisis management is a major issue to prevent emergency situations from turning into disasters. Quite often the inappropriate management of emergencies has created critical situations. In the event of a catastrophic event, it is human behaviour – and often-human behaviour alone – that determines the speed and efficacy of the crisis management efforts. Frequently speed and efficacy do not stem from the ignorance of procedures, but from the difficulty to operate in contexts where consistent damages are occurring, for the difficulty of managing emotional aspects. Training plays an important function to the preparation of the crisis manager.

Currently two main modalities are used for training purpose:

- The table top exercise (a group discussion guided by a simulated disaster);
- Real world simulation exercise (field tests replicating emergency situations).

Tabletop exercises are low cost and can be easily and frequently organized, but it cannot recreate the real atmosphere, in terms of stress, confusion and need to keep critical decisions in very little time. On the other hand, crisis managers trained through simulation exercises on the field can be very effective and can learn gain valuable skills, but such simulations are very expensive and cannot be easily and quickly organized. Notwithstanding these simulations are essentials to train the future crisis managers: 14 major simulation exercises of cooperation between European countries have been organized from since the end of 2002 up to now, each of them cost from €150.00 to €500.000.

Finally, in both cases, training currently focuses on single typology of critical infrastructure not taking into account the interdependency between different critical infrastructures. This often causes a situation where the decisions taken are correct when related to the single infrastructure under scrutiny, but are incorrect when considering their potential global effect on interlinked critical infrastructures.

Training for crisis decision makers – PANDORA's target group

When referring to planning connected to crisis management during emergency situations, we have in mind the intervention plans for those people that go directly to the operational level of response, see (Wilkins et al. 2008). In reality there are distinctly different levels of decision-making all of which are relevant in any crisis situation. The success of crisis management often depends not only on the ability to apply well-established procedures, but also on the effectiveness of high-level strategic choices. The ability of decision makers to anticipate the possible consequences of their actions (decisions) by means of flexible and forward-looking reasoning is also crucial to an effective response to a crisis. Figure 1 summarizes the three different levels corresponding to different roles of crisis decision makers:

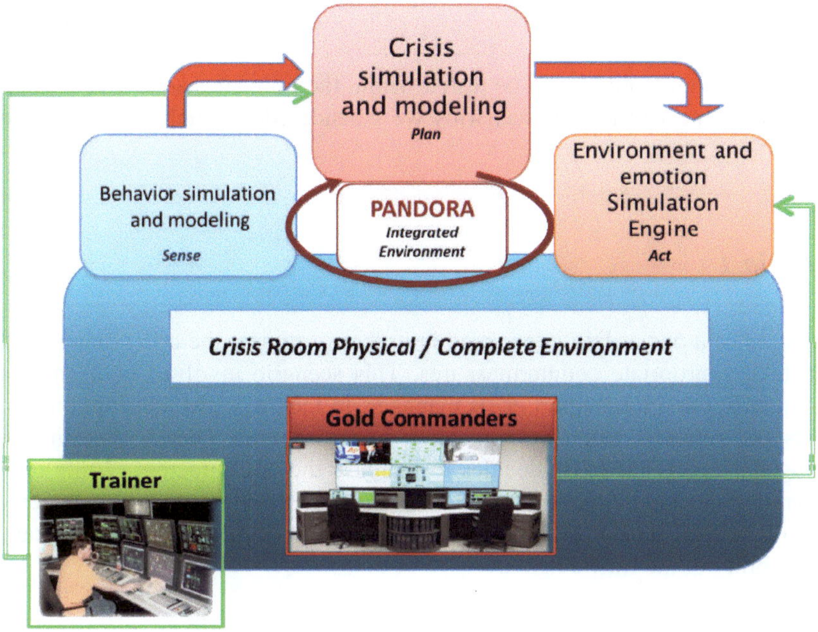

Fig. 8.1: Different decision makers in crisis management.

- At the operational level we have the operational or bronze level commanders, people operating within the detailed area of a crisis situation that perform practical activities and actions, the results of which are monitored and communicated to higher levels;
- At the tactical or silver level decision makers that are located close to but not within affected areas of the crisis are responsible for translating high level strategic decisions into actions by allocating tasks and resources down to the bronze level. At this level the anticipated results from the various allocated tasks are monitored and assessed for effectiveness.
- The strategic or gold level commanders identify the key issues of a critical situation and prioritize required activity from a detached and sufficiently high level of abstraction. Strategies for resolving the crisis are also decided and are then communicated to the lower levels for their detailed specification and implementation.

The choices at the strategic level are particularly important and critical for the success of the overall crisis response and specifically for devising strategies to contain and correct the developing situation by anticipating future consequences with decisions that try to avoid escalating of the crisis situation.

Possible scenarios

PANDORA main features will be tested within the pilot sites selected for the project some of the application scenarios we considered originally are briefly outlined.

Scenario 1

Simulation of a power line interrupted in order to estimate the crisis manager ability to take appropriate countermeasures. This scenario involved both an energy crisis manager and a transport crisis manager. In fact, the grid interruption has rebounds on transport and communication infrastructures. During the simulation training the expert modeller decides to increase the stress factors. While the energy crisis manager is trying to find a solution the transport crisis manager will have to face with accidents and fatalities in the transport sector due to for example unavailability of the traffic lights.

Scenario 2

This simulation involves two countries A and B. It starts with an accident that causes the trip of a 380kV line in the country A. The crisis manager of country A has many choices and each of them will have consequences inside the country A and on the country B. During the simulation the expert modeller introduces many stress factors creating a realistic situation. While the two crisis managers are trying to find a solution they can communicate, they can interact and any decision has a domino effect in each countries.

Bridging the gap

In short PANDORA aims at bridging the gap between table-top exercises and real world simulation exercises, while always proposing a global approach to crises management, providing a near-real training environment at affordable cost. In this context, the project will create an environment useful to measure the crisis manager against the management of a crisis in the completeness of:

- a realistic and complete simulation with timing coherent with the expected near real time;
- a simulation that reproduces the realistic emotional status;

- a simulation which might include different crises managers belonging to different sectors.

The focus on the emotional status of the crises manager in our project is because the knowledge of human behaviour, in all phases of emergency management, is critical in the development of effective emergency policies, plans and training programs. For many years, business continuity planners worked under a simple assumption: When a disaster strikes, people will follow plans and procedures. Psychologists and other behavioural scientists have found that this idea fails to consider the often-surprising behaviour of people during emergencies.

Considering that in a crisis, people will be part of the problem or part of the solution, the recent benchmarking study conducted by Continuity Insights Magazine and KPMG, revealed that 35% of respondents indicated that the "weakest link" in crises management was "people risks." Traditional business continuity plans do not adequately take to into account the many forces of human behaviour, especially when scenarios include extreme fear, harmful behaviours and survival responses. Planners often wrongly assumed that the organization's emergency plans will be automatically accepted, understood and acted upon by all. The principles of human psychology inform us that the behaviour of individuals and groups is shaped more by numerous intangible factors than by official or executive demand.

PANDORA environment, will take into account the behavioural status of crises managers and react to it, will equally foresee different levels of abstraction so to make possible its use in different kinds of crisis. The environment will be not totally automated but will be populated by several actors, among which a simulation director and some extras participating to de-structured simulations with third parties. It will be possible also to carry out training contemporary to many crisis managers of different sector: for instance, it will be possible to train a crisis manager of the energy sector simulating the fall of a high tension line and train a crisis manager of the transport sector in case the energy provision is interrupted. PNDORA's key users and the system architecture is presented in figure 8.2

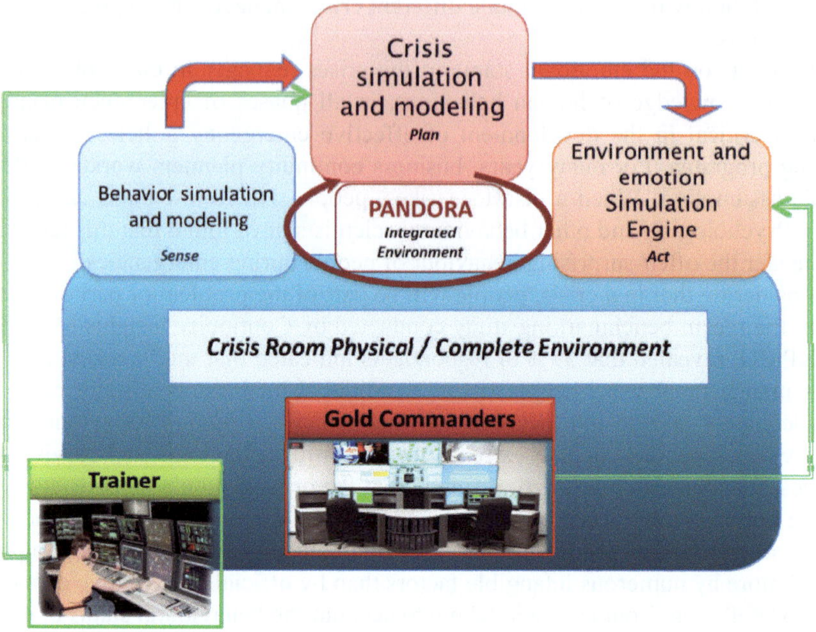

Fig. 8.2 - PNDORA's key users and the system architecture

- The actors
  - Gold commanders or better trainees, which are a group of people coming from different agencies in order to perform the training.
  - Trainer, which actives the exercise and monitors the progress of actions and environment during the training.
- The PANDORA system has 4 key components:
  - Behaviour simulation and modelling, which objective is to create model of each trainee in order to represent trainee's feature and actual behaviour.
  - Crisis simulation and modelling, which aims is to combine the information coming from the previous module and the knowledge about the critical, infrastructure domain in order to create a crisis scenario evolution to be simulated.
  - Environment and emotion simulation engine, which aims to effectively represents non–playable characters and environments for the simulation.
  - Crisis room, which is the "place" where the exercise is conducted, may be complete, portable or web, according to the selected use case.

User interface requirements

There are two types of users in PANDORA: trainers and trainees. Trainers will configure and control a crisis scenario that is represented in a 3D virtual environment (VE) Figure 3. In the customized 3D VE, an avatar will be controlled by a trainee or a program (NPC). The VE's timeline will be manipulated by the PANDORA's other components. Specific events (e.g. storm is coming, heavy rain is coming… according to a crisis scenario) will be generated over time from components and passed into the VE. Events will be presented to trainees via in-world text popup, PowerPoint slides, streaming videos, etc. Trainees/Avatars will collaborate with each other by typing, speaking or emailing to make decision to deal with the crisis. A trainer can also be an avatar in the VE to monitor and supervise trainees.

Fig. 8.3. In-world slide show and streaming video.

Technically, requirements can be summarized as below:

1. The VE is a wide-area distributed system. Trainees can log into the system anywhere from the world.
2. It is able to use different channels (slides, video, music, geographic maps, etc) to provide crisis information.
3. Avatars are able to communicate with each other by text, voice, emails, etc.
4. It can collaborate with PANDORA other components seamlessly.

Architecture

Figure 4 delineates a brief diagram presenting how the proposed user interface fit into the Pandora box.

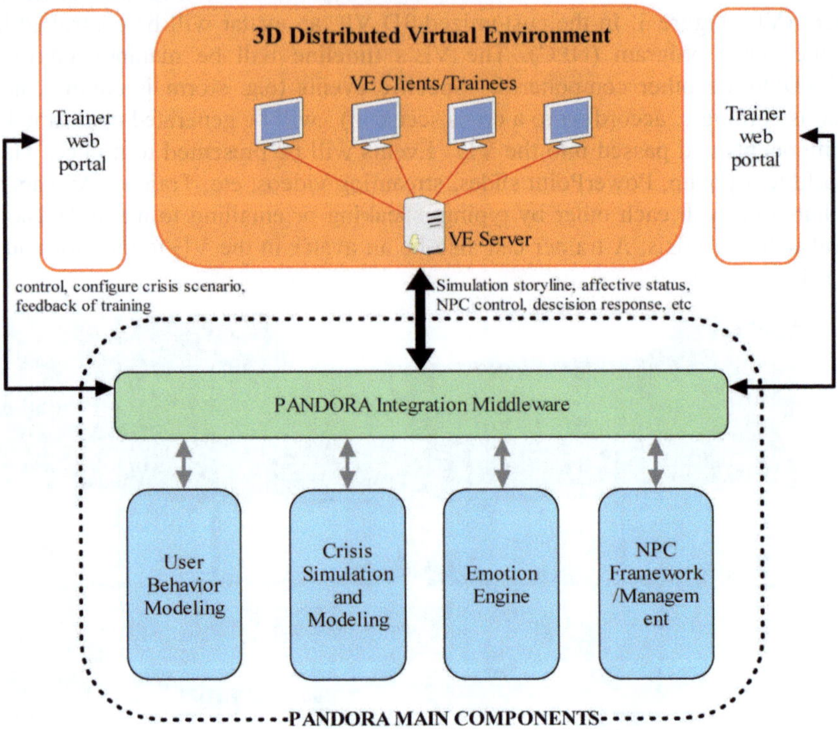

Fig. 8.4. PANDOR User Interface architecture.

The trainer web portal is a webpage interface for trainers to configure and monitor the training progress on the fly. The 3D Distributed Virtual Environment is the PANDORA trainee interface. It is the primary presentation box where all the crisis events, user control, and interactions are presented.

PANDORA distributed virtual environment (DVE)

PANDORA DVE simulates a 3D immersive crisis room where trainees can participate in the training from any geographic locations. Each trainee controls a 3D avatar with his/her keyboard, mouse and microphone. Trainees communicate with each other by typing/speaking to deal with a crisis scenario.

The 3D VE itself does not produce any events unless users make responses to specific events. Its functions are:

1. To represent objects and events passed from PANDORA components (e.g. Crisis Simulation, Emotion Engine, etc) into 3D models and animations;
2. To provide a realistic environment for trainee to react to these events;
3. To send user reactions back to relevant PANDORA components.

The VE receives event information pushed from PANDORA components through the middleware ontology translation (see the integration proposal) and interprets it to relevant animations. When users make any actions or responses, it sends such information back to relative components (through the middleware too), which will probably generate more events based on the responses.

Upon receiving event requests from components, the VE generates a timeline XML file that its native manipulating script can understand. Below is a XML file example (It is used in the demo video introduced in the next section). Of course we can add more tags and more attributes to represent every single event generated by any components. For example, an event "trainee 009 is nervous at time 100" generated by the Emotion component can be written as

<timestamp t="100", avatar id ="009", affective="nervous"></timestamp>

The VE manipulating script will then interpret it as "blushing" or other body animations for the avatar 009. What animations to be interpreted to for an event can be explicitly described by the requesting components or decided by the VE itself. An agreed event description format will also be needed so that components and the VE can understand each other.

Realising the PANDORA system

The PANDORA system design has followed a user-centered approach, based on a close cooperation with the training experts who have profoundly influenced the shaping of the system. Specifically, the Cabinet Office's Emergency Planning College (EPC) has synthesized their experience coming from training a wide range of senior decision makers and their leading expertise in emergency planning and crisis management. As end users representative in the PANDORA consortium, EPC has contributed to identify the main requirements for the innovative training environment, and is influencing the design and implementation choices.

A number of general constraints have emerged during a first phase of user requirement analysis:

- Support cooperative decision making: it has been immediately clear how training gold commanders implies teaching them to take joint decisions after cooperation.
- Training personalization: it has been underscored the role of personalized teaching even though within a group decision making context.

- Mixed-initiative interaction: it turned out as particularly important the need of a tool that empowers the trainer with further abilities rather than a pure video-game like type of immersive experience, hence the need to create a mixed-initiative environment in which the trainer is fully integrated in the “lesson loop”.

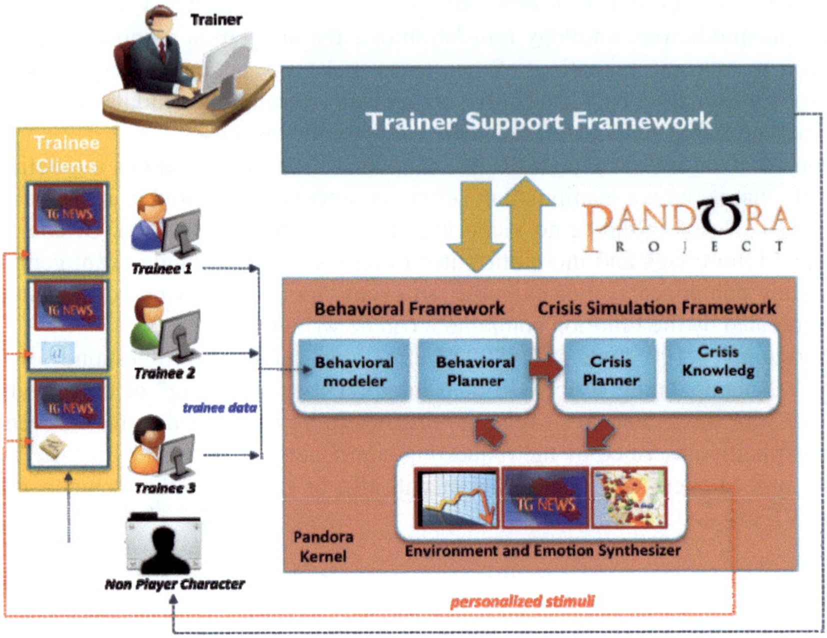

Fig. 8.5 The PANDORA-BOX General Architecture.

Figure 8.5 shows the main architectural idea pursued within the project to obtain a system called PANDORA-BOX whose first complete version has been officially demonstrated on March 2011. The system is composed of three environments: (a) a Trainer Support Framework allows the trainer to keep control of the training session and dynamically adjust the stimuli based on his/her experience; (b) distributed Trainee Clients can access the PANDORA-BOX and receive both collective and individual stimuli during a lesson; (c) a PANDORA kernel which is the main engine that generates the “lesson plan”, animates it in an engaging way and adjusts it on a continuous bases to keep peace with both the evolution of the specific group of people under training and their individual performance.

Specifically, a group of trainees, representative of different agencies involved in the resolution of a crisis (e.g., Civil Protection, Local Authorities, Health, Fire Rescue, Police, Transports and so on) have access to the training system through their training workstation. If some of the representative authorities are not present they are simulated by the PANDORA system through Non Player Character

(NPC), in which case, the trainer through the system synthesizes features and decisions.

The various participants in the training are characterized by different aspects, both in relation to the components closely linked to their role and responsibility, and for the particular ``affective states" they may exhibit during the training experience in response to the presented stimuli. Therefore, each trainee, by interacting with the system, feeds personal data to the PANDORA-BOX, which gathers this information to build a user model (Behavioural Model in the Figure 1). Based on this model, the system synthesizes a personalized training path that meets the specific needs and status of each trainee (Behavioural Planner). The output of this process is passed to a second module (the Crisis Planner), which on the basis of the Behavioural Module's indications, as well as the knowledge of the chosen guiding training scenario, synthesizes a sequence of stimuli appropriate for both the group (information shared among all trainees) and the individual trainees (information tailored to induce the "right level of stress").

The plan synthesized by the crisis planner is then given as input to the module called Environment and Emotion Synthesizer which is responsible for an effective rendering of the training temporal plan. In practice this module adds an additional level of ``realism" to the stimuli, by customizing the appropriate presentation mode (e.g., introducing noise on a phone call report) in order to achieve a high level of realism, stress and pressure. The use of advanced 3D scenario reproduction is also studied in the project.

Overall the PANDORA-BOX supports the loop:

- Trainer training – environment – trainee

This encourages the customization and adaptation based on the users' feedback as well as to keep in the loops goals and suggestions from the trainer. In the rest of the paper we underscore how we have inserted the timeline-based planning technology within the PANDORA-BOX and how the planning technology has become the unifying element of the overall system.

Using AI planning technology

Basic goal for the learning environment is to create and dynamically adapt a four hours lesson. The pursued idea is to represents lesson's content as a plan composed of different "messages" to be sent to trainees which have temporal features and causal relations among them. In \pan\ a lesson master plan is first synthesized starting from an abstract specification given by the Trainer, then it is animated, expanded and updated during its execution, in relations to new information gathered from trainees and their decisions. Specifically, the lesson master plan contains time-tagged activities that trigger multimedia events presented on the Trainee

Clients. A key point is represented by the reaction of trainees to lesson stimuli (e.g., the answer to a request to produce a joint decision on a specific critical point). “User reactions” internally represented in the plan trigger different evolutions of the current plan thus supporting dynamic adaptation.

The use of AI planning is quite natural for creating such a master plan. Previous work exists on the use of constraint reasoning for synthesizing multi-media presentations (e.g., (Jourdan, 1998)), the use of planning in story-telling (e.g., (Young, 1999)), etc. The main “technological idea” we have pursued in PANDORA is to use timeline-based technology to represent and manage heterogeneous information, a choice that naturally match of some of the manipulations which were specifically required to the master plan representation in the project. In particular two aspects offered an interesting challenge for timeline based technology: (a) the idea of doing planning, executing, re-planning in a continuous cycle; (b) the possibility of modelling a completely different type of information with respect to the ``usual" applicative domains in which timeline-based planning has been used (e.g., (Muscettola, 1994; Jonsson, 2000; Cesta, 2011)).

A timeline-based problem representation

Figure 8.6 exemplifies the basic modelling features and introduces some terminology for the \plan\ domain modelling. The main data structure is the timeline that, in generic terms, is a function of time over a finite domain. Possible values for a timeline are generically called “events”. Events are represented with a predicate holding over a time interval and characterized by start and end time .

Events can be linked each other through relations in order to reduce allowed values for their constituting parameters and thus decreasing allowed system behaviours. In general, relations can represent any logical combination of linear constraints among event parameters. According to the number of involved events, relations can be divided into unary, binary, and n-ary. For example, unary relations are used in PANDORA-BOX to fix initial scenario events' parameters placing them in time. Given an event e, an example of unary relation can be start-at(e, 15, 20) forcing starting time of event e to be constrained inside simulation time interval [15, 20]). Given two events e0 and e1, an example of binary relation can be ater(e0, e1, 100, 120), forcing starting time of event e1 constrained to be minimum 100 and maximum 120 time units after ending time of event e0.

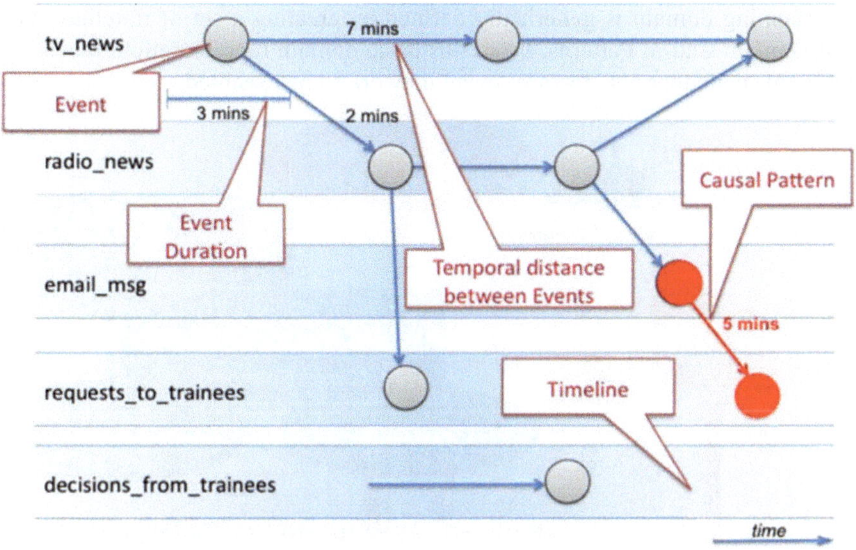

Fig. 8.6 The timeline-based plan data structure.

An Event Network is a hyper-graph having events as nodes and relations as hyper-edges. Through the concept of Event Network, the whole timeline-based planning procedure can be reduced to the process of reaching a target Event Network, which meets desired goal conditions, starting from an initial, already consistent, Event Network. In our case, goal conditions are characterized by high-level scenario events representing the abstract blueprint for the master plan while the initial Event Network is, trivially, an empty Event Network.

In the example of figure 8.6 we see an Event Network distributed over 5 timelines (three representing different media for giving ``active" information in a situation (tv_news, radio_news, email_msg), two more special purpose to ask input to trainees and for gathering such input (request_to_trainees, decisions_from_trainees).

A further basic ingredient in timeline modelling is the so-called "Causal Patterns" (see an example in figure 8.2). They are the way to express planning domain/causal rules in the current internal representation. Any given Event Network should be consistent with respect to the set of such specified causal patterns .

Patterns are defined through a logic implication reference – requirement; where reference is the event value that demands pattern application while requirement is the "consequence" of the presence of the reference value in the Event Network. Making use of a recursive definition, a requirement can be a target event value, representing a new value on the same or on another timeline, a relation among reference value and target values, a conjunction of requirements or a disjunction of requirements. Being relations, in the most general case, linear constraints, causal patterns allow great expressiveness that allows a PANDORA modeller to represent quite complex behaviours.

A planning domain is generically defined by creating a set of timelines and a set of Domain Causal Patterns. From this basic domain representation, receiving a set of goals a planner generates an event network to be executed.

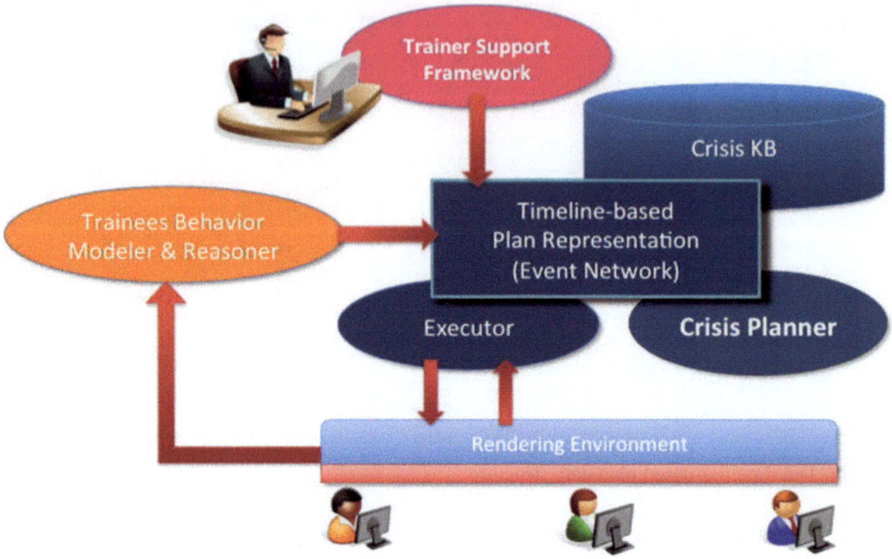

Fig. 8.7– The software architecture of the PANDORA-BOX

Opening the PANDORA's BOX

Having introduced several ingredients we now discuss how the general idea pursued in the PANDORA comprehensive cycle shown in figure 8.7 has been transformed during the project development in a complete implemented system that, within the project, is usually referred to as PANDORA-BOX.

Figure 8.7 shows the different modules that are combined together to create the software architecture of the innovative training environment pursued by PANDORA.

We distinguish among:

- The Trainer Support Framework
- The four blocks composing the core Crisis Simulation
- The Trainees Behavior Modeler and Reasoner responsible for the user modelling with respect to Trainees
- A generic block called Rendering Environment that roughly summarizes work done in in two workpackages dedicated to produce the Emotion Engine, the NPC Framemework, and the Physical Environment to set the whole training experience.

The picture again contains simplification some parts but allows us to summarize some important aspect:

- The trainer through the Trainer Support Framework define the Scenario, an abstract plan that acts as a set of goals for the planning problem specification in the
- Within the Simulation module the subdivision of work between Event Network and Crisis KB. The Event Network acts as a front-end (run time engine for lesson/plan enactment) while the CKB acts as a back-end (background knowledge for the simulation, e.g., the domain knowledge for the crisis planner)
- The Crisis Planner is responsible for the connection of the CKB and the Event Network, for creating the real lesson plan starting from the domain theory and the goals arriving from the trainer, for adapting the plan during the lesson enactment according to input from the trainees, from the behavioural reasoning and from new decisions from the trainer
- The Executor receives a lesson/plan and dispatches it according to increasing time for the rendering toward the specific environment. Notice that the Executor creates the first continuous loop with the trainees because this module is responsible for registering in the timeline framework the decisions coming from the trainees' class.
- The Trainer Behaviour Modeller and Reasoner also uses a timeline representation communicates with the Event Network posting values on specific timelines (for example after analysing the data gathered from the trainees and reasoning upon them the behavioural reasoner may set a timeline induced_stress for any of the trainees enforcing the Crisis Planner to insert some personalized stimulant for each of the trainees). This is the second continuous loop around the trainees as a combined action Behaviour and Crisis Reasoner (Cortellessa et al, 2011).
- It is worth saying that also the Trainer can post new goal trough specific interactive supports from the Trainer Support Framework and through the Event Network intervene on line to modify the course of event adapted incrementally by the planner.
- It is also worth commenting that the Crisis Planner deeply uses the causal patterns stored in the CKB not only for expanding the initial lesson plan but also for adapting it during the lesson.

Conclusions – progress so far

A prototype of the complete system was produced in early December 2010 while a first robust version of the PANDORA-BOX was officially was presented to the EU project officers during the mid-term project review in March 2011.

Many improvements are scheduled in the remaining life-time of the project. Our next steps will be to provide a tool for Knowledge and Scenario Authoring that allows incremental creation and/or editing of crisis Scenarios. We will be also considering how we can achieve better realism for PANDORA's environment. In order to achieve a high degree of realism, stress and pressure, the use of a 3D environment will be explored with the purpose to render a Crisis Room with all trainees together, even if for logistic reasons they are in different locations during the training.

Acknowledgments The PANDORA project is supported by EU FP7 under the joint call ICT/Security (GA.225387) and is monitored by REA (Research Executive Agency). Authors are indebted to all the project partners for the stimulating work environment. We would particularly like to thank Dr. Yasmine Arafa, Dr. Hao Liu, Prof. Cornelia Boldyreff for their work and contribution to development of PANDORA's 3D virtual environment and integration tasks and Gabriella Cortellessa and Riccardo De Benedictis for joint work on using planning in PANDORA. Authors are indebted to all the project partners for the stimulating work environment. The PANDORA web site is: http://www.pandoraproject.eu/

References

1. Atkin, A. (2004), "Playing at Reality: Exploring the Potential of the Digital Game as a Medium for Science Communication", Published by the Australian National University, PhD Thesis.
2. Chan, W-H(2007), "Serious Games=Serious Training"; Published in FCW.com as a cover story May 7, 2007.
3. Harrison, P. (2007), "Games 3.0: Developing and Creating for the 3rd Age of Video Games" Keynote of Phil Harrison, President of Worldwide Studios, Sony Computer Entertainment to Games Developers Conference 2007
4. Ochalla, B. (2007), "Who Says Video Games Have to be Fun? The Rise of Serious Games", Published by Gamasutra, June 29th 2007, www.gamasutra.com.
5. Marecki, J., Schurr, N., Tambe, M., Scerri, P., (2009), Analyzing Dangers in Multiagent Rescue Using DEFACTO, Safety and Security in Multiagent Systems, M. Barley, H.
6. Mouratidis, A. Unruh, D. Spears, P. Scerri, F. Massacci (Eds), Lecture Notes in Artificial Intelligence, vol. 4324, pp 241 -257
7. Smith, H. (2001), "The Future of Game Design: Moving Beyond Deus Ex and Other Dated Paradigms", delivered lecture in Multimedia International Market, in Montreal, October 2001
8. Smith, J.L., Brokaw, J.T., (2008), Agent Based Simulation of Human Movements during Emergency Evacuations of Facilities, Proceedings of the 2008 Structures Congress.
9. Wooldridge, M., Jennings, N.R., (1995), Agent Theories, Architectures, and Languages: A Survey, Intelligent Agents, Wooldridge, Jennings (eds.), Springer-Verlag, pp 1-22.
10. Zyda, M. (2006), "Educating the Next Generation of Game Developers", Journal of Computer, Published by IEEE Computer Society, p:30-34.
11. Jourdan, M.; Layaida, N.; and Roisin, C. 1998. A Survey on Authoring Techniques for Temporal Scenarios of Multi- media Documents. In Furht, B., ed., Handbook of Internet and Multimedia Systems and Applications - part 1: Tools and Standards. CRC Press. 469–490.
12. Young, R. M. (1999). Notes on the Use of Plan Structures in the Creation of Interactive Plot. Working Notes of the AAAI Fall Symposium on ``Narrative Intelligence", Cape Cod, MA.

13. Muscettola, N. 1994. HSTS: Integrating Planning and Scheduling. In Zweben, M. and Fox, M.S., ed., Intelligent Scheduling. Morgan Kauffmann.
14. Jonsson, A.; Morris, P.; Muscettola, N.; Rajan, K.; and Smith, B. 2000. Planning in Interplanetary Space: The- ory and Practice. In AIPS-00. Proceedings of the Fifth Int. Conf. on Artificial Intelligence Planning and Scheduling.
15. Cesta, A.; Cortellessa, G.; Fratini, S.; and Oddi, A. 2011. MrSPOCK: Steps in Developing an End-to-End Space Ap- plication. Computational Intelligence 27(1):83–102.
16. Cortellessa, G.; D'Amico, R.; Pagani, M.; Tiberio, L.; De Benedictis, R.; Bernardi, G.; and Cesta, A. 2011. Mod- eling Users of Crisis Training Environments by Integrating Psychological and Physiological Data. In IEA/AIE 2011, Part II,, volume LNAI 6704, 79–88.

Chapter 9: Choices and Voices – A Serious Game for Preventing Violent Extremism

Mitra Memarzia and Kam Star

Abstract Choices and Voices is an interactive simulation encouraging young people to explore and discuss the underlying issues and adverse influences, which can lead to divisions and tensions in communities. In various scenarios the player faces a number of moral dilemmas in which their decisions define their own outcomes, as well as those of their friends and family. Although the game offers the same range of choices to start with, each player makes a different set of decisions that substantially alter the outcome of their game. The structured group discussions in response to the game further emphasise how real life decisions can have significant consequences.

Background

Evidence shows that the long-term solution to tackling violent extremism lies in prevention. The most effective way to prevent young people from turning to violence is to encourage open and honest conversations on attitudes, ideas, choices and consequences in a safe and positive environment.

Local Authorities and the UK Local Government Association (LGA) took on a vital role in strengthening communities through Preventing Violent Extremism (PVE) under the PREVENT strand of the Government's counter-terrorism strategy (CONTEST). Cross-Government responsibility for PREVENT was shared between the Home Office, Communities and Local Government with the principal objective being: "To prevent people becoming or supporting terrorists or violent extremists".

The PVE agenda funded a range of community projects initially through the PVE pathfinder fund in 2007/08 and became an increasingly important part of the core services delivered by local authorities. The projects that were piloted during this period led to a range of innovative and engaging initiatives, and further developed towards an extensive range of projects throughout 2008-09 with many projects continuing their legacy to the present day. One such project is Choices and Voices, an interactive resource designed by the award winning Serious Games

Company, PlayGen, which is aimed at 12 to 16 year olds and is being used in many schools across the UK.

Choices and Voices was instigated and supported by West Midlands Police, developed by PlayGen in collaboration with Birmingham University's School of Education and relevant academics, the Department for Children, Schools and Families (DCSF) and a number of regional schools. It has been rigorously researched and is in full accordance with the National Curriculum, DCSF's National Strategy, and covers specific areas within the Citizenship, PSHE and SEAL curriculum.

A focused research and development phase was undertaken with the objective of creating a resource for schools to make a positive contribution to the prevention of violent extremism in young people. The aim was to provide an inspiring and interactive experience that acted as a catalyst and a focus to discuss, debate, and unpick arguments with the aim to ultimately stop young people getting to the point where they may even contemplate cruelty and violence. This was achieved by developing an interactive resource based on social scenarios that require them to make choices, discuss consequences and understand different points of view.

At specific points in the scenarios, pupils are presented with challenging decisions that form the focal point for class discussion. Positive messages are woven throughout the narrative, and group discussions encourage students to extract the positive ideas and to reflect on their merits.

A brief overview of serious games

The term "serious game" was firstly used by Clark Abt in his 1970 book Serious Games to differentiate between games for fun and games for learning. In that book, he mainly referred to the use of board and card games. Although he did not refer to computer games, he proposed a definition that can be considered applicable in the computer age:

> "Reduced to its formal essence, a game is an activity among two or more independent decision-makers seeking to achieve their objectives in some limiting context. A more conventional definition would say that a game is a context with rules among adversaries trying to win objectives. We are concerned with serious games in the sense that these games have an explicit and carefully thought-out educational purpose and are not intended to be played primarily for amusement."

The "serious game" term as we intend today was firstly used in 2002, with the start of the Serious Game Initiative lead by David Rejeski and Ben Sawyer in the US, and taken up in Europe by the formation of the Serious Games movement including the Serious Games Institute in the UK.

SGs were initially conceived to train people for tasks in particular jobs, such as training army personnel, or training insurance salesmen. More recently, serious games are being developed to tackle a range of behavioural and attitudinal issues.

In 2005, the World Food Programme (2004) developed "Food Force", sought to take advantage of the popularity of computer games to educate children about hunger and the work of the aid agency. A further example is the game designed with the help of the New York Fire Department, aimed at training fire fighters on how to deal with conventional, environmental, biological and terror-based incidents while functioning as a team where the players play the game through networked computers communicating through headsets to complete cooperative tasks (Entertainment Technology Center and Carnegie Mellon University, 2005).

Serious Games Interactive has developed Global Conflicts: Palestine, an immersive role-playing simulation that gives the player the chance to explore the Israeli-Palestinian conflict first-hand. Through the diverse stories students engage within the game and learn about issues related to conflicts in terrorism, human rights and media's role.

PlayGen has continued to develop a wide range of serious games for tackling deep rooted issues. In 2009 PlayGen developed "Anti-Money Laundering game", used by financial institutions to reduce money laundering that sometime fuels terrorism. In 2010 "What should we tell the children" was developed in collaboration with Coventry University Health and Life Sciences, a game for parents and children to tackle teenage pregnancy. In 2010 following the success of the original C&V games, discussed in this article, PlayGen developed the Primary school version, designed for 6 to 11 year olds.

SGs offer an enormous potential, because a large and growing population is familiar with playing games, that can present users with realistic and compelling challenges. They are highly stimulating and capable of processing information and capturing players' concentration span for long durations. Through exploring gaming technologies, SGs are able to contextualize the player's experience in a stimulating and realistic environment.

> "Games embody well-established principles and models of learning. For instance, games are effective partly because the learning takes place within a meaningful (to the game) context. What you must learn is directly related to the environment in which you learn and demonstrate it; thus, the learning is not only relevant but applied and practiced within that context. Learning that occurs in meaningful and relevant contexts is more effective than learning that occurs outside of those contexts, as is the case with most formal instruction. Researchers refer to this principle as situated cognition and have demonstrated its effectiveness in many studies over the last fifteen years. Researchers have also pointed out that play is a primary socialization and learning mechanism common to all human cultures and many animal species". Richard Van Eck, Digital Game-Based Learning: 2006

Don Menn (1993) claims that students can only remember 10 per cent of what they read, but almost 90 per cent, if they engage in the job themselves, even if only as a simulation, and this assertion has been supported by evidence from recent studies on the effectiveness of game-based learning (Jarvis and de Freitas, 2009). Effective SG's challenge players' sense of a given situation and provide compelling contexts where the player can become fully involved. This important element can be used to create the connection between the gaming experience and the everyday experiences outside of the game. SG scenarios can in this way greatly enhance the relationship between possible choices and their outcomes, leading to self-realisation of consequences of and attitudes and behaviours.

Choices and Voices research and development

The research and development phase of the project revealed 3 key elements that may lead to violent extremism; experiences, mechanisms and attitudes, which became focal points within each scenario.

- Experiences: C&V incorporates the understanding of key experiences that may lead to violent extremism.
  - Underachievement
  - Resilience
  - Being easily lead
  - Seduced by: adventure /secrecy/ belonging
  - Camaraderie
  - Migration
  - Life changes
  - Bullying
  - Social exclusion
  - Peer Pressure
  - Alienation/ Isolation
  - Exposure to violence
  - Trauma and Fragility
  - Theological distortion
  - Humiliation
- Mechanisms: C&V incorporates an understanding of the mechanisms that may lead to extremism.
  - A disadvantaged position and discrimination are seen not as mistakes in a good system but as the expression of an essentially bad system
  - A disadvantaged situation is seen as an expression of dominant cultural – religious contract and of power politics.
  - The notion that 'religious' identity must be developed in an enclave that is opposed to modern society
- Attitudes: C&V incorporates an understanding of psychological attitudes that may lead to extremist behaviour
  - The need for cognitive closure
  - The desire for a definite answer to a particular topic, as opposed to confusion, ambiguity or a subjective view of the world.
  - The need for purpose, love and respect
  - The predisposition to unquestioned belief that everything has a purpose.
  - Unquestionable respect for self proclaimed authority

- Following other peoples authority without questioning the basis of their interpretation
  - The need to be unique and special. This is the desire to be the only true saviour of believers of destiny of being the chosen one.

Throughout the interactive experience and outlined in the teacher's guide are a range of Positive Attitudes and Behaviours that are also in keeping with the National Curriculum's Citizenship requirements. These are outlined as:

- Commonality:
  - It is important to emphasise commonality between young people and to develop an awareness of shared life experiences, grievances and goals. However, although commonality is important, it is vital not to replace theories of difference with impractical and general theories of commonality such as 'Britishness'. Teachers and Facilitators are signposted to encourage pupils to develop an understanding of their commonality on their own.
- Working together for common goals:
  - Creating opportunities for young people to work cohesively together towards a safe and inspiring community will limit the tendency for violence and the application of extreme notions of difference. Young people are encouraged to work together on the grievances and concerns they share. Choices and Voices is designed to encourage cohesion and illustrate the value of working together.
- Promoting honest and critical conversations:
  - Honest and open conversation about religious groups and cultural differences is essential to the development of positive attitudes within multicultural environments. Using interactive games such as Choices and Voices, young people can be engaged and inspired to act positively within their community.

The Choices and Voices scenarios

Choices and Voices is divided into two short scenarios, with each scenario split into a series of acts and scenes. The scenarios take place in a diverse multicultural community in the West Midlands and the player is a local resident and school pupil, with consequent versions made to reflect a range of other regions.

Fig. 9.1. Choices and voices scenarios

The pupils interact with characters in a virtual community that reflects real life situations, set in a potentially volatile location with a multicultural population. Their decisions will lead to other events unfolding, and the information they gather depends on the approach they take. It is important that they can make choices in any way they choose, ie: they can make the wrong choices in a safe environment and individuals will determine a variety of outcomes, that will range from the negative to the positive, vividly demonstrating the consequences of different styles of engagement. These outcomes become the focus for the all important group discussion. At the end of each scenario pupils are given feedback and key decisions they have made are highlighted and explained. Key positive messages regarding engagement with one's community, its leaders and the police are woven into the scenarios. Group discussions give pupils the opportunity to reflect on why certain interactions and decisions gave very different results.

In Scenario 1 the player is 'led' through the interactive story. A new cultural group of people are settling within the player's community and the player's friends, who have negative opinions of the unnamed group, are planning to attack their community meeting with eggs. They want the player to participate and have told the player not to tell anyone. The player has the opportunity to warn authorities about this attack and a more dangerous attack that follows. Scenario 1 includes issues of peer pressure and the seductive power of adventure and the sense of belonging it can engender.

Players encounter examples of theological distortion and misrepresentation and the characters display a need for cognitive closure. In response to these negative features, the scenario emphasises the characters' commonality and the importance of contributing to a safe and cohesive environment. These are all possible discussion points.

In the second scenario, the player is 'leading' the group. With this responsibility, they must consider each choice on offer very carefully, as the success of the group depends entirely on their personal choices. A large-scale regeneration is planned for a local park and the young people are unhappy. The player wants to stop the development and so must decide between violent or peaceful protest. Scenario 2 includes examples of an unquestioning respect for a self-proclaimed authority and the characters exhibit a need to feel unique or special. Positive aspects include working together for a common goal and committing to honest and critical dialogue. Again these are the primary discussion points from this scenario. The aim is to counter the spread of misinformation, negative ideas and attitudes by offering an interactive session in which students are presented with a series of choices, encouraging them to develop their understanding of consequences.

Character profiles

Name: Athena

Characteristics: Unstable home with lack of parental contact. Looks for ways to rebel to substitute purpose. Easily swayed to take part in unlawful activities, often under the radar as good at covering her tracks.

Primary Traits: Intelligent, rebel

Secondary Traits: Lacks purpose, deceptive

Name: Ilan

Characteristics: Aggressive and can create havoc. Constantly on the lookout for confrontations toprove his power. Deprived background, violent parents and traumatic childhood.

Primary traits: Angry, judgemental

Secondary traits: Self-justified, reactionary

Choices and Voices lesson plans

In order to ensure that the resource is useful to schools, an extensive review of the National Curriculum for key stages 3 and 4 was carried out in collaboration with the DCSF and their remit within the PVE agenda. Through working closely with teachers and school based officers, the teacher's guide accompanying the interactive online scenarios clearly outlines these specific areas and offers structured lesson plans. A summary of the research that underpins the scenarios as well as questions, suggested points for discussion and extended home study options is included in the pack. This assures that the resource is both easy to use and accessible to teachers and facilitators who may not be informed about the concepts in PVE.

Examples of group engagement

Teachers:

> "There is a lot of potential for a deeper and longer enquiry to take place. Its very versatile like that." adding that the game "gives the freedom to relate to real-life issues".

School Based Officer:

> "Its great to see them engage with something so quickly."
> "It's a great product, I can see a lot of schools using this. It's important to look through the guide before hand, there is a lot of useful information in there."

Pupils:

> "The game was very interactive and it felt like you was in the game."
> "The game was very good at showing the consequences of making bad decisions, it could have involved more scenarios"
> "I think this programme really helped me. It helped me in many ways to think about choices. It helped me to understand what good and bad can come out of choices."
> "I liked how it was set in Birmingham. It made the scenarios seem very realistic, like it could be here!"
> "I think this game was very good and different from the others. I like the idea that if I make different choices, the situation changes."
> "It reflects on the choices you may have to make in real life."

A team at the School of Education, University of Birmingham, carried out research. Lessons using the game were observed, including how the game was introduced and how the teacher or police officer followed up the game immediately afterwards. Teachers were given a questionnaire about their experience of using the game, and focus groups discussions with students were held. Brief points from the longer report were that:

1. Pupils enjoyed playing the game, appreciating the interactive nature and seeing what happened to their decisions. They often wanted to play it again to see what would be the consequences of different decisions and paths. This showed engagement with the game and appreciation of the issues involved.
2. The game deliberately did not specifically focus on religion or the far right, nor use the term extremism or extremist. The question is whether pupils would make the connection. One said 'As far as the video is concerned, extremism didn't really come across'. However, the problem of peer pressure was keenly recognised, and pupils felt that this was central. Joining extremist groups or

acting in an extremist way happened 'possibly when you were with friends' and had 'no time to think'. The focus of the game on such peer pressure clearly resonated with pupils and there was much discussion on being drawn into things you know are wrong.

3. The focus and impact depends therefore greatly on how the game is used by teachers immediately afterwards and for any follow up work. Sometimes the focus was on peer pressure, other times violence, and other times on how to achieve change in the community. Some pupils felt that 'deeper' issues related to religious extremism should not in fact be aired, as 'someone could get freaked out'. In this sense the game provides a good medium for a teacher who knows their class to take in an appropriate direction without people being disturbed straight away. It will be important that teachers do not use the opportunity for didactic moralising after the game,
4. The game cannot on its own be expected to change attitudes overnight. A few pupils in one school still thought that violence did work. Yet the key aim was fulfilled of making pupils reflect on actions and their consequences, in that discussions were lively. Some of these discussion revolved around how 'realistic' the game was, and how it could be made more realistic, but others developed themes of right and wrong, and thinking about 'hanging around with people who might influence me'. It seemed to give a legitimation to 'doing the right thing'. Above all, the game pointed up for pupils that life is about decisions (which seems obvious to adults, but not necessarily to pupils in the course of their daily lives). This enabled a sense of control and is in itself an important learning experience.

Conclusion

Serious games can be effectively used as an engaging and accessible tool to open discussion and meaningful debate on violent extremism. Through combining a serious game that brings to life and highlights repercussions of the players' decisions, and a framework that enables structured group discussion, it is possible to encourage open and honest conversations on attitudes, ideas, choices and consequences in a safe and positive environment.

For many the Preventing Violent Extremism agenda appeared to present many risks particularly a danger of being accused of racially or religiously discriminatory behaviour. Choices and Voices took a serious and sensitive issue, and provided a tool that gives guidance and confidence to teachers. Young people have the opportunity now to engage in the type of debate and discussion, which will ensure the future safety and cohesion of all our communities. Serious Games are being increasingly used to target a wide range of law-enforcement issues, from reducing anti-social behaviour to training on interrogation techniques and from tackling violent crime to helping spot money laundering that maybe being used to fund terrorism. When designed and delivered appropriately, they can offer a 21st century method for better engagement and tackling underlying grievances. Serious games can open the door to addressing the root causes of issues more effectively.

References

Richard Van Eck, Digital Game-Based Learning: It's Not Just the Digital Natives Who Are Restless, 2006

Clark C. Abt, Serious Games, Viking Press, 1970

Challenging Violence in Schools: an issue of masculinities, Martin Mills, Open University Press, 2001.

Education and Conflict, Lynn Davies, Rutledge Falmer, 2004

Educating against Extremism, Lynn Davies, Trentham, 2008

Evaluation of an Immersive Learning Programme, Jarvis, S. & de Freitas, S. (2009). ISBN: 978-0-7695-3588-3.

The Challenge of Teaching Controversial Issues, Edited byt Bilary Claire and Cathie Holden, Trentham, 2007

Useful websites

http://www.choicesandvoices.com
https://www.education.gov.uk/publications/standard/publicationDetail/Page1/288113
http://www.cohesioninstitute.org.uk/
Playable demo of Choices and Voices : http://playgen.com/choices-and-voices

Section 3: Social, Organisational and Policy Aspects of ICT and Strategic Intelligence Management

Section 3: Social, Organisational and Policy Aspects of ICT and Strategic Intelligence Management

Chapter 10: Strategic Intelligence Management for Combating Crime and Terrorism

Babak Akhgar and Simeon J. Yates

Abstract In this chapter we propose a conceptual framework for use by Law Enforcement Agencies when developing methodologies to best strategically manage intelligence in the context of crime and terrorism detection and prevention. Conceptually we define strategic intelligence management as: "A term that reflects an evaluable framework for a complex matrix of individual or collective mental constructs (thoughts, visions, ideas, insights, learning processes, experiences, goals, expertise, values, perceptions, and expectations) held by individuals that provides specific guidance for specific actions in pursuit of particular ends. This includes the rationale for the steps and stages of the methodology and the user's goals and objectives, which should reflect the methodology's overall goals and objectives. Therefore for the purposes of this chapter we extend Akhgar's (1999) definition of KM and define it in the SIM context as: "a process of creating value added Learning Processes (i.e. knowledge) so that knowledge becomes the strategic resource of a law enforcement agency with measurable and quantifiable value in successfully combating a crime or act of terrorism". From this we propose a conceptual template for the construction of a methodology (CTCM) in this domain and consider its application in an example case.

Introduction

In this chapter we will discuss Strategic Intelligence Management (SIM) and its application in law enforcement contexts from an informatics and strategic management perspective. Our aim is to explore methodological approaches to SIM and put forward a paradigm based on an epistemological (rather than ontological) approach to Intelligence Management. In this chapter, we focus on a process view of SIM with particular attention to law enforcement agencies activities in combating crime and terrorism through the use of ICT.

From our perspective the prerequisite for successful Intelligence Management, is applied and domain specific Knowledge Management (KM). The core foundation of KM is built upon a continuum by which data – a set of facts or observations – are first turned into information – an interpretation of the data within a particular context – and then information into knowledge – an abstraction of a learning process (see: Akhgar, 1999). Extending the later we define intelligence in the context of law enforcement agencies as a process of utilising the knowledge created, obtained or extracted for particular course of action.

Akhgar's (1999) view of knowledge is driven from an epistemological notion of logic. The foundation of the latter is deeply grounded in ideas of Farabi and Sohrevardi who were Persian Scholars/Philosophers from 10th and 12th centuries. Therefore for the purposes of this chapter we extend Akhgar's (1999) definition of KM and define it in the SIM context as:

> "A process of creating value added Learning Processes (i.e. knowledge) so that knowledge becomes the strategic resource of a law enforcement agency with measurable and quantifiable value in successfully combating a crime or act of terrorism".

An alternative perspective on KM applications

There are a wide range of technologies available to support KM although there is no definitive market leader. Akhgar and Siddiqi (2001) suggest a taxonomical categorisation of KM applications in terms of their core functionalities, which include:

- Gathering
- Representing,
- Organising/Visualising
- Contributing
- Distributing
- Collaborating
- Refining

From the philosophical perspective many current KM applications and tools are predominately 'ontology' driven either by design or by their core assumptions. Therefore the dominant method of gathering, organising, representing and distributing knowledge are through explicit relationships defined among different concepts through the use of an 'ontology' or controlled vocabulary. The controlled vocabulary enables representations and facilitates automatic reasoning and inferences. In ontology driven KM solutions, for a given problem there can be a set of pre-defined solutions with fixed and pre-defined value propositions.

Within Ontology driven solutions the mode of knowledge can be viewed as analogous to one where we consider knowledge as the dependent variable (K) of a basic production function (f) such that:

$$K = f(x_1, x_2, x_3, x_{n-1}, x_n)$$

Where the independent variables (x_1, x_2 *etc.*) are defined as static factors that do not change over time. Knowledge is therefore the sum at any point of the combined effects of these factors. As with production functions in microeconomics, in assuming that that the maximum output technologically possible from a given set of inputs is achieved, the approach abstracts from the realities inherently associated with any particular knowledge production and management process.

Given the dynamic nature of the environment in which Law Enforcement Agencies (LEAs) operate with constant changes in the modus operandi of criminals and terrorists, ontology driven solutions can have limited impact and return on investment (ROI) for LEAs. This is due to the fact that, by nature, ontology based systems only provide a “solution” to “a problem” based on highly structured and static relationships.

Furthermore if we look at a simple Intelligence type classifications used by LEAs (e.g. IMINT, SIGINT, ELINT, HUMINT in the UK context) the current ontological solutions fail to create a holistic representation and single knowledge asset – a combined intelligence representation – useable for elements of the investigation, planning or execution of an operation. Intelligence of this type in law enforcement agencies data repositories can be ‘fused’ in two general ways. The first involves ‘direct’ associations and reasoning chains and the second is ‘indirect’. Semantically configured, the direct method usually results in a small number of potential conclusions or solutions. The indirect approach usually results in a larger potential number of conclusions. The indirect approach is useful for ‘web crawling’ type activities in virtually combined, distributed and mixed datasets (for example in cross border collaboration as in the context of the Odyssey project – see chapter 2).

In order to address the above we propose the Epistemologically Driven KM approach as the underlying principal of SIM. Here no ‘correct’ solution can be sought. Instead different value added processes for understanding and learning about real world dynamic problems (e.g. criminal activities) should be considered. Figure 10.1 below is a representation of the philosophical and technological barriers that exist between ontological KM solutions and our proposed epistemological approach. We believe the epistemological approach can satisfy the canonical set of requirements needed for the law enforcement agencies activities.

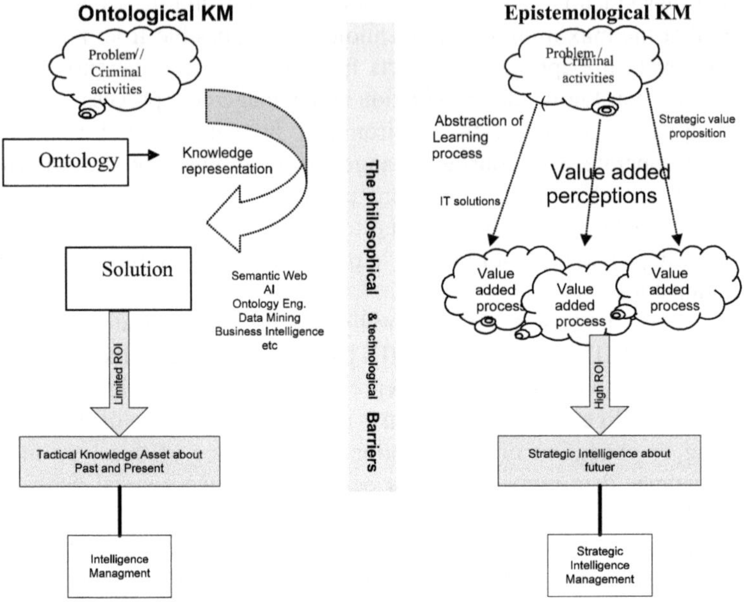

Fig. 10.1. Epistemological Perspective of Knowledge Management

In our proposition the KM solutions are not merely tactical representations of domain knowledge based on a pre-defined functional representation of knowledge. In the context of a criminal investigation or the design of an operation ontology based functional representations are at best concerned with "What", "How", "When", "Where" and "Whom. Rather KM solutions need to be an inter-related set of multidimensional functions and underlying logic rooted in the abstraction of human or machine learning processes. As well as attempting to answer the above questions these solutions have to push the boundaries during an investigation or when planning an operation to discover "Why", "What if", "What next", and to produce pro-active alerts. Alerts are particularly important when it comes to "Prevention" and "Detection" functions of LEAs. It should be noted that by 'value added processes' we are referring to all activities and services needed and their synchronization for development of Strategic Intelligence.

Strategic Intelligence Management (SIM)

Law enforcement agencies regard deployment of their Intelligence Management and KM cycles as one of their key strategic initiatives which can potentially provide the necessary basis for sustainable competitive advantage over criminal and terrorist activities. From the ICT perspective, there are numerous methodological approaches for KM deployment, predominantly driven from software vendors or consulting firms promoting their services. The lack of an end-to-end holistic approach for SIM deployment that is grounded in a sound methodological foundation is clearly evident in the current market place (Akhgar and Yates 2011).

In the previous sections we have elaborated on two types of KM deployment approaches - epistemological and ontological. We argued that although the ontological approaches for KM deployment provide substantive benefit and advantages to Strategic Intelligence, in order to fully realize KM potential, law enforcement agencies need to adopt epistemological approaches. One of the critical success factors identified by Akhgar et al (2009) for an epistemological approach is the formulation of a SIM strategy and provision of a generic methodological approach capable of dealing with complex requirements of combating crime and terrorism. However before we address our proposed methodological solution, it is necessary to further define SIM and the SIM formulation process.

Conceptually we define SIM as:

> "A term that reflects an evaluable framework for a complex matrix of individual or collective mental constructs (thoughts, visions, ideas, insights, learning processes, experiences, goals, expertise, values, perceptions, and expectations) held by individuals that provides specific guidance for specific actions in pursuit of particular ends. This is undertaken by utilising knowledge within LEAs extended value systems (location, communication platforms, social media, legal requirements, jurisdiction, political and social constrains).

Thus SIM formulation can be defined as:

> "A pragmatic, action-oriented and result driven process of transforming LEA knowledge utilisation from current status to the desired status based on combined Intelligence and knowledge life cycle which include the processes of collection, analysis, creation, transformation, collaboration, visualisation, storage, evaluation, refinement and assessment."

Conceptual template for the construction of a methodology

Formulation of SIM requires a methodological approach. Our approach is based on a review of a number of publically available intelligence models (e.g. UK NIM, EU IMM) and earlier research by Tolavanen (1998) and Akhgar (2003). In this context of 'method engineering' we have used a conceptual template for the construction of a methodology (CTCM) in order to identify and elaborate the core methodological components needed for SIM. CTCM core elements are illustrated in figure 10.2

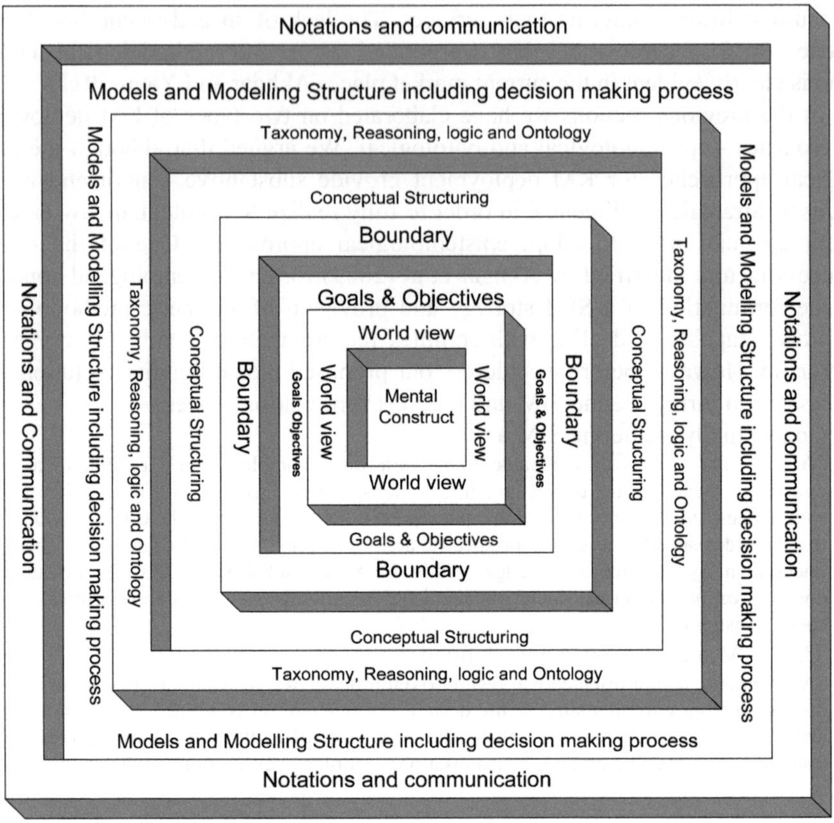

Fig. 10.2. A conceptual template for construction of a methodology

According to the CTCM (Figure 10.2) a methodology is based on a number of problem frames (Jackson, 1995) or layers. The shape [original idea of the shape drive from the research by Tolavanen 1998] of the CTCM emphasises that different layers are neither exclusive nor orthogonal (mutually independent). Each layer complements the others and all are required to construct a methodology. Each layer has two facets: a) a conceptual description; and b) an interface projection (see figure 10.3).

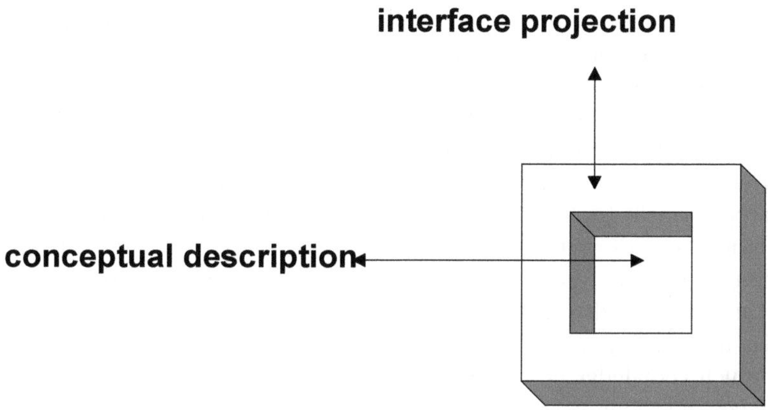

Fig. 10.3. CTCM Fragment

The conceptual description is the 'underlying logic' and the interface projection is the instantiation of that logic. In essence the conceptual description represents the absolute view of the object/idea/representation and the interface projection represents the operational view. Below, we describe the core components of this CTCM and how it could be used to construct a methodology for SIM.

Mental constructlayer

The mental construct (MC) layer of the actant creating the methodology is the heart of the CTCM. The underlying philosophical paradigm of the methodology derives from this layer. However in law enforcement contexts there is usually more than one person or system (several actants) involved in the development of methodologies. Particularly when dealing with complex and multi-agency operations or investigations. Hence a question will rise about whose set of mental constructs will be used?

Within the methodology development environment a range of processes will require the production of an overview of the collective set of mental constructs for in play for the specific investigation or action. The collective "representation" of the set of methodology creators' mental constructs will form the layer of CTCM. However as the research by Nuseibeh (1990) shows in the context of human intellectual architecture and group dynamics the dominant thought processing elements (in relation to the group) of individuals will form the group mental construct (GMC).

The group mental construct (GMC) is a different mental construct than the individual actants MCs; rather it is the representation of dominated factors within each MC. For example different knowledge sets and ethical values from individuals will be projected through the GMC; although there are other elements that might be influential in the formation of the GMC such as political pressure and national security. The projection of the methodology creator(s) mental constructs will be communicated through the description of a World-View. This projection of MC onto the environment creates a semantic representation of the underlying philosophy and the perception of the methodology from methodology creator(s) perspective. It includes all the values, perceptions, understandings and knowledge of the target domain (in this case a criminal or terrorist group). In the context of LEA activity the GMC may force the set of actants working on an investigation or prevention activity (e.g. an investigation team) to address such questions as:

- What are the value drivers of the criminal/terrorist group?
- Is there any ideology?
- How much knowledge do we have about the ideology?
- How accurate is our information and knowledge about the ideology?
- Is there any pattern to behaviours?
- What are our constraints when dealing with the problem situation?
- How will the end game form?
- What are the consequences of our actions?
- How do we obtain the required intelligence?
- What are the legal issues?
- What are the critical success factors in reducing vulnerability to a terrorist and organised crime attacks?
- Are we seeking hard solutions (e.g. technology focused) or soft solutions (e.g. community engagement) for this problem?
- Are our actions ethical?
- What are our ethical guidelines and codes of conduct?

Goals and objectives

The next layer in the CTCM is the goals and objectives layer. Methodologies are not only used to describe the problem domain in the course of an investigation or planning of an operation, but they also should help to improve the "current situation" (before intervention). Before we discuss this layer of the CTCM we have to emphasise that goals and objectives should be based around a clear separation between the uses of the words "goals" and "objectives". Whereby the goals represent the desired outcome in the future – the purpose of the SIM methodology in law enforcement problem solving context – objectives are the points along the way that inform the methodology user if they area on the right track. Objectives identify the critical success factors of an investigation process. This layer of the CTCM is concerned with the contextualisation of the problem situation and its domain. It is used to frame our understanding of a problem. Jackson (1995) refers to this as the "problem frame". It deals with all the aspects of the real world one needs to consider and understand. For example the interrelationship between intelligence components such as the HUMINT and ELINT elements or people linkage directly or otherwise in a course of an investigation. This includes identification of the problem and its type in order to develop goals and objectives. The projection of a methodology aims and objectives is communicated to the methodology user through the boundary element of the CTCM. In them methodology construction context it should provide a clear understanding of "what is in" and "what is out" based on the methodology goals and objectives. This is illustrated in figure 10.4.

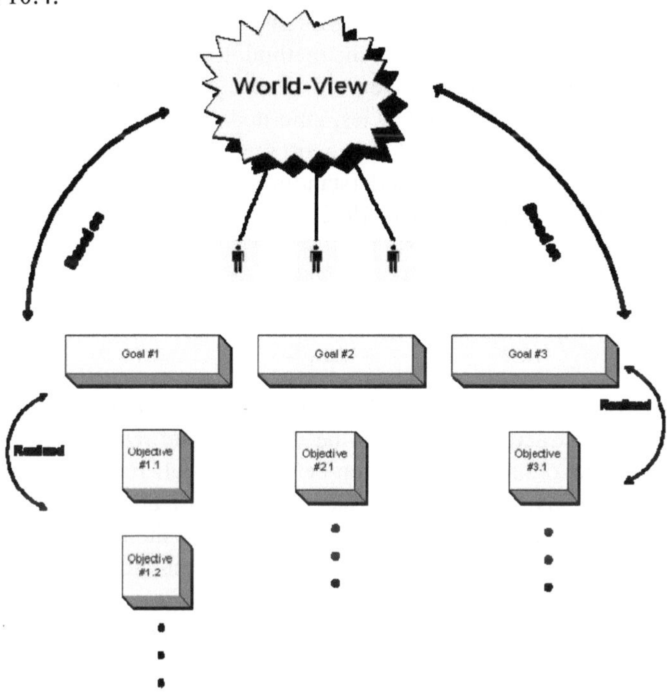

Fig. 10.4. Boundary construction for the CTCM

Conceptual structuring

The next layer of the CTCM is the conceptual structuring. The rationale provided by Jayaratna (1994) asserts that in the context of methodology construction we use structuring [verb] rather than structure [noun] to describe the linkages and organization of concepts. Following this then, during methodology construction it is impossible to simply and statically analyse and completely represent the goals and objectives of the methodology and required actions. It is therefore necessary to restrict attention to a smaller number of concepts and the key meaningful relationship between them. This is particularly important for envisaging the clustering of intelligence captured during an operation and creating a logical and conclusive link between the items of intelligence. The conceptual structuring layer covers procedural guidelines and service descriptions, which describe how the process of achieving the methodology's goals and objectives should be carried out. This is usually based on a national framework or directive such as UK NIM model. The conceptual structuring of a methodology in CTCM is communicated with them methodology user through its taxonomy, reasoning, logic and ontology. This includes the rationale for the steps and stages of the methodology and the user's goals and objectives, which should reflect the methodology's overall goals and objectives as identified in the previous layer. IT should also communicate the key properties (such as the history, dependencies, inherited, events, instantiation, composition and decomposition, states, and emergent, services and roles and responsibilities) needed for planning, tactical understanding and strategic execution of an investigation or an operation (Tolavanen, 1993 and Jayaratna 1994)

Models and the modelling structure

This layer deals with Models and the Modelling structure. Ontology defined as part of the conceptual structuring layer can be validated and represented globally by using models and taxonomical interaction between models represented through modelling structure. Hence models can be seen as a simplification of the reality or snap view of what is perceived as reality. The latter also should also be implemented for the decision making processes needed within the goals and objectives of the methodology. Jayaratna (1994) stated that models are embedded in the methodologies and their role, type and form help to determine what aspects of reality are captured and understood. In the methodology construction process, models are used to try to gain understanding, and the model's complexity increases as we learn more about the underlying problem domain. For example in a criminal drug trafficking activity the proceeds of the operation may be linked to terrorist activities; therefore our modelling of the drug supply chain may include a clear understanding of a particular terrorist cell. Therefore a combined drug trafficking and terrorism model and modelling structure maybe needed to address the issue. The purpose of creating a model in CTCM is to help law enforcement agents understand, describe, communicate, analyses, or create scenarios with regard to a specific issue of concern

Notations and communication

In the CTCM, models and modelling structure are communicated with the user via a notation. What models and modelling structure are defined based on an epistemological view as part of the conceptual structuring can be discussed and represented only by a notation or set of inter-related notions (see chapter 2 for example of the Odyssey project's Gun Crime analysis notation). The combination of models, modelling structure and notations provides a communication platform in the methodology. The notations can range from formal mathematical representation (e.g. Z) to highly unstructured representation such as rich pictures. Communication standards, both formal and de facto exist in the practice of LEAs. As with any area of professional communication cultural norms and practices have developed within the day-to-day working of LEAs. This is often driven by legal requirements or by formal or de facto standards imported through the use of specific software or the market dominance of specific technologies. For example many crime analysts and investigating officers within LEAs make use of networked graph representations of the links between objects of evidence, people and locations to quickly describe findings or hypotheses. The communication strategies, formats, notations and content used in the CTCM need to fit with the accepted and understood standards known to the methodology creators and users.

Possible scenario

A group of terrorists inspired by a fundamentalist religious ideology decide to undertake acts of social terror in order to gain international attention. They intend to commit acts of homicide by planting bombs on the rail transport network in a major European City. They plan a series of co-ordinated explosions on trains packed with commuters to create mass loss of life and chaos on the rail network. They use mobile phones including text massages, social network web sites and e-mail to plan the attacks and obtain the necessary resources; such as information on locations, technical know-how, financing of the operation, and target identification. Stolen credit card information, other false identity documents and sleeper agents are used to create the financial resources needed to commit the act of terrorism. Bombs were to be detonated by mobile phone technology triggering a detonator in an explosive pack left on the trains. In one case an attacker was prepared to explode his own bomb whilst it was in a bag he was carrying. Training for the attacks was co-ordinated and delivered in a foreign country for the group; from where they communicated with people in Europe using multiple languages and coded communication protocols.

In the above simplistic scenario we can apply CTCM for SIM from 4 different strategic perspectives: prevent, pursue, protect and prepare. Following the constituent elements of the CTCM the first step is identification of group mental constructs (for each of the above strategies or a collective view of them). This needs to be done within law enforcement agency as well as for the terrorist group, and the potential target victims. We have to create a clear and methodical view of the possible perpetrator of the crime, their ideological stands (if known), value propositions, mode of operation, decision making process, command structure both formal and informal and other elements needed for each of the above strategies. At the next level using boundary construction method, goals and objectives should be identified. The latter can be instrumental for any protect or prepare type strategy.

Having now identified the relevant mental constructs, which the methodology users will be, the methodology application domain (for example terrorism prevention) as well as the aims and objectives of the action (specific incident prevention) the next set is the formalisation of the knowledge packages and their interrelationship. This might include a taxonomy of the communication used within the terrorist group, locations, events, social media feeds, traces, DNA profiles, existing information packages such as CCTV footage, data from law enforcement agencies own ICT platforms, all other types of INTEL. A holistic and integrated model of the latter can form the ontological representation of the problem situation enabling staff from related agencies staff to take appropriate and informed decisions. Finally a relevant communication platform including ICT needs to be created using appropriate notions, not only for the execution of the strategy but also for any altering system needed during the monitoring operation of the potential terrorist activities. For example such a platform might alert LEA staff of network traffic in a particular chat room, provide location alerts, note changes in suspects extended communication network, possible sleeper cell activation, and situation awareness alerts from other agencies.

Conclusion

The goal of this chapter has been to try and capture how specific methodologies for combating crime and terrorism might be developed using a conceptual template – itself informed by ideas from KM. Though one solution might be a highly integrated ICT system, either in general or specific to a domain (for example gun crime – see chapter 2), many real systems in use by LEAs involve a mix of ICT, organisational systems and practices, multiple communications media and data sources. New forms of ICT for the support of investigations (see chapter 6), communication (see chapter 13), data capture (see chapter 7), training (see chapters 8 and 9) and also knowledge elicitation (see chapter 2) add to the complexity (see chapter 5) of the domains in which LEAs function. A systematic approach to KM and a strategic approach to intelligence management are therefore needed in this context. A lack of systematic strategic intelligence management of available information and intelligence has real and profound human consequences (see chapter 11). In this chapter we have discussed the notion of SIM from theoretical perspectives. We have put forward a number of definitions which might enable user community to construct their own representation of SIM. We have presented a model to enable law enforcement agencies to develop methodologies for implementation and execution of SIM.

References

Akhgar, B (1999) Strategic information systems beyond technology, A knowledge management perspective. SHU Presentation.

Akhgar, B and Crosland I (2000); An investigation into the extent to which knowledge management technologies can promote knowledge sharing, Sheffield Hallam University M.Sc. Thesis

Akhgar, B (2003); Strategic Information Systems, from Concept to Code, WSG 2003.

Akhgar, B and Siddiqi J (2001); A framework for the delivery of web-centric knowledge management applications, Internet Computing IC'2001. Vol. 1 page 47. CSREA Press

Akhgar, B and Yates, S (2011); Strategic Intelligence Management, presentation for 3Int Conf on KM. THE/IR

Checkland, P and Holwell, S (1998) Information, Systems and Information Systems: Making sense of the field. John Wiley & Sons, England

Farabi, a (950); Terminology of Logic, Translation into Persian by Hassan Malekshahi (Tehran 1998).

Harris, K, Austin, T, Fenn, J, Hayward, S, and Cushman, A (1999) The impact of knowledge management on Enterprise architecture, Strategic analysis report, Gartner Group

Jackson, M. (1995); Software Requirements and Specifications - a lexicon of practice, principles and prejudices. Wokingham, Addison-Wesley.

Jayaratna, N (1994/1996); Understanding and Evaluating Methodologies, NIMSA, A systemic Framework, McGraw-Hill Book company

Nuseibeh, S (1990); Management philosophy, Avicenna Perspective on epistemology. Arayeh Publication. Fifth Edition.

Tolavanen, J (1998); Incremental Method Engineering with Modeling Tools, Theoretical Principles and Empirical Evidence

Chapter 11: Human Trafficking – The Importance of Knowledge Information Exchange

Glynn Rankin and Nick Kinsella

Abstract Trafficking in persons is a complex and growing global problem that requires a comprehensive cross sector response. It occurs across and within national borders. It affects virtually every country either as a country of origin, transit or destination for victims. It involves the exploitation of people and the fundamental breach of their human rights. Every year, thousands of men, women and children fall into the control of traffickers, in their own countries and abroad. Trafficking in Human Beings, (THB) involves the exploitation of people through force, coercion, threat, fraud or deception and may include acts generally defined as human rights abuses. Trafficking takes many forms, trafficked persons are exploited into prostitution, forced labour and services, slavery-like practices, and their body organs may be removed and sold. Human trafficking can be identified by the coming together of three factors: First, the act, (the recruitment, transportation, transfer, harbouring or receipt of persons); Second, the means, (the threat, use of force or other forms of coercion) and third, the purpose, (i.e. exploitation). In the case of children the use of threat or force in achieving these three factors is not required. Improving current data/intelligence systems and the ability to harmonise and use the data and exchange information is advantageous and would enable in-formed national action strategies and planning at both strategic and tactical level; improved monitoring and evaluation; targeted and informed awareness and prevention campaigns; enhanced training; targeted victim care and provision; identification of links between source and destination countries; improved and informed investigations and prosecutions.

Introduction

> 'I believe that trafficking of persons, particularly women and children, for forced and exploitative labour, including for sexual exploitation, is one of the most egregious violations of human rights that the United Nations now confronts. It is widespread and growing'. Kofi Annan, Secretary-General of the United Nations, (forward to the United Nations Convention against Transnational Organised Crime).

Trafficking in persons is a complex and growing global problem that requires a comprehensive cross sector response. It occurs across and within national borders. It affects virtually every country either as a country of origin, transit or destination for victims. It involves the exploitation of people and the fundamental breach of their human rights.

Every year, thousands of men, women and children fall into the control of traffickers, in their own countries and abroad. Trafficking in Human Beings, (THB) involves the exploitation of people through force, coercion, threat, fraud or deception and may include acts generally defined as human rights abuses. Trafficking takes many forms, trafficked persons are exploited into prostitution, forced labour and services, slavery-like practices, and their body organs may be removed and sold. Children are trafficked for many forms of abuse including, sexual exploitation, forced labour, domestic servitude, organised begging, street crime and ritual abuse. According to UNICEF, as many as two million children are subjected to prostitution in the global commercial sex trade. International covenants and protocols obligate criminalization of the commercial sexual exploitation of children.

Many regard this trade in human beings as the ‘modern slave trade’. This trade in human misery has many differences however to the slave trade of two hundred years ago. Two hundred years ago, in the days of William Wilberforce and other leading abolitionists, the slave trade was visible. Governments, courts, supported this horrendous trade and even in some cases the church. Today, public opinion and the opinions of governments has altered, the trafficking we see in the twenty first century is a covert crime, conducted by criminals in networks that cross local and national borders. The covert nature of the crime makes it much harder both to detect and to gage the true scale of the activity. Intelligence therefore becomes vital in the struggle to defeat the traffickers and support victims. Likewise, the data that in many instances was so meticulously kept two hundred years ago by slave owners is absent today. Governments, civil society and the public at large have a duty to improve our knowledge on the scale of the issue to ensure a more effective response.

There has been a great deal of focus on improving this data knowledge gap and some estimates have been forthcoming; much more needs to be done however, before we can be confident in the accuracy of knowledge and predictions of scale and type of activity undertaken. According to the 2008 report by the International Labour Organisation[16] (ILO) an estimated 2.4 million people fall victim to human trafficking annually. Human trafficking is increasingly developing into a profit-generating form of organised crime. According to the ILO study, criminal networks generate revenues of 26.6 billion Euros per year with the “human being as a commodity”. Trafficking in human beings now ranks third in terms of the generation of illegal revenues after illegal drug trafficking and the arms trade.

Women and children are particularly affected by human trafficking. Poverty, social exclusion, the effects of globalisation and displacement following conflicts

---

[16] ILO Action against Trafficking in Human Beings Report, 2008

are all factors impacting on individuals that increase the potential risk of being trafficked. According to the United Nations Office on Drugs and Crime, (UNODC) 2008 report[17] the annual flow of new victims (based on a two year turnover) is 70,000 in a market volume of 140,000 that is worth US$3 billion per year.

The 2010 Trafficking in Persons (TIP) report records the following data on global scale:

- Adults and children in forced labour, bonded labour, and forced prostitution around the world: 12.3 million
- Successful trafficking prosecutions in 2009: 4,166
- Successful prosecutions related to forced labour: 335
- Victims identified: 49,105
- Ratio of convicted offenders to victims identified, as a percentage: 8.5
- Ratio of victims identified to estimated victims, as a percentage: 0.4
- Countries that have yet to convict a trafficker under laws in compliance with the Palermo Protocol: 62
- Countries without laws, policies, or regulations to prevent victims' deportation: 104
- Prevalence of trafficking victims in the world: 1.8 per 1,000 inhabitants
- Prevalence of trafficking victims in Asia and the Pacific: 3 per 1,000 inhabitants

In 2009, as part of 'Operation Pentameter 2', a national campaign in the United Kingdom targeting trafficking, the Association of Chief Police Officers of England and Wales, (ACPO), sponsored 'Project Acumen', a project targeted at identifying the scale of sex trafficking within the UK. The police led enquiry reported in the summer of 2010 on the sexual exploitation of foreign migrants only and estimated that there are 2600 trafficked women in the UK. The report highlighted that these women are highly vulnerable. A further 9200 women were considered to be vulnerable to the trafficking scenario. The difficulty in such work was shown when the project failed to identify any victims from Africa, a fact that contradicted the 'hard' data recorded within the National Referral Mechanism (NRM) of the United Kingdom. The project also excluded UK national victims from the project terms of reference, yet in the NRM data of the UK, British nationals are the largest group conclusively identified as victims of trafficking.

What is Human Trafficking?

To build an effective response there must be clarity on both what constitutes human trafficking and also what doesn't. Governments have, and are, being urged by the United Nations and other bodies to take effective action to prevent and

[17] UNODC Trafficking in Persons to Europe for Sexual Exploitation Report, 2008

counter human trafficking and support victims. To this end the United Nations has taken a lead role in countering trafficking by facilitating greater understanding of the problem and facilitating international shared definitions and responses.

The internationally recognised definition of human trafficking is contained within the United Nations Convention against Transnational Organized Crime, adopted by General Assembly resolution 55/25 of 15 November 2000. The convention entered into force on 29 September 2003 and is supplemented by three separate protocols, each of which focuses on a particular criminal activity. The Protocol to Prevent, Suppress and Punish Trafficking in Persons, Especially Women and Children; was adopted by General Assembly resolution 55/25 and entered into force on 25 December 2003.

> 'It is the first global legally binding instrument with an agreed definition on trafficking in persons. The intention behind this definition is to facilitate convergence in national approaches with regard to the establishment of domestic criminal offences that would support efficient international cooperation in investigating and prosecuting trafficking in person's cases. An additional objective of the Protocol is to protect and assist the victims of trafficking in persons with full respect for their human rights.'

According to Article 2 of annex 2 of the protocol, the purposes of the Protocol are:

> (a) To prevent and combat trafficking in persons, paying particular attention to women and children;
> (b) To protect and assist the victims of such trafficking, with full respect for their human rights; and
> (c) To promote cooperation among States Parties in order to meet those objectives.

Article 3 defines trafficking as:

> For the purposes of this Protocol:
> (a) "Trafficking in persons" shall mean the recruitment, transportation, transfer, harbouring or receipt of persons, by means of the threat or use of force or other forms of coercion, of abduction, of fraud, of deception, of the abuse of power or of a position of vulnerability or of the giving or receiving of payments or benefits to achieve the consent of a person having control over another person, for the purpose of exploitation. Exploitation shall include, at a minimum, the exploitation of the prostitution of others or other forms of sexual exploitation, forced labour or services, slavery or practices similar to slavery, servitude or the removal of organs;
> (b) The consent of a victim of trafficking in persons to the intended exploitation set forth in subparagraph (a) of this article shall be irrelevant where any of the means set forth in subparagraph (a) have been used;
> (c) The recruitment, transportation, transfer, harbouring or receipt of a child for the purpose of exploitation shall be considered "trafficking in persons" even if this does not involve any of the means set forth in subparagraph (a) of this article;
> (d) "Child" shall mean any person under eighteen years of age.

Human trafficking can therefore be identified by the coming together of three factors:

1. First, the act, (the recruitment, transportation, transfer, harbouring or receipt of persons)
2. Second, the means, (the threat, use of force or other forms of coercion)
3. Third, the purpose, (i.e. exploitation)

In the case of children the use of threat or force in achieving these three factors is not required.

What form does Human Trafficking take?

The 2010 TIP report records the major forms of trafficking and exploitation include:

- Forced Labour
- Sex Trafficking
- Bonded Labour
- Debt Bondage among Migrant Labourers
- Involuntary Domestic Servitude
- Forced Child Labour
- Child Soldiers
- Child Sex Trafficking

Forced labour

Recent studies show the majority of human trafficking in the world takes the form of forced labour. The ILO estimates that for every trafficking victim subjected to forced prostitution, nine people are forced to work. Also known as involuntary servitude, forced labour may result when unscrupulous employers exploit workers made more vulnerable by high rates of unemployment, poverty, crime, discrimination, corruption, political conflict, or cultural acceptance of the practice. Immigrants are particularly vulnerable, but individuals also may be forced into labour in their own countries. Female victims of forced or bonded labour, especially women and girls in domestic servitude, are often sexually exploited as well.

The European Court of Human Rights has interpreted "forced labour" as comprising two elements; involuntariness and unjustifiable or oppressive character. Forced Labour represents a severe violation of human freedom practices similar to slavery, debt bondage and serfdom. For example:

- A woman and her two sons were convicted of human trafficking in their Indian restaurant in 2010. They were found guilty of conspiracy to traffic persons into the UK for purposes of exploitation. They brought nine men from India and Pakistan to the UK and made them work long hours for low wages. Their passports were confiscated and they were subjected to physical and verbal threats.
- Eighteen pensioners with dementia living in a care home were victims of trafficking where working a "modern day slaves". The victims were brought from Mauritius to the UK by the traffickers, a couple who owned the care home, and

forced to work up to 90 hours a week against their will. The traffickers were jailed and ordered to pay a £450,000 confiscation order.

Sex trafficking

Sex trafficking comprises a smaller but still significant portion of overall human trafficking. When an adult is coerced, forced, or deceived into prostitution – or maintained in prostitution through coercion – that person is a victim of trafficking. All of those involved in recruiting, transporting, harbouring, receiving, or obtaining the person for that purpose have committed a trafficking crime. Sex trafficking can also occur within debt bondage, as women and girls are forced to continue in prostitution through the use of unlawful "debt" purportedly incurred through their transportation, recruitment, or even their crude "sale" – which exploiters insist they must pay off before they can be free. It is critical to understand that a person's initial consent to participate in prostitution is not legally determinative: if they are thereafter held in service through psychological manipulation or physical force, they are trafficking victims and should receive the benefits outlined in the Palermo Protocol and applicable domestic laws. For example:

- The victim was an 18-year-old Lithuanian trough an acquaintance in Lithuania, she was offered a job in a hotel in London (her cousin had come to London 3 months earlier but had disappeared). She flew to London with two other women where they were met by three men and a woman. The men took the passports from each of the young women. The next day the three were separated. In the evening one of the men raped her. The next day she was sold to a man and taken to his home. He beat her and told her that she would be working as a prostitute. He said he has paid £4,000 for her. He raped her. The following day she was taken to a brothel and made to work as a prostitute where one of the gang kept guard over her. She told her story to all the men who had sex with her to no avail. The next day she was taken to the same flat and put to work again. Again she told the punters that she had been kidnapped but no help was offered. Later, she escaped through a bathroom window and climbed down a tree. She went to the first house and asked the occupier to call the police. He did so. Police raided the premises that afternoon and made arrests.
- Two victims from Lithuania, aged 21 and 23, believed they were travelling to the UK to work as cleaners. The first victim arrived at Heathrow in July and the second in August. The traffickers met them at the airport, they were both taken to Sheffield, their passports taken from them and held against their will. They were raped repeatedly, made to work in saunas and massage parlours.

Bonded labour

One form of force or coercion is the use of a bond, or debt. Often referred to as "bonded labour" or "debt bondage," the practice has long been prohibited under U.S. law by its Spanish name – peonage – and the Palermo Protocol requires its criminalization as a form of trafficking in persons. Workers around the world fall victim to debt bondage when traffickers or recruiters unlawfully exploit an initial debt the worker assumed as part of the terms of employment. Workers may also inherit debt in more traditional systems of bonded labour. In South Asia, for example, it is estimated that there are millions of trafficking victims working to pay off their ancestors' debts.

Debt bondage among migrant labourers

Abuses of contracts and hazardous conditions of employment for migrant labourers do not necessarily constitute human trafficking. However, the attribution of illegal costs and debts on these labourers in the source country, often with the support of labour agencies and employers in the destination country, can contribute to a situation of debt bondage. This is the case even when the worker's status in the country is tied to the employer as a guest worker in the context of employment-based temporary work programs.

Involuntary domestic servitude

A unique form of forced labour is the involuntary servitude of domestic workers, whose workplace is informal, connected to their off-duty living quarters, and not often shared with other workers. Such an environment, which often socially isolates domestic workers, is conducive to non-consensual exploitation since authorities cannot inspect private property as easily as they can inspect formal workplaces. Investigators and service providers report many cases of untreated illnesses and, tragically, widespread sexual abuse, which in some cases may be symptoms of a situation of involuntary servitude.

Trafficking for domestic servitude covers a range of situations, all of which share certain features: subjugation and an obligation to provide work for a private individual, low or no salary, no days off, psychological and/or physical violence, limited or restricted freedom of movement, and the impossibility of a private life.

Be it an adult or a child, the trafficked person usually lives in the house of the family and is constantly at their disposal or mercy[18]. For example:

- A UK pensioner was convicted of trafficking and exploiting an African victim who she used as a slave. She was imprisoned and ordered to pay £25,000 compensation. A UK pensioner was convicted of trafficking and exploiting an African victim who she used as a slave. She was imprisoned and ordered to pay£25,000 compensation.

Forced child labour

Most international organizations and national laws recognize children may legally engage in certain forms of work. There is a growing consensus, however, that the worst forms of child labour should be eradicated. The sale and trafficking of children and their entrapment in bonded and forced labour are among these worst forms of child labour, and these are forms of trafficking. A child can be a victim of human trafficking regardless of the location of that non-consensual exploitation. Indicators of possible forced labour of a child include situations in which the child appears to be in the custody of a non-family member who has the child perform work that financially benefits someone outside the child's family and does not offer the child the option of leaving. Anti-trafficking responses should supplement, not replace, traditional actions against child labour, such as remediation and education. However, when children are enslaved, their abusers should not escape criminal punishment by virtue of longstanding administrative responses to child labour practices.

Child soldiers

Child soldiering can be a manifestation of human trafficking where it involves the unlawful recruitment or use of children – through force, fraud, or coercion – as combatants or for labour or sexual exploitation by armed forces. Perpetrators may be government forces, paramilitary organizations, or rebel groups. Many children are forcibly abducted to be used as combatants. Others are made unlawfully to work as porters, cooks, guards, servants, messengers, or spies. Young girls can be forced to marry or have sex with male combatants. Both male and female child soldiers are often sexually abused and are at high risk of contracting sexually transmitted diseases.

---

[18] See: (Unprotected Work, Invisible Exploitation: Trafficking for the Purpose of Domestic Servitude. OSCE, Vienna (2010)

Child sex trafficking

International covenants and protocols obligate criminalization of the commercial sexual exploitation of children. The use of children in the commercial sex trade is prohibited under the Palermo Protocol as well as by legislation in countries around the world. There can be no exceptions and no cultural or socioeconomic rationalizations preventing the rescue of children from sexual servitude. Sex trafficking has devastating consequences for minors, including long-lasting physical and psychological trauma, disease (including HIV/ AIDS), drug addiction, unwanted pregnancy, malnutrition, social ostracism, and possible death. In addition to those forms mentioned in the TIP report above, there is also the threat of organ harvesting, where victims are trafficked in order to sell their body parts and organs for transplant.

Evidence of these different forms of trafficking within the EU, can be seen in the National Referral Mechanism data of the United Kingdom, (principally a destination country). The National Referral Mechanism, (NRM,) is a framework for identifying victims of human trafficking and ensuring they receive the appropriate care via a two stage decision making process of satisfying a 'Reasonable grounds' and 'Conclusive Grounds' test. An agreed cadre of authorised agencies, including the Police, UK Borders Agency, Social Services and certain NGOs, who encounter a potential victim of human trafficking, can refer them to the Competent Authority.

This data also clearly demonstrates the significant number of source countries and the impact of trafficking on children. The table 11.3 shows a breakdown of minor referrals by exploitation type, Reasonable Grounds (RG) and Conclusive Grounds (CG) decisions. Conclusive Grounds decisions are only considered when a positive Reasonable Grounds decision has been made. In this period, there were 217 positive RG Decisions with the table reflecting exploitation of minors.

Exploitation Type	Referrals at 31/12/10	Positive RG Decision	Positive CG Decision
Domestic Servitude	175	102	42
Labour Exploitation	267	183	122
Sexual Exploitation	438	235	121
Unknown exploitation	52	7	2
Total	932	527	287

Table 11.1. UK National referral mechanism -Statistical Data 1st April 2009 – 31st December 2010

Nationality	Referrals as at 31/12/10	Positive RG Decision	Positive CG Decision
Nigeria	216	102	40
China	149	71	24
Vietnam	120	77	26
Slovakia	57	50	39
Czech Republic	54	43	38
UK	51	49	44
Uganda	42	23	12
Romania	40	30	25
India	37	27	6
Albania	30	15	11
Bangladesh	26	18	10
Sierra Leone	26	17	10
Zimbabwe	26	13	3
Lithuania	21	18	12
Somalia	21	10	6
Total	916	563	306

Table 11.2. Source countries: UK National referral mechanism -Statistical Data 1st April 2009 – 31st December 2010

Exploitation Type	Age Range at Date of Referral	Referrals at: 31/12/10	Positive RG Decision	Positive CG Decision
Sexual Exploitation	Under 10	0	0	0
	10 to 11	0	0	0
	12 to 15	37	33	25
	16 to 17	56	41	29
	Over 18	6	5	5
Labour Exploitation	Under 10	6	5	1
	10 to 11	1	1	1
	12 to 15	33	24	9
	16 to 17	53	36	15
	Over 18	5	0	0
Domestic Servitude	Under 10	2	1	1
	10 to 11	1	1	1
	12 to 15	17	15	11
	16 to 17	20	17	11
	Over 18	4	3	1
Unknown Exploitation	Under 10	13	4	0
	10 to 11	7	2	0
	12 to 15	23	10	6
	16 to 17	36	18	5
	Over 18	2	1	0
Total	322	217	121	

Table 11.3. Age and nature of exploitation: UK National referral mechanism -Statistical Data 1st April 2009 – 31st December 2010

The difference between Human Trafficking and people smuggling

A distinction needs to be made between THB and people smuggling, the two terms are often used interchangeably, but it is important to distinguish between them. People smuggling is trans-national and is illegal migration involving the organised transport of persons across an international border, usually in exchange for a sum of money. The financial component of a people smuggling transaction may be a one-time fee paid to the smuggler before arrival or instalment payments after arrival. The relationship between trafficker and victim does not end upon arrival at destination, as the victim may be subjected to debt bondage (forced labour to pay off a debt). THB occurs both across international borders and within national boundaries. It is a complex problem brought about by inter-related economic, social, cultural, political and personal factors.

THB is an illegal business and criminal activity with individual, informal networks and national and trans-national organised crime groups engaging in trafficking because of high profits and low risks. It is believed that those criminals involved in THB are, most likely, engaged in other illegal activities including drug and gun trafficking and money laundering. If this assumption is correct then particular attention needs to be given to the criminal justice system.

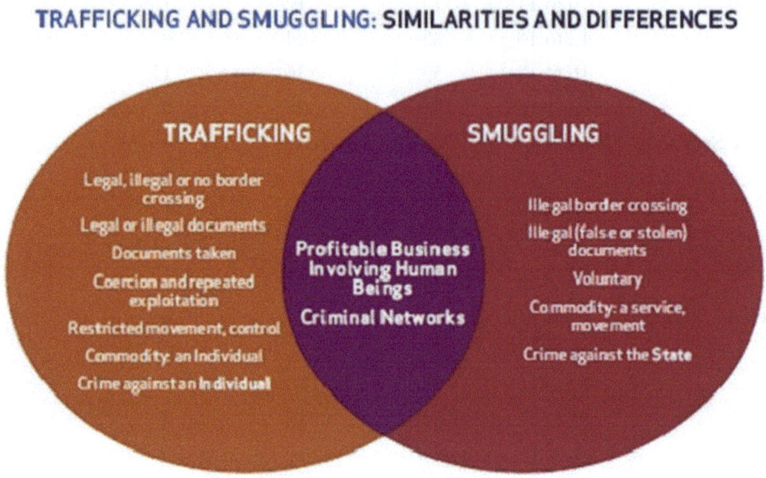

Fig. 11.1. Trafficking and smuggling: similarities and differences

The knowledge of the individual in many cases is different between a person who is smuggled and one who is trafficked. In many cases, (but not all – see debt bondage comment above), a smuggled individual knows they are being smuggled. In contrast a victim of trafficking will, in most scenarios, be unaware of what awaits them until they arrive at their destination.

It is important that the differences between the two activities are accurately understood. The confusion between the two frequently leads to trafficking being seen as, (and contextualised within), an immigration issue rather than a human rights and broader policy issue that requires a broader policy response across governments. This difficulty has been highlighted consistently and was again highlighted within the 2010 Trafficking in Persons report where it refers to:

Dismantling the "3D" approach to Human Trafficking

In the 10 years since the passage of the Palermo Protocol with its "3P" paradigm of prevention, protection and prosecution, a competing, more unfortunate, paradigm seems to persist in impeding greater anti-trafficking progress: the "3D" phenomenon of detention, deportation and disempowerment.

The use of this approach in detaining and deporting trafficking victims is most often the outgrowth of immigration policies or archaic laws that have yet to fully appreciate the phenomenon of modern slavery. However, some of the manifestations of this response are new, appearing only in the last few years and affecting many more women than men.

In such a response, governments may act out of self-interest in ridding themselves of potential burdens. Or they may act in what they claim is the best interest of foreign victims. This usually includes detaining the victims for a short period of time and then deporting them to their country of origin without offering them credible opportunities to seek legal redress (including civil restitution), adequate psychological repair, longer term residency and work, or relocation to a third country. Attempts to hold identified trafficking victims in detention-based facilities governments describe as "shelters" – no matter how comfortable and safe they may be – disempower victims at a critical time when they need a restored sense of individual freedom. Detention models undercut any rapport service providers or investigators might build with victims. Research and law enforcement practice indicates that initial trauma lasts for months and that victims can only give a partial account of their experiences in the early stages of an investigation; a response based on detention and repatriation – even if initial statements have been reduced to video or affidavit – will likely prevent law enforcement from arriving at critical facts.

Sending victims back to their countries of origin without informing them of a full range of options not only exposes them to possible trauma associated with being identified as a trafficking victim, but it also risks returning them to the same condition and exposing them to the same or even more enhanced pressures that contributed to their initial trafficking experience, thus raising the prospects for their re-trafficking. Furthermore, when a country jails and repatriates victims without screening or protection, NGOs are deterred from bringing their clients to the government's attention.

Improving knowledge and understanding of Human Trafficking

THB is a complex problem requiring a comprehensive response. It is important to ascertain the scope and scale of the problem to determine any appropriate response. This requires identifying the differing types of trafficking; are countries source, transit, destination countries or potentially all three? What criminality is involved in THB? More information is required across the key knowledge areas that assist in developing an accurate understanding of the problem. Accurate information on the 'Who, Why, Where, When, What and how' of trafficking is essential. It is crucial that knowledge and understanding of the problem is improved to enable the development of a more effective response.

The UNODC consider that globally 2.5 million people are trafficked within and across borders annually. Further UNODC estimates place the number of people trafficked into Europe at 250,000 per year.

The numbers of trafficked people within the EU (European Union) is large and the costs in human, economic and social terms are enormous. THB is predominantly a gendered crime with approximately 80 per cent of transnational victims thought to be women and girls and up to 50 per cent of victims are thought to be children.

The International Labour Organisation (ILO) estimates that 32 per cent of all victims were trafficked into forced labour, while 43 per cent were trafficked for sexual exploitation and 25 per cent a mixture of both. As with other forms of contemporary slavery, human trafficking is rooted in patterns of discrimination, inequality, social exclusion and poverty and typically affects the most vulnerable members of society.

THB is by its nature transnational, although it is not transnational by definition, and cannot be addressed without international cooperation. The UN Special Rapporteur on trafficking in persons, especially women and children, has stated that "an effective means for combating trafficking in persons will require enhanced information sharing between States through bilateral and multilateral cooperation and increased data collection capacities.

THB can often involve, amongst other things, organized crime networks (OCNs), corruption and a range of other inter-related criminal activities and therefore has high social and economic costs. It can weaken political, social and financial institutions and can debilitate economic development, growth and sustainability; it can undermine the rule of law and break down social cohesion. Globally, the ILO estimates the annual profits generated from THB could be as high as 39 billion US dollars.

Although human trafficking has serious impacts on both individuals, as victims, and Nation States as origin, transit and destination countries, conviction rates currently remain low in most European countries and are below one conviction per 100,000 people.

To successfully combat THB it is necessary to enhance data collection to promote trans-border cooperation, develop a capacity to collect, analyse and ultimately share relevant THB information and data. Knowledge can take the form of either intelligence or data and understanding THB is central to tackling the problem more effectively. Knowledge, from whatever source, is a key requirement in the architecture of that response.

The European Parliament resolution on 10th February 2010 on preventing trafficking in human beings stated:

> "whereas currently there is no precise data on this phenomenon and the available figures appear to underestimate its real scope, as it is a form of crime that takes place underground and is often undetected or wrongly identified: whereas more research must be done on how trafficking takes place, who commits it, how demand drives the supply of services from victims and who falls victim to it and why, and on ways to discourage demand: whereas cooperation and exchanges of information between the Member States and third countries need to be stepped up".

Within the same resolution a call was made on the Council and the Commission to take action to obtain as much information as possible.

The Council of the European Union stated:

> "Without information and statistics, it is difficult to determine the extent of THB and prepare the appropriate policies and operational and legislative responses and ensure effective implementation of initiatives. Therefore, a serious effort within the EU external dimension on THB should promote a move towards a clearer understanding of the root causes, factors in countries of destination facilitating THB, current trends with regard to victims, traffickers and criminal networks, their modus operandi, travel routes and different forms of exploitation".

Due to the covert nature of the crime and the methods used by traffickers to control victims include threats of denunciations to the authorities, threats of violence to both the victim and the victim's family and the actual use of violence – accurate identification of victims is a difficult issue. Victims and survivors of trafficking can provide invaluable and accurate data and intelligence. Harmonisation of processes to assist in the identification of victims would be a significant and positive development that would facilitate the opportunity for effective debriefing, lead to improved intelligence gathering and development, a more targeted intervention approach and the recovery of further victims and perhaps the disruption of traffickers before exploitation takes place.

The Delphi method is used to reach consensus on the indicators of human trafficking. It was developed in the 1950's and has since been widely used in the social, medical and political sciences. In 2001 the ILO established the 'Special Action Programme to Combat Forced Labour including human trafficking. This programme has assisted governments in implementing new laws, developed new training materials and also designed new practical tools to assist in the identification of victims of human trafficking. This work has resulted in the development of four sets of 'operational indicators' relating to forced labour and sexual exploitation of both adults and children. Each individual set of indicators is structured around the component parts of the trafficking definition. Each indicator is also 'weighted' as strong, medium or weak. Overall this system provides an improved and effective process that assists in victim identification.

The Importance of data and intelligence in combating Human Trafficking

Opinion Number 07/2010 of the Group of Experts on Trafficking in Human Beings of the European Commission stated that:

> "Data collection, research and policy definition. Shared knowledge is of fundamental importance in order to plan and revise policies and action. Therefore some specific issues must be tackled. Define parameters for collecting data on THB, using comparable indicators, based on the conclusions of the projects funded by the EU and other relevant information, involving the National Rapporteurs or equivalent mechanisms and their informal network. This would promote a clearer view of the dimension of the phenomenon across the Member States and also provide qualitative information about the different forms and sectors of exploitation and methods of recruitment that would help identify those areas where more specific action is needed" (p.8).

When we refer to knowledge we commonly mean the collection of data and intelligence. Data is defined; by the Wikipedia dictionary:

> "as facts and statistics collected together for reference or analysis. Things known as facts, making the basis for reasoning or calculation".

Intelligence is defined by the Wikipedia dictionary as:

> "the ability to acquire and to apply knowledge and skills. The collection of information of value. Allows thought and reason of intelligence collected".

Improving current data/intelligence systems and the ability to harmonise and use the data and exchange information is advantageous and would enable informed national action strategies and planning at both strategic and tactical level; improved monitoring and evaluation; targeted and informed awareness and prevention campaigns; enhanced training; targeted victim care and provision; identification of links between source and destination countries; improved and informed investigations and prosecutions.

It is a primary objective of all countries to improve their understanding of the phenomenon of THB by developing comprehensive data. Governments, inter-government, non-government and law enforcement agencies all understand the need to collect data and the importance of data is now seen as a key requirement in combatting THB.

The Irish government in their National Action Plan to Prevent and Combat Trafficking of Human beings in Ireland 2009-2012, Objective (3.1.3) is;

> "To improve our understanding of the nature and scale of the problem by developing a comprehensive data and research strategy".

The objective of the Anti-Human Trafficking Unit (AHTU) is:

> "by engaging with relevant Government and non-governmental stakeholders in data capture and research this should help to provide a more comprehensive picture of the scale of and trends in human trafficking and therefore inform policy making."

The AHTU of the Department of Justice, Equality and Law Reform, (now the Department of Justice and Equality), implemented this data collection strategy in January 2009. Anew data strategy is due to be published in May 2011.

The strategy was implemented in conjunction with both governmental and non-governmental agencies.

> "Data is being collected and analysed for the purposes of informing policy development, improving victim support services and guiding counter-trafficking measures. The information collected will include data on victims and traffickers".

The AHTU has attempted to improve its knowledge of the nature and extent of human trafficking in Ireland by collecting standardised data from State Agencies and non-Governmental Organisations with regard to the type of exploitation experienced, gender, age, region or origin and immigration status of alleged victims. Information is also gathered on the criminal justice response in terms of trafficking related arrests, prosecutions and convictions.

A more detailed analysis of alleged victims shows that adult female victims of sexual exploitation from Western Africa form the largest group of those trafficked to Ireland, though the 2010 figures show a significant rise in the number of adult female victims of sexual exploitation from EU Member States. This type of information on the nature, scale and trends of human trafficking is vital for policy makers in Ireland enabling them to tailor services, implement legislative responses and engage in targeted awareness raising in response to observable trends.

The AHTU Data Strategy has been designed to be compatible with data systems currently being developed at EU level. As standardised data is collected over the next few years, trends can be mapped with a possibility for trafficking data to be linked to other social and economic data with a view to providing a more in-depth understanding of the phenomenon.

The International Organization for Migration (IOM) is using a unique tool to monitor the assistance and collect information on the victims of trafficking (VoTs) it assists. Implemented in 2000, and thus incorporating more than eight years of experience, the IOM Global Human Trafficking Information Management System is the largest global database on victims of trafficking containing only primary data on 12,500 registered victims of more than 80 different nationalities trafficked to more than 90 destination countries. It is a standardized anti-trafficking data-management tool and is actively used throughout all regions of the world.

While initially designed as a case management tool for IOM counter-trafficking direct assistance programmes, the IOM Global database quickly demonstrated its added value to research and evaluation. At an IOM-led UN.GIFT expert research meeting in Cairo, Egypt, 2009, the merits of the IOM Global database were further highlighted and the system was upheld as a model of good practice for the systematic collection of human trafficking data.

The International Centre for Migration Policy Development, (ICMPD), in the SEE, (South-East Europe), implemented two projects connected with a database creation for THB: "Data Collection and Information Management – Trafficking" and "Data Collection and Information Management, (DCIM), – Trafficking Phase II". The capacities of SEE countries to efficiently implement national action plans and strategies and thus properly address the problem of trafficking in persons needed to be strengthened. One of the main issues concerns the basic precondition for developing and revising national responses to trafficking, (both national action plans and strategies; the systematic collection and management of statistical data relevant to trafficking in persons. These projects specifically addressed the improvement of the availability of reliable and standardised data and information management.

The ICMPD project "Data Collection and Information Management – Trafficking Phase II" (DCIM 11) had an overall objective to build upon the achievements of the first phase of the DCIM Programme, and to strengthen the capacities of participating institutions to monitor, evaluate and review their National Anti-Trafficking Responses. It aimed to build up the capacities of the participating institutions to process, analyse, present and consequently transform into relevant programmatic information and activities the information contained in the DCIM databases. Whilst ensuring that the criteria and methods for analysing and presenting THB statistical data were regionally harmonised and corresponded to the commonly accepted international standard.

Under these projects the ICMPD further aims to contribute to the harmonisation and improved quality and reliability of data related to trafficking in persons in SEE countries in the areas of prevention, protection and prosecution. It is anticipated that in the course of the project a uniform data system as well as a database will be developed for each participating country/territory and installed within the relevant national institutions.

Footer - The 21 month 'Programme for the Enhancement of Anti-trafficking Responses in South-Eastern Europe, Data Collection and Information Management (DCIM) – Phase 2: Data Processing, Maintenance and Analysis', which concluded in August 2010, is the follow-up project to DCIM Phase I. The DCIM Phase 2 project aims to extend continued technical support to 12 dedicated participating institutions from the preceding project. It combines capacity building relevant to the presentation, maintenance and analysis of the information contained in the databases, with a study concerning the transnational exchange of THB records. Participating countries were Albania, Bosnia and Herzegovina, Croatia, Kosovo, Macedonia, Montenegro, and Serbia

The Council of the European Union stated; "The EU should continue to promote the establishment of National Rapporteurs or equivalent mechanisms and coordination structures with a view to improving the exchange of information and in turn the understanding of the THB phenomenon for the mutual benefit of the EU, third countries, regions and organization's at international level.

Opinion Number 07/2010 of the Group of Experts on Trafficking in Human Beings of the European Commission stated that;

> "Fundamental to increasing the levels of investigations into the organised criminality that lies behind trafficking is the dissemination of information and intelligence amongst the law enforcement authorities of the Member States and with competent EU agencies such as Europol and Eurojust".

Establishing a National Rapporteur or equivalent Mechanism is an important step toward implementing 1) comprehensive qualitative and quantitative data collection, research and analysis of the trafficking situation in the participating State concerned, and 2) a systematic analysis of the effectiveness of measures and policies undertaken to prevent and combat THB. Footer - (Efforts to Combat Trafficking Human Beings in the OSCE Area: Co-ordination and Reporting Mechanisms. OSCE (2008) Vienna pp57)

The collecting and sharing information identifies new trends and patterns to enable THB to be combatted. In the Law Enforcement Agency, (LEA), sphere intelligence is an important factor and agencies that both collect and share information are central to successful operations.

The collecting and sharing of information identifies new trends and patterns to enable THB to be combatted. In the Law Enforcement Agency, (LEA), sphere intelligence is an important factor and agencies that both collect and share information are central to successful operations.

The collection, development and exchange of information and intelligence and the use of such 'data' in intelligence reporting (situation reports, threat assessments, profiling, etc.) is a fundamental element of policing and crime investigation.

Intelligence collection needs to be a thorough and continuous information-gathering and research process and the European Criminal Intelligence Model (ECIM) provides a sound methodology for this process at both national and international levels.

Accurate intelligence provides a platform to scope and analyse crime, to identify knowledge gaps, to develop effective and sustainable policies and to inform policy makers. Without this, the level and scale of the crime and the impact of any response to the crime cannot be accurately measured.

The collection of data must be accompanied by regular reporting. The development of a common methodology for reporting by law enforcement authorities of Member States on the nature and extent of their trafficking problem and the effectiveness of their responses would be helpful. It is noted that the Council has called for work to be done on data collection, so as to make 'comparable national statistical data … available'.

The National Rapporteur, or equivalent mechanism in the Member State, has a clear role in gathering relevant information and statistical data. National data-producing bodies such as law enforcement authorities need to be actively engaged in their own information and intelligence gathering, for both current and future domestic use, and to assist other Member States and relevant EU organisations.

> The European Commission's Stockholm Programme, stated; "The European Council invites Europol, with the support of Member States, to step up intelligence gathering and strategic analysis, to be carried out in cooperation with countries of origin and transit".

Europol is a central information hub that supports and enhances LEA operations and utilises intelligence to support and inform the LEA operations of Member States. It uses Analytical Work Files (AWF), which are databases on specific crime areas which are linked to specific forms of operational support. An AWF is a tool to store, process and analyse factual information, ("hard data"), and intelligence, ("soft data"). It also publishes, bi-annually, an Organised Crime Threat Assessment (OCTA). THB is one of the organised crime activities that are reported upon within the OCTA.

On May 4th, in The Hague, upon publication of the 2011 OCTA, the Europol Director Rob Wainwright said:

> "The bi–annual report, which assesses current and expected trends in organised crime affecting the European Union, explores how a new criminal landscape is emerging, marked increasingly by highly mobile and flexible groups operating in multiple jurisdictions and criminal sectors. Organised crime is a multi–billion euro business in Europe and it is growing in scale. The further expansion of Internet and mobile technologies, the proliferation of illicit trafficking routes and methods as well as opportunities offered by the global economic crisis, have all contributed to the development of a more potent threat from organised crime. Europol's OCTA is the definitive EU assessment of organised crime activity. Ministers, police chiefs, and policy makers will use it to set priorities and establish effective response measures. Europol looks forward to continuing to play a significant role in the fight against organised crime".

Interpol provides all member countries with instant, direct access, to a wide range of criminal information. It is the world's largest international police organization, with 188 member countries. Created in 1923, it facilitates cross-border police co-operation, and supports and assists all organizations, authorities and services whose mission is to prevent or combat international crime. . THB is one of INTERPOL's six priority crime areas and there is an INTERPOL Working Group on Human Trafficking.

INTERPOL's mission is to assist law enforcement agencies in each of its 188 member countries to combat all forms of transnational crime. Guided by four core functions, INTERPOL provides a high-tech infrastructure of technical and operational support to enable police forces around the world to meet the growing challenges of crime in the 21st century. INTERPOL aims to end the abuse and exploitation of human beings for financial gain. Women from developing countries and young children all over the world are especially vulnerable to trafficking, smuggling or sexual exploitation.

Child sexual exploitation on the Internet ranges from posed photos to visual recordings of brutal sexual crimes. One of INTERPOL's main tools for helping police fight this type of crime is the International Child Sexual Exploitation Image database (ICSE DB). Containing hundreds of thousands of images of child sexual abuse submitted by member countries, the ICSE DB facilitates the sharing of images and information thereby assisting law enforcement agencies with the identification of new victims.

Threat assessments based upon intelligence are also key tools in the fight against organised crime, including THB, used within Nation States. In the United Kingdom, (UK), there are threat assessments that consider organised crime and THB which are published annually; there are also specific assessments on THB only that are published when the intelligence is available.

In the UK the Serious and Organised Crime Agency (SOCA) publish the annual Strategic Threat Assessment (STA) of Organised Crime annually. The assessment describes the threats to the UK by organised crime and considers how these threats may develop. Having identified the key threats, a 'National Intelligence Requirement' is produced that stimulates a cross agency 'National Intelligence collection Plan,' prioritizing the collection of information and intelligence against the key intelligence gaps identified in the STA. In November 2010, the Child Exploitation Online Protection (CEOP) published an assessment on child trafficking within the UK. The document is an assessment of the current intelligence picture of child trafficking into, within and through the UK. It aims to build on the findings of CEOP's 2007 Scoping Report and the 2009 STA. The 2009 STA focused on the period 1 March 2007 to 29 February 2008. This assessment brings knowledge up to date by focusing on data collected during the period 1 March 2009 to 28 February 2010. This report aims to inform the reader of the latest trends, themes and patterns in child trafficking. It examines the profiles of child victims and trafficking networks, discusses the methodologies employed and identifies the enablers of trafficking.

Within the UK, the National Intelligence Model, (NIM), is used by LEA. It takes an intelligence led, problem solving approach to crime and disorder. It promotes partnership working and uses the management of information and intelligence to operate at three levels of policing, International, National and Local. The NIM became the policy of the Association of Chief Police Officers (ACPO) in 2000. Under the Police Reform Act (2002) it provides a statutory basis for the introduction of minimum standards and basic principles. (NPIA website)

Conclusion

A vital part of any effective strategy to combat THB is the establishment of a collective response to data and/or intelligence sharing. This should be across all sectors and should not just be confined to government and law enforcement. By collecting information in a systematic structure from all sectors and harmonising data, this exchange of knowledge, can enable the establishment of holistic national action strategies and subsequently effective national action plans, with informed monitoring and evaluation. Targeted and informed multi-agency awareness and prevention campaigns, enhanced victim care and protection and the improved identification of victims of THB. Improved and informed investigations and an increased number of prosecutions. Informed intelligence assessments both on an international and national level that will enable LEAs to target and eradicate those organised criminals involved in THB. It will also enable enhanced training and provide a platform for qualified research.

It is important that all Nation States, whilst taking cognisance of any liberty and privacy issues co-operate on the development of their different operating systems for the collection of data, and work towards a harmonised system. In accord with the European Commission's Stockholm Programme that encourages EU Member states to develop both "an information systems architecture that guarantees interoperability, consistency and adaption to needs".

The European Parliament resolution on 10th February 2010 on preventing trafficking in human beings stated:

> "Calls on the Council and the Commission, in order to obtain as much information as possible, to take action with a view to; - an annual publication of a joint report by Europol, Eurojust and Frontex, to be presented to the EP and the national parliaments as well as the Commission and the Council. This joint report, the presentation of which should be followed by a public hearing with NGOs and civil society so that they can add their expertise, should promote work towards a better understanding of…Developing a common EU template for the collection and collation of data relating to all aspects of trafficking in human beings, including age and gender, to be used in both the Member States and third countries, while complying with relevant legislation on data protection and the rights of the data subject".

Harmonised systems need to include not only a standardised approach to the collection, management and analysis of data, but also comparable and definable terminology and indicators that encourage compatibility and promote data sharing. This will enable the dissemination and sharing of reliable transnational data, create a common data collection methodology and establish and promote improved analytical capabilities that will ensure improved transnational cooperation and coordination of data sharing within Nation States.

Article 19 Of the EU Directive to fight human trafficking states:

> Member States shall take the necessary measures to establish national rapporteurs or equivalent mechanisms. The tasks of such mechanisms shall include the carrying out of assessments of trends in trafficking in human beings, the measuring of results of anti-trafficking actions, including the gathering of statistics in close cooperation with relevant civil society organisations active in this field, and reporting by such a reference on the occasion of their official publication. The methods of making such reference shall be laid down by the Member States.

Chapter 12: Cybercrime Profiling and Trend Analysis

Hamid Jahankhani and Ameer Al-Nemrat

Abstract A significant percentage of the populace do not consider or understand "what and how" cybercrime is committed, nor how they might be a victim of it, and many fear they might unconsciously be part of the process, i.e. they don't understand how to behave online. Reducing the opportunities for cybercrime is not a simple task. It will require co-operation between many players, and fundamental changes in common attitudes and practices. When considering legal implications of the misuse of technologies, it is worth noting that crossing national borders results in a change in the laws that people are subject to. Some countries do not consider hacking and online identity theft as high priority crimes. Similarly, the technological divide leaves gaps in the laws in those countries that are less technologically advanced. The aim of this chapter is to examine the relationship between online behaviour and computer victimisation. Understanding the trends of cybercrime and the strategies employed by cyber criminals in order to commit cybercrime will help to identify the steps that needs be taken to prevent such criminal activities.

Introduction

The Internet can be considered a double-edged sword because, while offering a range of benefits, it provides criminals with the opportunity to extend their work to areas and places previously unimaginable. Therefore, all countries face the same challenges on how to fight cybercrime and how to effectively promote security to their citizens and organisations.

This chapter explores individuals who do or do not take precautions to guard themselves against cybercrime, and examines how their perception of law influences their actions towards incidents of cybercrime. Here, 'guardianship' refers to actions or procedures that individuals take to ensure that any given computer is secure before they go online, and is linked to the awareness of risks associated with the use of the Internet that an individual might have.

Environmental crime theories are popular because of their success in solving traditional crime. Life-style Routine Activity Theory (LRAT) is a good example of these traditional crime theories. The particular interest here is how to benefit from these crime theories in the fight against cybercrime victimisation. The conceptual model and theoretical basis suggests that it is not only computer-related Formal Social Control (FSC) aspects which can have an impact upon an individual's perception of online activities, but also posits that an individual's awareness of cybercrime can influence their online behaviours.

What has been done to tackle cybercrime?

The Law has an important role to play in governing our societies because self-precaution taking by individuals, while essential, to protect them is not sufficient. However, the rule of law in order to be efficient must be enforced.

The cyber law in many countries is still in its infancy which made these countries, in one hand, struggling to cope with these types of crime to protect their infrastructures resources, and their individuals, (Jahankhani, 2010). On the other hand, these countries become increasingly less able to compete in the new economy. McConnell (2000) conducted an international survey of a global network of information technology policy officials to determine the state of cyber security laws around the world. The surveyed countries were asked to provide laws that would be used to prosecute criminal acts involving both private and public sector computers.

> "Over fifty national governments responded with recent pieces of legislation, copies of updated statutes, draft legislation, or statements that no concrete course of action has been planned to respond to a cyber-attack on the public or private sector. Countries were provided the opportunity to review the presentation of the results in draft, and this report reflects their comments. Countries that provided legislation were evaluated to determine whether their criminal statutes had been extended into cyberspace to cover ten different types of cybercrime in four categories: data-related crimes, including interception, modification, and theft; network-related crimes, including interference and sabotage; crimes of access, including hacking and virus distribution; and associated computer-related crimes, including aiding and abetting cyber criminals, computer fraud, and computer forgery. Thirty-three of the countries surveyed have not yet updated their laws to address any type of cybercrime. Of the remaining countries, nine have enacted legislation to address five or fewer types of cybercrime, and ten have updated their laws to prosecute against six or more of the ten types of cybercrime" (McConnell, 2000:4).

However, despite that McConnell's report is 11 years old. This chapter uses this report to highlight how little progress has been made in 11 years.

Formal Social Control - legislations

In 1990 the UK created its own law, The Computer Misuse Act, which predates the Internet and is partly based on unauthorised access which is incompatible with, and unclear regarding, today's technologies (Sommer, 2004). However, changes have been made to the original Act. The 2006 Police and Justice Act made some changes to some of the criminal offences in Sections 1 and 3, and inserted a new offence regarding articles for use in the commission of offences. These changes were primarily intended to implement the European Council Framework Decision on Attacks against Information Systems (Bainbridge, 2007).

The Identity Cards Act 2006 delineates a new offence: being in possession or control of false identity documents; genuine documents that have been improperly obtained; or documents issued to another person without reasonable cause. The offence is now punishable with a maximum penalty of two years imprisonment (APPG, 2007). The Fraud Act (2006) has replaced several pieces of pre-existing fraud legislation, creating a single overarching fraud offence. The Act focuses on dishonesty, and was ahead of its time in encompassing Internet fraud, the use of bankcards to purchase goods and services, and confidence tricks such as 'phishing'. Section 6 of the Act makes a person guilty of an offence if he is in possession of any article for use in the course of, or in connection with, any fraud. Those convicted under the Act face a maximum five years imprisonment (APPG 2007).

However, the same Act makes clear no offence in relation to the offering of a document for sale. This is a particular problem as a number of websites are offering documents for sale under the banner of 'novelty' or 'toy' documents, which seem to be simply high-quality versions of the originals that can readily be used to commit identity theft. The Association of Chief Police Officers (ACPO) identified over fifty Internet sites that offer these counterfeit documents for sale. These include Passports, Birth Certificates, P45s and wage slips (APPG 2007).

Yet the UK was one of the first countries to have its own specialist squad of computer crime cops (Sommer, 2004). Below is a timeline of key events in the UK's response to "cybercrime":

- 1985-Metropolitan Police Computer Crime UNIT (CCU) established.
- 1996- National Criminal Intelligence Service (NCIS) start project Trawler.
- Mid-1990's Customs and Excise, the Serious Fraud Office and the Inland Revenue have computer investigation resources.
- 2001- National Hi-tech crime unit established.

The National Hi-Tech Crime Unit was merged last year into part of SOCA (Serious and Organised Crime Agency). Warren (2007) reports that Ollie Ross, Head of Research at Corporate IT Forum, commented: "A lot of trust was built up between large businesses and the NHTCU, and that took a lot of time to develop…Just as the structure seemed to have reached fruition, it was taken away, and nothing has filled its place. There is no reporting mechanism now.

Furthermore, CIFAS, The UK's Fraud Prevention Service, revealed in their 2006 study "Identity Fraud: What about the victims?" that over a third of identity fraud victims consider the police response to their incident report to be either "bad" or "very bad". Furthermore, a leading security expert has criticised the UK government for ignoring recommendations on tackling cybercrime from peers in the House of Lords (Leyden, 2007). Lord Broers, who chaired the committee's Internet security sessions, said:

> "In our report we raised concerns that public confidence in the Internet could be undermined if more was not done to prevent and prosecute e-crime. We felt that the government and the police were failing to meet their responsibilities and were quite unreasonably leaving individual users to fend for themselves" (Williams, 2008)

Informal Social Control - educating the public

There are number of professional organisations setup to provide training and investigative resources for cybercrime. These agencies work independently, as well as with regional law enforcement agencies. There are also various kinds of organisations that exist to warn consumers and businesses of the risks of cybercrime, and to increase awareness among people to prevent and limit victimisation. The work of these organisations varies from one to another. Some organisations focus on fighting organised cybercrime, while others purport to increase the level of protection, prevention, and awareness against cybercrime in general. Some organisations are specific in their focus, and aim to educate parents of the potential dangers facing their children when they use the Internet. Internet Watch Foundation (IWF) is an example of such an organisation, which also offers victims support in the identification and location of the perpetrators, and coordinates with law enforcement agencies in attempts to arrest the offender.

Most of these professional organisations offer advice and methods in preventing victimisation, and most also have their own mechanisms for reporting crime, where those who believe that they have been victimised can fill in an incident form. Alternatively, the victim will be directed to another agency specialising in their specific cybercrime type. Furthermore, some groups, like Get Safe Online (GSO), teach the consumers the potential dangers of getting online, and provide advice to minimise the chances of victimisation. Some organisations focus on legal and policy issues, and offer a wide range of white papers for researchers from different disciplines to gain better understanding of cyber-related issues and policy.

Cybercrime victimisation

Cybercrimes are on the rise, and the number of Internet crime victims is increasing every year. The Symantec Global Internet Security Threat Report provides an annual overview and analysis of worldwide Internet threat activity, a review of known vulnerabilities, and highlights examples of malicious code.

Trends in phishing and spam are also assessed, as are observed activities on underground economy servers. Symantec In their 2009 report (A) stated that more than ever before, attackers are financially motivated and focused on compromising end users.

> "In 2008, 78 per cent of confidential information threats exported user data, and 76 per cent used a keystroke-logging component to steal information such as online banking account credentials. Additionally, 76 per cent of phishing lures targeted brands in the financial services sector and this sector also had the most identities exposed due to data breaches. Similarly, 12 per cent of all data breaches that occurred in 2008 exposed credit card information. In 2008 the average cost per incident of a data breach in the United States was $6.7 million—which is an increase of 5 per cent from 2007—and lost business amounted to an average of $4.6 million", (Symantec 2009 A).

The IC3 (Internet Crime Complaint Centre) report in 2008 also highlighted many of the current trends and patterns in cybercrime.

> "The data indicates that instances involving Internet crime are on the increase as seen with the record number complaints submitted; 275,284, in 2008; up from 206,884 in 2007; 207,492 complaints in 2006; and 231,493 in 2005. This total includes many different fraud types and non-fraudulent complaints. However, research indicates that only one in seven incidents of fraud ever make their way to the attention of enforcement or regulatory agencies. The total dollar loss from all referred cases of fraud was $264.6 million up from $239.1 million in 2007".

A report on cybercrime in the UK shows that the estimated total number of cybercrimes in 2007 has increased overall by 9% from 2006, (Symantec 2008 A). Online financial fraud has increased significantly since 2006. However, looking at cybercrime in absolute terms, the bulk of this increase comes from online offences against persons who form part of the greater number of individuals using the Internet year on year, in particular, social networking sites (see Fafinski and Minassian – Garlik Power Stuff, 2008).

Once cyber criminals have gained access to financial information or other personal details—such as names, addresses, and government identification numbers—they frequently sell this information on the underground economic market (Symantec 2009). A prime example of this type of underground professional organization is the Russian Business Network (RBN). The RBN reputedly specializes in the distribution of malicious code, hosting malicious websites, and other malicious activity. The RBN has been credited with creating approximately half of the phishing incidents that occurred worldwide last year. It is also thought to be associated with a significant amount of the malicious activities on the Internet in 2007 (Symantec 2009).

According to Symantec Report 2008 (B), "the most popular item for sale on underground economy servers in 2008 was credit card information, accounting for 32 per cent of the total". This is most likely a consequence of the numerous ways in which credit card information can be stolen, and the fact that stolen card data can be easily cashed out. According to Symantec 2008 (A):

> "this is because the underground economy has a well-established `infrastructure for monetizing such information, again indicating the increased sophistication of the underground economy. Also, because of the large quantity of credit card numbers available, the price for each card can be as low as 6 cents when they are purchased in

bulk. Some groups in the underground economy also specialize in manufacturing blank plastic cards with magnetic stripes destined to be encoded with stolen credit card and bankcard data... The manufacture and distribution of these cards requires a well-organized level of sophistication since the cards are often produced in one country, imprinted, and then shipped to the countries from where the stolen data originated."

Finally, from the examples above a summary can be reached: that the changes in the cybercrime landscape—such as the increasing complexity and sophistication of attacks, the evolution of attackers and attack patterns, and malicious activities being pushed to emerging countries—show not just the benefits of, but also the need for, increased cooperation among security companies, governments, academics, and other organizations and individuals to combat these changes.

Theoretical perspectives

In the last three decades, theories of crime have been greatly informed by an influx of thinking that supersedes criminology's traditionally myopic focus on offenders. Most notably, Lifestyle Routine Activity Theory (LRAT) has significantly influenced thinking about criminal victimisation and crime rates. LRAT consists of exposure/lifestyle theory and routine activity theory (Cohen and Felson, 1979), and work relating to environmental theory (Bratingham and Bratingham, 1980). The role of victims and other targets, and their interaction with the environment or context, are now understood to play major role in determining the opportunity structure in which offences occur and aggregate crime rates are determined (Farrell et al. 2005).

The particular interest of this chapter is how to benefit from these crime theories in the fight against cybercrime victimisation. Several empirical studies have attempted to apply these crime theories to cyberspace, such as Holt et al (2009), who has examined the publicity of lifestyle-routine activity theory (LRAT) for cybercrime victimisation; Williams (2008) who has used Charles Tittle's Control Balance Theory to understand computer crime and deviance; and Choi (2008) who has conducted an empirical assessment of computer crime victimisation and integrated theory. The previous studies have employed LRAT to prevent computer victimisation, relying on the tenet of "Capable Guardianship" which is, according to Choi's study, the process of installing the security software in the machine used to connect to the Internet. No previous studies have taken individuals' awareness into account as an essential factor contributing towards the reduction of cybercrime victimisation. The LRAT's tenet of "Capable Guardianship' should consider "individuals 'awareness" as a new factor in reducing cybercrime victimisation. Therefore, a theoretical model, which is an expansion of the LRAT that seeks to fill this gap, is proposed here. In order to justify this study, it is necessary to give a demonstration of how the theoretical perspectives could be transferred to cyberspace before introducing the model.

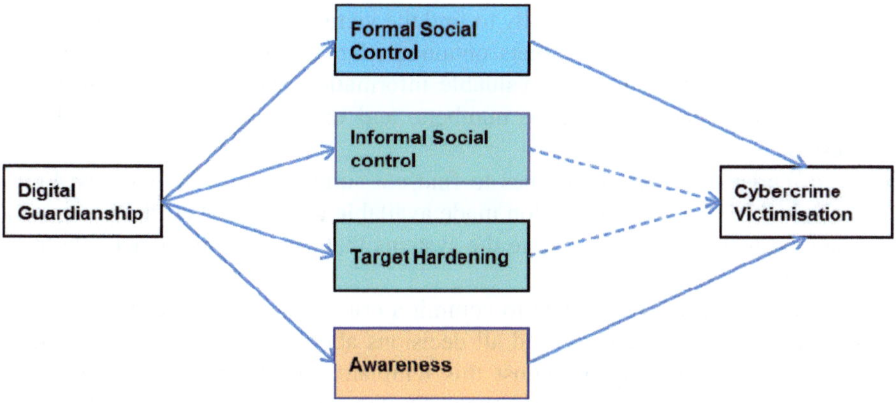

Fig. 12.1. Proposed Structural Model

Environmental crime theory

Brantingham and Brantingham (1991) suggest that crime has four dimensions: the victim, the offender, a spatial dimension and a legal dimension. Concentrating on the spatial element of crime is significant to the understanding of the behaviour of offenders. A crime space can be intentionally or unintentionally chosen by either the victim or the offender according to their lifestyles. Several things have an effect on the crime rate of an area. For example, 'socio-economic status' of an area – how middle class, or rich, or poor people are and what type of security is available to them.

Brantingham and Brantingham (1991) proposed a theoretical model based on the notion of opportunity and motivation, the key features of which are as follows:

- Strength and sources of motivation are diverse and varied; there are some people who are specifically motivated to commit offences. The hackers' social ethic is based upon three principles; firstly, the belief that sharing any information, including that which is about the weather or a novel, is good; secondly, that hackers have an ethical duty to share the information with which they work; thirdly, that hackers should facilitate access to computers wherever possible (Chance, 2005).
- Commission of crime depends on the location, target and victim's position in time and space. The initial step in commissioning crime in cyberspace is footprinting (also known as enumeration). The primary objective of this is to locate and learn the nature of the potential target. An attacker, for example, is able to obtains huge amounts of information readily available online from web sites such as Google, Whois, and Dig.

- An offender may search carefully to find the victim, depending on their motivation. The list of potential targets obtained from the footprinting process provides the attacker with more valuable information about the potential target, such as their name, telephone numbers, and their range of possible IP addresses.
- An offender uses signals or cues to find out suitable targets or victims; From the valuable store of information made available to the attacker, they can use a scanning technique to determine the systems that are alive and reachable from the Internet.
- An offender makes a template to commit a crime based on the experience and sequence of the given cues, and all decisions about whether to leave or attack future targets are judged against this template. The template could be constructed consciously or unconsciously. On the one hand, there are cyberspace attacks which do not require any technical skills on the part of the attacker. Attacking methods can depend more heavily on the interaction of human factors, such as in the case of a social engineering attack. On the other hand, there are also attacks that require the attacker to be technically skilled, for example, in firewall intrusion, or traffic sniffing and analysis.
- Once the model is established, it influences the future behaviour of an offender and becomes self-reinforcing;
- Several crime templates could be constructed based upon the diversity of targets and victims. People have some universal behaviour traits which help to identify the templates.

Rational choice perspective theory

This theory, assumes that those who commit crimes do so intentionally and purposively. The aim of a criminal act is to obtain benefit for the offender. 'Benefit' can be defined as any type of intangible assets such as cash and goods, but an exploration of the term can lead to the consideration of other forms of benefit, such as prestige, fun, excitement, sexual gratification, and domination (Willison, 2006)".

Rational Choice Perspective Theory takes into consideration the criminal's decision-making process and the factors that influence such a process. The criminal's decision-making process varies and differs from one offence to another. Analysis is therefore needed to identify the nature of the offence, leading to improved understanding of the steps taken by criminals leading up to their crime. The Rational Choice perspective Theory categorises criminal choices into two 'decision groups': Involvement; and Event.

Involvement decisions consist of three stages which are connected to the criminal career. The offender must take a decisions about starting crime activities, whether or not to continue these activities over a period of time, and when, if at all, to cease offending (Willison, 2006). Event decisions refer to the series of decisions made by the perpetrator during the commission of the crime process. For example, in domestic burglary, the burglar's choices could involve the choices of target, the point of entry, and which items to steal (Willison, 2006).

In Cyberspace, an attacker has to go through a progression of steps when attacking a particular system, just as the analogous physical robbery is carried out. The robber will try to gather enough information about the potential target such as area, street, and population. These steps are known as; information gathering or reconnaissance; scanning and gaining access; and finally, covering up. The first step is a preparatory step for the attacks, as by collecting intelligence information about the target, the attacker opens security holes. In doing so, the perpetrator will be able to find out a surprising amount of information, such as the account name and address, and which operating systems are in place. The second step is the attacker's gaining of access to the systems, who could have numerous different ends to his means, such as to control, theft, or damage. The last step occurs after the attack, where the attacker covers up his attack to avoid detection.

For example, in July 2008, a small company with less than 6 employees, selling quality model cars, was infiltrated online by hackers who altered online prices on the site's catalogue. The hacker's were able to set any price they wanted for any product, and they did so, reducing prices to one tenth of the original.

Obviously, the company suffered substantial losses as a direct result of the attack. Fortunately, they recovered from the event quickly and prevented a recurrence by employing a specialist e-commerce oriented consultancy. This involved additional expense, but less than the amount they lost in the hacking attack.

Lifestyle Routine Activity Theory

Scholars argue that in light of its success combating various forms of street crime delinquency, LRAT may be useful in preventing cybercrime (Pease 2001; Holt et al 2009). However, Yar (2005, cited in Holt et al, 2009) argues that the "virtual environments are spatially and temporally disconnected, limiting the "wholesale application" of the basic theoretical constructs of this theory". However, Holt et al (2009) states that the research conducted in this field usually explored the relationship between online deviance and victimisation. According to Holt et al, Yar (2005) provided no assessment of this relationship in his critique. However, such a debate is outside the realm of this thesis, which relies upon the argument that LRAT is applicable to cyberspace in order to gain a theoretical understanding of cybercrime victimisation.

The increase in the volume of cybercrime victimisation could be therefore explained by changes in the routine activities of people's everyday lives. For instance, according to the report by the insurance group CCP, cited in BBC 2010,

40% of victims of house burglary were targeted because of the amount of information available about them on social web sites. These websites, such as Facebook, allow individuals to share pictures - for example, of holiday snaps - and other personal information with their friends, thus exposing their potential as a target to be burglarised.

With the advent of the Internet people have changed the way in which they communicate or interact with others, shop, entertain, and do business. The Internet is available almost everywhere. People not only have access to it in their homes and workplaces, but also in more public domain such as airports, libraries, shopping centres, and cybercafés. Some of these Internet portals are free, whilst others charge a small fee, but either way, access is possible globally. Cybercafés are located world-wide, and one reporter comments that:

> There are thousands of Internet cafés of all shapes and size, all over the world from city centres to small villages to the depths of the jungle and even on remote mountains sides. From simple beginnings the Internet café concept has brought access and communication to local people and travellers alike and it's hard to imagine life without them (Calson 2004)

However, cybercafés tend to be clustered in major population centres and locations. There are risks associated with using the Internet, and these risks are greater when individuals are not aware of them. When the Internet is accessed from a cybercafé, these risks could even go so far as to be duplicated as a result of the limited security measures available or possible in these instances.

> Most of the cybercafés today are operated by users with little or no security or system administration expertise. They do not understand the nature of the threats they face, have little idea of what constitutes a reasonable security policy, and know little of the remedies which they can take. Instead, they rely solely on software, which is demonstrably inadequate. Such systems can easily be used by attackers to attack other systems without the knowledge of the operator.(Mohammad 2008)

An application of LRAT as proposed by Cohen and Felson (1979) would suggest that crime is likely to occur when three factors converge. These factors are:

1. Motivated offenders
2. Suitable targets
3. The absence of capable guardians against violation.

This research believes that a cybercafé is the most common location for cybercrime because it holds the prime conditions of all three factors. The theoretical analysis of this thesis will pay attention to these factors, and will attempt to prove that such convergence being possible in one place could lead to a large increase in cybercrime rates.

John Stewart's small scale study of UK cybercafés (cited in Calson 2004), commented that:

> They all have a regular customer base, with over 50% of customers coming in at least once a month and many more regularly. Users are very mixed, male and female, young and old, although there is a marked bias towards younger people using the cafes.

For example, In Jordan, a study by Mohammed Al-khadi, a professor in the Press Department at Yarmouk University indicated that the 18-22 age bracket constitutes the highest percentages of cybercafés visitors in Amman and Irbid, the biggest two cities in Jordan. The study also shows that text based web chatting constitutes some 85% of Internet use (openarab.net 2008).

Furthermore, John Springhall (cited in Calson 2004), stated that cybercafés where youth gather pose a number of issues. Issue of "youth endangerment" addresses the concern that young people are inadequately supervised online in cybercafés, and can thus come into contact (online or face-to-face) with older predators. Another concern resides in cybercafé owners who do not rigidly prohibit entry to those who are underage, or block machine monitoring from their machines for cases of absence of guardianship.

Cybercafés are also an obvious location for offenders and victims to knowingly and unknowingly converge or gain exposure to improper content. Additionally, there are no safeguards in place whereby users have to prove their genuine identity before going online, as they can easily give fake or false identification details. Finally, although there are techniques for tracing the devices used by criminals, it is more difficult to trace them back to a cybercafé as each computer can have multiple users.

Cohen and Felson argue that "the absence of one of these three factors (offender, target, and absence of a capable guardian) will be sufficient in preventing the successful completion of a direct-contact predatory crime" (Cohen and Felson, 1979: 589). Indeed, in the available literature to date, many researchers support the notion that the likelihood of property victimisation has a parallel relationship with the victim's frequent absence from the home (Choi 2008). LRAT suggests that victimisation is most likely when individuals: are placed in higher risk settings; are in close proximity to motivated offenders, such as in Cybercafés; appear to be attractive targets to criminals; and lack a capable guardian (Cohen and Felson 1979; Miethe and Meier, 1987; Holt et al, 2009).

There are a large number of sophisticated cybercafé users who have the ability to intercept and/or modify any information sent from one user to another. These sophisticated users are also likely to be able to introduce their own traffic on to the network, in an attempt to fool the receivers that they are legitimate senders (or vice versa). As Mustaine and Tewksbury (2000) claim, the strength of LRAT is based on the idea that crime does not randomly occur in a society, but follows regular patterns regarding situation and behaviour, examining how these interact with individual characteristics and behaviours.

Although LRAT has gained popularity as an approach to test trends in crime rates, there are few empirical studies to further test and develop the elements of its discourse. According to Bennett (1991), LRAT is a "crime-specific" theory.

Cyberspace consists of websites hosted by digital communities (chat rooms, online classrooms, social networking websites) that link all online users together via the World Wide Web. Internet users can have access to anywhere and everywhere, surpassing all physical boundaries at the click of a mouse. This ease with which national borders can be crossed has subsequently armed cyber criminals with a mobility far exceeding the mobility of offenders in the 'real', physical world (Stalder, 1998, Choi, 2008).

LRAT would suggest that all criminal events occur in a particular place at a particular time. Cohen and Felson (1979, cited in Choi, 2008) assert that "the synchronization of a perpetrator's rhythms with those of a victim's" facilitate a convergence of a potential offender and a target. Cohen and Felson also believe that examining how and why criminal offences occur in particular places may be useful and important to a study of cybercrime victimisation. This argument relies on the notion that cyber criminals often search for suitable and valuable targets in specific types of social arenas (cybercafés) or through websites with dense user populations (Piazza, 2006).

Castells (2002) asserts that cyberspace creates a shared and common social environment, which extends the traditional world and reflects its socioeconomic and cultural dimensions. Online users from differing social demographics have different purposes for the Internet, demonstrated by their varied website choices which can often be predicted based upon their interests, social values and cultural dimensions. A higher density of Internet connectivity indicates the proximity of cyber criminals and cybercrime victims (Yar, 2005). In fact, it has been established that individuals are most likely to be targeted as victims if they visit numerous social networking websites, as lots of diverse people meeting on a universal platform raises issues of cultural and social values (Jahankhani, 2011).

Crime victimisation is mainly determined by the accessibility dimension, which links to the level of capable guardianship, regardless of the target desirability (Cohen et al; Yar, 2005; Choi 2008).

The third element of LRAT is capable guardianship. A guardian refers to a person who can preserve a suitable target from risks exactly as was intended by its authorised owner. Guardianship can be subdivided into three categories: formal, and informal social controls and target hardening activities (Cohen, Klugel, and Land, 1981; Choi 2008).

Formal social control is the first category of guardianship, whereby law enforcement plays the role of the guardian persona. In cyberspace, as mentioned earlier, law enforcement agencies should do more in protecting individuals from being victimised by cyber criminals. Difficulties arise in prosecuting cyber criminals because of the intangible nature of cybercrime activities that do not match nicely with traditional criminal statuses such as theft (Tiernan 2000). Also, the ability of cyber criminals to hack private and public computer systems and cause huge damage to these hacked systems without prosecution has weakened the reliability of formal social control as a method of guardianship (Tiernan, 2000). In addition, Rosenblatt (1996) argued that only a small number of law enforcement officers are equipped with the knowledge necessary to process digital evidence needed for an effective cybercrime investigation.

The second category of guardianship is informal social control which could be defined in the traditional world as, for example, parents, relatives, teachers, friends and other individuals who can participate in surveillance and protection tasks, in the manner of security personnel. In cyberspace, informal social guardianship, involves semi-public and public groups, private network organisations, and information security professionals (Yar, 2005).

Moitra (2005) argues that despite the criminal justice system gearing its policies towards cybercrime initiatives, "these initiatives are not yet fully viable". An example of this would be self-regulation and cooperative measures by private and semi-public organisations against child pornography to increase public awareness in order to minimise cybercrime. Wilkinson (ACPO) comments, "one of my big beliefs is that everyone expects so much of the police in this [the policing of cybercrime], but actually we all have a role to play. The big institutions have a role to play, the great big technology companies, and the banks (Goodwin, 2007)".

There are a lot of hurdles in implementing formal and informal social control groups so that they can maintain effective guardianship in cyberspace, since cyber criminals can commit cybercrime from anywhere, at anytime, and get away the from crime scene because of the difficulties of policing cyberspace (Yar, 2005). Thus, informal social control is like formal social control in that it has little impact on cybercrime victimisation (Choi, 2008).

Despite the various cybercrime categories reserved specifically for conduct that falls within the Computer Misuse Act 1990 (as amended by the Police and Justice Act 2006), UK cybercrime has rebounded to worrying levels not seen since 2006, as a result of the recession and consumer complacency, according to Garlik's annual UK Cybercrime report, now in its third year (Fafinski and Minassian 2009).

> One possible explanation for the sharp rise in cybercrime lies in the consumer reaction to it. Identity theft in particular received a great deal of media and public attention in 2006. As a result, many consumers took the first steps to protect themselves, buying shredders and anti-malware software to feel secure but have since become too complacent and as a result have been hit by the next wave of cybercrime. (Fafinski and Minassian 2009)

The third and final element of capable guardianship is target hardening. In the real world target hardening is defined as the increasing of the level of security measures via physical security, in order to remove all the excuses for crime. In doing so, numbers of victimisations decrease (Cornish and Clarke, 2003; Willison, 2006). For example, anti-robbery screens, to increase resistance against criminals; multiple clerks in convenience stores, to increase the risks; and removable car radios, to reduce the rewards.

Cyberspace is not so different from the 'real' world, as physical security measures are similar to those used in computer security to protect a system from cyber criminals. Today, no one should take the gamble of not equipping their computer with the many kinds of available software, such as firewalls, and anti-virus and anti-spyware software, to protect it from cyber criminals. Failure to do so will lower the level of guardianship and can potentially lead to online victimisations (Choi, 2008). Indeed, in computers connected to the external world via the Internet, security software is crucial to protect the computer's systems from hackers and criminals, and enhances the level of guardianship in cyberspace. Unfortunately, "absolute security is unattainable in practice. Even if complete security were achievable, security measures will only be applied on the basis of a cost-benefit rationalisation" (Rowligson, 2007).

From the discussion of the three elements of LRAT, and in particular the discussion of the three sub-elements of capable guardianships, it can be concluded that none of the above strategies can play a very effective role in reducing cybercrime victimisation or can guard against cybercriminal activities when operating in isolation. However, the above analysis has highlighted the important role of guardianship as the crucial weapon to win the battle against cyber criminals. It has also provided evidence about the limitation of formal social control (by law enforcement agencies) in dealing with such crime. Furthermore, it has also clarified the need to bring together the debates over cyberspace governance and take into account the fact "That the law in isolation only has a limited direct impact upon behaviour, but does have the capacity to shape the environment in which behaviour takes place" (Greenlaf 1998; Wall 2007).

In addition to this, the analysis of target hardening in cyberspace as one of the capable guardianship pillars has shown the need for "the use of technological means to change the physical environment of criminal opportunity in order to reduce it" (Wall, 2007). "As threats shift and change, it is essential for consumers to take steps towards their own safety: even if they think that it is 'someone else's problem', it is not. Consumers need to be smart online and stay one step ahead of the cyber criminals (Fafinski and Minassian 2009)".

Wall asserts, that "there seems to be an implicit assumption within the computer security community that users have to be protected from themselves, to prevent them from becoming either victims or offenders" (Wall, 2008). In this chapter it is posited that the law has not sent a clear message to online users about the punishment, which they might face if they engage in any deviant behaviours, which may in turn affect their decision to support or resist criminalisation.

The policing of cybercrime is essential to its reduction, yet law enforcement agencies do not have the means to police cybercrime effectively.

This chapter has so far acknowledged the importance of awareness as an element in reducing cybercrime victimisation in our society. It therefore seems appropriate to introduce "user awareness" as a new category within theoretical capable guardianship, accompanying formal social control, informal social control, and target hardening. This research strongly believes that this new category could be the missing fourth of guardianship.

This new pillar will strengthen the guardianship discourse in its fight to reduce cybercrime victimisation. In order to support the argument that "user awareness" is a crucial key element which needs to be added to the capable guardian, it must work in coalition with other elements.

Conclusions

LRAT focuses on the victims' "daily social activity" rather than on individual offenders' characteristics or causal variables (Choi, 2008)". It suggests that victimisation is a result of the daily living patterns of the victims (Choi, 2008). It also suggests that exposure to certain places at certain times increases the risk of victimisation. The victimisation literature has shown that risk of victimisation increases when people spend more time in public places. Cohen et al (1981) define exposure as "the physical visibility and accessibility of persons or objects to potential offenders at any given time or place".

The rapid increase in computer Internet usage in our life has changed the way we communicate or interact with one another. Instead of posting letters we send emails; instead of using corded telephones to speak to friends, people are chatting live online. In other words, the everyday carrying out of routine has dramatically altered, to the extent that most people cannot imagine life without the Internet. Relying heavily on Web access to perform daily tasks and activities seems like a natural state of affairs. The Internet and the accessibility it provides give people the supernatural feeling of being simultaneously conducting operations whilst also being invisible. However, Sukhai (2004) believes that this cloak of invisibility may lead individuals to perform actions that they would not do in public or in person – actions which might be morally wrong or linked to some deviant or illegal behaviour.

References

APPG, 2007." Identity_ Fraud Report12. Available online: http://www.idfraud.org.uk [Access Oct.2010].

BBC, Thursday, 21 January 2010 "Young Facing online Fraud Risks http://news.bbc.co.uk/1/hi/business/8470631.stm. [Accessed March 2011]

Bennett, Richard R. 1991. Routine Activities: A Cross- National Assessment of a Criminological Perspective. Social Forces, 70: pp 147-163.

Bainbridge, D., (2007)."Criminal law tackles computer fraud and misuse". Computer Law & Security Report. 23(3) pp. 276-281.

Brantingham, P.L., and Brantingham, P.J,. (1991). Notes on the geometry of crime, in Environmental Criminology, USA: Wavelend Press Inc.

Brantingham, P.J., and Brantingham, P.L. (1984) Patterns in crime. New York: Macmillan.

Castells, M. (2002). The internet galaxy: Reflections on the Internet, business, and society. Oxford, United Kingdom: Oxford University Press.

Calson Analytics (2004). cybercafés and telecentres. (http://www.calson.com.au/cafenote.htm. [Accessed Feb. 2011]

Chance, T., (2005), The Hacker Ethic and Meaningful Work . MA Philosophy candidate University of Reading

Choi, Choi-shick Computer Crime Victimization and Integrated Theory: An Empirical Assessment, International Journal of Cyber Criminology, 0974 – 2891 January-June 2008, Vol 2 (1): 308–333

Cohen, L. E., & Felson, M., (1979). Social change and crime rate trends: A routine activity approach. American Sociological Review, 44, pp 588-608

Cohen, L. E., Felson, M., & Land, K, (1981). Social inequality and predatory criminal victimisation: An exposition and a test of a formal theory. American Sociological Review, 46, pp 505-524.

Fafinski S. &Minassian N.; (2009) "UK Cybercrime Report". Invenio Research. Garlic powerful stuff.
http://www.garlik.com/press.php?id=613-GRLK_PRD [Accessed Feb 2010]

Fafinski, S. & Minassian, N., (2008). UK Cybercrime Report. Garlik Power Stuff. London. http://www.garlik.com/static_pdfs/cybercrime_report_2008.pdf {Accessed May 2011]

Farrell, G. et al. 2005 "Of Targets and Supertargets: A routine Activity Theory of High Crime Rates" Internet Journal of Criminology(IJC). http://www.internetjournalofcriminology.com/Farrell,%20Clark,%20Ellingworth%20&%20Pease%20-%20Supertargets [Accessed April 2011]

Holt et al, (2009). Examining the applicability of lifestyle-routine activity theory for cybercrime victimisation. Deviant Behaviour, 30: pp 1-25.

Hamid Jahankhani, Ameer Al-Nemrat, Cybercrime victimisations/ criminalisation and Punishment, 6th International Conference on Global Security, Safety and Sustainability, Communications in Computer and Information Science, CCIS, Springer Proceedings of the 6th ICGS3-10, 1-3 September 10, Braga, Portual.

Leyden, J. (2007). UK.gov lambasted for ignoring peers' cybercrime report", Channel & Register. http://m.channelregister.co.uk/2007/10/30/ukgov_cybercrime_response [Accessed March 2011]

Miethe, Terance; Stafford, Mark C.; and Long, J. Scott. 1987. Social Differentiation in Criminal Victimisation: A Test of Routine Activities/ Life style Theories. American Sociological Review, 52:pp 184-194.

McConnell Report, (2000). Cyber Crime and Punishment? Archaic Laws Threaten Global Information. www.mcconnellinternational.com [Accessed March 2011]

Mohammad L.; A, (2008). Cybercafé Systems Security. Security and Software for cybercafé, 1-17. Ed. Esharenana E. Adomi. IGI Global

Pease, K. (2001)." Crime future and foresight", In Wall, D.S. (Ed) Crime and the Internet. London, Routledge.

Piazza, P. (2006). Technofile:Antisocial networking sites. Security Management, 1-5.

Rowlingston, R., 2007. Towards A Strategy for E-Crime Prevention. IN ICGeS Global e Security.3rd edn. London

Rosenblatt, K. S. (1996), High-technology crime. San Jose, CA: KSK.

Sukhai N. B, 2004, " Hacking and Cybercrime", Information Security Curriculum Development. 1(1): 128-132.

Sommer, P., (2004). The future for the policing cybercrime. Computer Fraud & Security . 2004(1):pp 8-12.

Symantec Global Internet Security Threat Report Trends for 2008 (A); Volume XIV, Published April 2009 http://eval.symantec.com/mktginfo/enterprise/white_papers/b-whitepaper_internet_security_threat_report_xiv_04-2009.en-us.pdf [Accessed May 2011]

Symantec Report on Rogue Security Software, July 08 – June 09 (B), Published October 2009 http://eval.symantec.com/mktginfo/enterprise/white_papers/bsymc_report_on_rogue_security_software_WP_20100385.en-us.pdf [Accessed Jan 2011]

Tiernan, B. (2000). E-tailing. Chicago: Dearborn.

Wall, D. (2007), Hunting Shooting, and Phishing: New Cybercrime Challenges for Cybercanadians in The 21st Century. The ECCLES Centre for American Studies.http://bl.uk/ecclescentre 2009

Waren, P., (2007)."Lack of concern over growing cybercrime angers UK Businesses", The Guardian, Thursday July 19. 2007. Available at: www.guardian.co.uk/technology/2007/jul/19/crime.gurdianweeklytechnologysection

Williams, K.S., (2008). "Using Title's Control Balance Theory to understand computer crime and deviance", International Review of Law Computers & Technology. 22(1), pp. 145-155.

Willison, R., (2006). Understanding the offender/environment dynamic for computer crimes. Information technology and people, 19 (2), pp. 170-186.

Willison, R., (2006). Understanding the perpetration of employee computer crime in the organisational context.http://ir.lib.cbs.dk/downloaded/ISBN/x656517364.pdf [Accessed March 2011]

Yar, M. (2006). Cybercrime And Society. Sage Publication Ltd. London

Yar, M (2005). The Novelty of "Cybercrime": An Assessment in Light of Routine Activity Theory. European Journal of Criminology 2005; 2; 407

Chapter 13: Up Close and Personal – The Interplay between Information Technology and Human Agency in the Policing of the 2011 Sheffield Anti-Lib Dem Protest

Kerry McSeveny and David Waddington

Abstract This chapter constitutes a case study of South Yorkshire Police's (SYP's) handling of a protest outside the Sheffield City Hall venue of a Liberal Democrat party conference on 11-12 March 2011. The demonstration occurred in the wake of a number of high-profile official reports advocating a more permissive approach to protest policing. The chapter describes and analyses two particular aspects of SYP's 'Operation Obelisk': the use of social media (such as Twitter and Facebook) to keep the general public informed of ongoing or impending police activities as part of a 'no surprises' approach; and the deployment of a Police Liaison Team, part of whose responsibility was to complement CCTV surveillance by feeding information on the mood and activities of the crowd to a remote command cell. The study concludes that such technological innovations have a vital role to play in complementing – and moderating the negative impact of – more established methods of policing political protest.

Introduction

The Metropolitan Police Service's (MPS's) handling of the anti-G20 demonstration in London on 1 April 2009 attracted widespread public criticism and indignation. Mass media coverage of the event emphasised how police officers had reacted to protesters in a sometimes violent and allegedly indiscriminate manner, and had resorted to the controversial tactic of 'kettling' (corralling or 'containing') demonstrators into a confined space and detaining them for several hours (Greer and McLaughlin, 2010; Rosie and Gorringe, 2009). An official inquiry undertaken by Her Majesty's Chief Inspector of Constabulary subsequently called on the police to adopt a more permissive approach to managing political protest, committed to facilitating, rather than nullifying, the right to protest (HMCIC, 2009a and b). This message appears to have been heeded by the Association of Chief Police Officers and Association of Chief Police Officers in Scotland, whose

Manual of Guidance on Keeping the Peace (ACPO/ACPOS, 2010) stipulates that crowd order tactics and strategy must be designed and implemented in such a way as to facilitate protest, adequately differentiate between the 'innocent' and 'guilty', and generally remain in keeping with a 'no surprises' approach to engaging with the public.

More recent protests by UK university students, in opposition to proposed funding cuts in further and higher education, have emphasised how police attempts to achieve these objectives have been complicated by the growing ubiquity of social media and the ways in which it is being utilised, both in the mobilisation of dissent and as a means of keeping participants informed while demonstrations are in progress. This was exemplified by a 50,000-strong student march through central London in November 2010, during which a small 'breakaway' group occupied and inflicted substantial damage on the Conservative Party's headquarters at Millbank House (Stott et al., 2010). In the weeks leading up to the march, the MPS had appealed for protest organisers to contact them with their plans but this was to underestimate the extent to which such action had been mobilised 'organically' – i.e. via the social media of Facebook and Twitter. With little idea of what sort of numbers to expect, the police initially assigned only 225 officers to contain the tens of thousands descending on the capital (Lewis and Taylor, 2010).

According to the *Daily Mail*, this was the UK's first-ever digitally co-ordinated event of its kind - the 'ultimate in modern protest':

> And as the students took to the streets Twitter went into overdrive receiving more than 100 tweets a minute. Real-time images of burning placards, rioting students and words of encouragement were beamed around the world as the Metropolitan Police used Twitter to communicate with students. At 5.30pm yesterday the police tweeted: 'For the safety of themselves & others we advise anyone on the roof to come down.' Their first message, sent at 4.30pm read: 'Anyone who engages in crime will be arrested.' The messages were sent to two Twitter pages, the official demonstration page and the page set up for the action at Millbank. The local effect of Twitter messages created 'flash-mobs' with thousands directed to riot hotspots such as Millbank. (Loveys, 2010)

Stott et al. (2010, p. 17) have since criticised the way the MPS used social media on this occasion on the grounds that the messages they transmitted were 'hardly calculated to inspire compliance or interact with the dynamics of legitimacy' and suggested a need for 'more training in these softer skills of communication and dialogue and more thought as to how such messages might be communicated, to who, and by whom'. These views chime with Copitch and Fox's general observation that: 'The real challenge for the police will be finding a way to embrace the spirit of the new social media in such a way that the content that is developed is convincing and feels authentic to the users of social media' (2010, p. 48).

In a recent evaluation of developments in police public order strategy, tactics and training since the publication of its G20 inquiry, Her Majesty's Inspectorate of Constabulary (HMIC, 2011, pp. 6-7) commented on the modern need for police commanders to be able to adapt their tactics to sudden changes in protester behaviour inspired by social media. Among those questions identified by the HMIC as requiring 'urgent consideration' were:

- How might the police participate in and utilise social media to help them achieve their objective of maintaining the peace?
- How might they use 'modern communication mechanisms' to communicate more effectively with different sections of the crowd?
- How can the police ensure the greater availability and accuracy of information, before, during and after protest activity, so as to enable both demonstrators and the general public to make better informed decisions?

This chapter examines the way in which one particular UK police force, the South Yorkshire constabulary, has endeavoured to adapt its methods of protest management in line with recent priorities established by the HMCIC, HMIC and ACPO/ACPOS documents, alluded to above. The chapter utilises in-depth interviews with eleven police personnel and three protest organisers, combined with participant observation (both on- and offline) to provide a case study of South Yorkshire Police's (SYP's) employment of social media mechanisms and a 'Police Liaison Team' to manage a demonstration staged outside the Liberal Democratic Party conference in Sheffield on 11-12 March 2011. In keeping with the overall theme of the book, we shall be focusing especially on SYP's use of information technology (notably, mobile phone, computer-mediated and Closed Circuit Television), and on related aspects of human judgement and decision-making, as they attempted to improve the flow and quality of communication, not only between the police and civilians, but also between 'remote' and 'front-line' police commanders.

An overview of the anti-Lib Dem protest

The decision to hold the 'Lib Dem' conference in Sheffield had been made some twelve months before it actually occurred, in what was widely interpreted as an act of benevolence towards the city by the party's leader, Nick Clegg, MP for Sheffield Hallam. Due to the failure of any major party to achieve an overall majority of seats in the May 2010 General Election, the Lib Dems had since formed a Coalition Government with the Conservative Party, with Mr Clegg rising to the rank of Deputy Prime Minister. Shortly after assuming power, the Lib Dems provoked intense political criticism by jointly authorising major public sector spending cuts and endorsing a large increase in student higher education fees – a measure that the party had promised it would never resort to were it to enter government (BBC, 2010).

Student opposition in Sheffield to these cuts and the raising of tuition fees was manifested in a major protest march, a sit-in at the University of Sheffield, and a mass lobby by students belonging to the city's two universities (the other being Sheffield Hallam) outside Mr Clegg's constituency office (*The Star*, 25 November

& 1 December 2010). Speaking at the protest march on 24 November, one of the organisers maintained: 'The people of Sheffield deserve MPs who keep their promises. We will be taking our campaign out of campuses and to the public. Mr Clegg campaigned directly for the student vote in Hallam by attacking plans to raise tuition fees and he is now reneging on that promise.' (*The Star*, 25 November 2010).

It was in this increasingly highly-charged political context that, on 24 February 2011, SYP first outlined its security plans for the conference. This was to involve the erection of an eight-foot-tall, part-concrete, part-metal fence (which the media quickly dubbed a 'ring of steel'), around the conference venue of Sheffield City Hall. (*The Star*, 24 February 2011). This protective barrier was designed in such a way as to be lower in height on the bottom side of the venue, where protesters were due to gather, to enable them to see the people they were hoping to address. One senior officer involved in 'Operation Obelisk' explained that the fenced-off space in front of the hall was necessary to provide conference delegates with somewhere to assemble in the event of an emergency evacuation (ibid.).

Police 'guesstimates' suggested that anywhere between 5,000 and10,000 protesters might be attending the event, and that 1,000 officers would be on duty. The local evening newspaper, *The Star*, informed its readers that: 'South Yorkshire Police are to unleash a new high-tech defence against potential rioters – Twitter. A force "protest liaison team" is being set up to communicate to protesters outside the Liberal Democrats' spring conference at Sheffield City Hall. The team will reach protesters through the social media network, Twitter, accessible to many via mobile phones.' In expanding on the police thinking, a senior commander explained how: 'We want to try to defuse any that may be caused by people sending inflammatory messages from the protest...We want to be able to counter that with our own messages – it reduces tension' (ibid.).

The two days of protest passed off without any notable instances of disorder. On the Friday afternoon of 11 March, some 800 protesters gathered outside the City Hall and began chanting slogans. All the while, the crowd remained visibly tolerant of a dozen or more 'police liaison' officers (decked out in distinctive blue tabards) who freely mingled in their midst. The relatively good-natured tone of the demonstration was undisturbed by a sudden decision by one Lib Dem delegate to enter the crowd for the purpose of discussion. He quickly had his say and left without there being any cause for police involvement. As darkness began to fall, 200 protesters suddenly broke off and ran to the top end of the square (having realised that this was the point at which a stream of Lib Dem delegates were entering the hall). The verbal baiting that ensued was mildly abusive, though not deemed sufficiently threatening as to warrant police intervention.

The following morning's march followed the short route from Devonshire Green, through the town centre to the rallying point of Barker's Pool (in front of the City Hall) where an estimated crowd of 5,000 gradually assembled. The Police Liaison Team was once again conspicuous and, afterwards, it was acknowledged by the protest organisers we interviewed that the co-operative and good-humoured attitude of these officers made a significant contribution to the generally cordial and relaxed atmosphere that prevailed.

Midway through the afternoon, a group of some 12 to 15 teenage demonstrators began using the broken off handles of their wooden placards to beat out a loud, repetitive noise on a section of perimeter fencing. However, the police made no attempt to intervene (*The Star*, 14 March 2011). Shortly afterwards, a small group of equally youthful protesters briefly entered the Boots and Topshop stores on Fargate and the Nat West bank on High Street. Each of these institutions had been singled out beforehand on the website, 'Rage Against the Lib Dems and Tax Evaders', either as chain stores which were allegedly guilty of tax evasion, or as banks which had recently been rescued from financial collapse by taxpayers' money and/or had paid out what were considered to be unjustifiably large bonuses to executives (ibid.). The police responded to these incursions by ejecting the individuals concerned and trapping them inside a 'corral', before marching them off to the main protest area and releasing them. The only arrest of the afternoon occurred when a 20-year-old man lit up a flare and scaled the protective barrier, whereupon he was intercepted by a small group of police officers and taken into custody (ibid.).

An SYP Chief Superintendent subsequently lauded the co-operative attitude of the demonstrators as having been a key reason for the peaceful outcome. In his view, the perimeter fence had been another decisive factor, insofar as it virtually ruled out any likelihood of lines of police and protesters coming into contact. The Chief Superintendent also made a point of praising the efforts of social media officers and the Police Liaison Team. He maintained that the latter had helped keep the crowd as well-informed as possible, thereby ensuring that there was no risk of protestors being surprised or disconcerted by police activities. Meanwhile, the former had skilfully employed such devices as Twitter and Facebook to dispel rumours (e.g. that the police were deploying snipers on nearby rooftops) and allay widespread fears that the police were intent on 'kettling' demonstrators (ibid.).

In the next two sections, we dwell in more detail on the nature and consequences of the work undertaken by the social media and police liaison teams, starting with the latter.

The work of the police liaison team

Our first major illustration of the way in which the interplay between communication technology and human agency played a significant part in the police management of the anti-Lib Dem protest concerns the use of Close Circuit Television (CCTV) to monitor the crowd and aid reactive decision-making. This process was heavily dependent for its effectiveness on the work of a specially constituted Police Liaison Team (PLT).

Command structure

The PLT comprised fifteen police personnel (a Chief Inspector, Inspector and Acting inspector, who were all specially trained police negotiators, and twelve Police Constables). The Chief Inspector was also a qualified Advanced Public Order Commander, and was appointed PLT Bronze Commander. This role complemented those of other senior colleagues (e.g. the Public Order Bronze for the City Hall) which also involved the direct supervision and direction of junior officers assigned to particular tasks and/or protest zones.

Prior to the demonstration, Bronze and the Acting Inspector each liaised with representatives of the main protest groups (e.g. the presidents of the two local university Student Unions, and delegates for the Sheffield 'Anti Cuts Alliance' and 'Right to Work' campaigns) with the intentions of explaining the police strategy, negotiating the protest route, and generally trying to establish a close police-protester rapport.

During the protest itself, the PLT divided into three smaller teams, each led by one of the trio of senior officers, but all ultimately responsible to Bronze. The junior members of the PLT were all hand-picked on the basis that they were known to be approachable and considered extremely skilled in communicating with the public. One of their main purposes as a group was to mingle with the crowd and thus ensure that the protesters were kept as well-informed as possible (in line with the 'no surprises' approach). Their second major function involved feeding 'real-time' intelligence on the mood and activities of the crowd to a remote Silver Command team, led by a 'Silver' Superintendent and his assistant 'Negotiator/Co-ordinator', a female colleague of equal rank.

The Silver Command chiefly relied on CCTV footage and radio interconnections as their basis for directing and co-ordinating the activities of Bronze Commanders on the ground. In this way, the PLT was seen as having the potential to enhance the quality of active risk assessment and, therefore, to help offset the possibility of any police interventions likely to be perceived by protesters as unwarranted, illegitimate and undifferentiating.

Practical interventions

There were several practical examples of this process, the first of which occurred on Friday, 11 March. The incident in question concerns the sudden appearance among the crowd of the Lib Dem delegate who was clearly intent on addressing his political adversaries. Although initially shouted down, this interloper was afforded a brief opportunity to speak - thanks largely to a handful of protesters who insisted that the delegate be given his say. While this was happening, the PLT Bronze Commander looked on nearby, clearly engaging in two-way radio communication with his Silver counterparts. Junior colleagues had also quietly manoeuvred themselves into close proximity of the incident, but all concerned were determined not to intervene unless absolutely necessary - a piece of judgement that was clearly vindicated:

> So, when [the delegate] walked into the crowd, on the first day which was the Friday, the negotiator-co-ordinator had an open channel to [the PLT Bronze Commander], who was actually saying, 'Don't react! Don't react! There's actually some self-policing going on in the crowd. Don't deploy.' The Negotiator/Co-ordinator was then taking all this onboard and saying, 'Hold fast! There's some self-policing going on. There's some people telling others to be quiet and let him speak.' Whereas, if you'd relied solely on CCTV, which is a bit one-dimensional, or observations from afar from a public order commander, and without all that, we'd have probably put a serial in there, thinking we'd got to rescue him because it didn't look very good on camera, to be fair. So that's how we developed that picture while the whole thing was happening before our eyes. They were observing a person they'd identified as being influential in the crowd conduct an element of self-policing. It gave us that vital open communication channel (Silver Commander)

The main demonstration on the following day yielded further instances where interventions by the PLT helped to improve the quality of remote decision making. The fist such occasion arose when Silver directed his Public Order Bronze to place a number of PSUs on standby alert in response to the group of youths who were beating sticks against the fencing. Taken in isolation, CCTV pictures suggested that this might be the prelude to a mass raid on the secure conference zone. However, the Silver Commander resisted a strong inclination to send in the PSUs and decided to first contact the PLT Bronze Liaison officer for a ground-level impression of the mood and behaviour of the relevant section of the crowd. Bronze's feedback quickly reassured the Silver Command that, whilst undoubtedly noisy, the youths had no real intention of trying to scale the fence. Thus, the decision was taken not to deploy resources.

A similar example occurred, later on Saturday afternoon, when CCTV cameras captured the activity of a small cluster of protesters who appeared to be defacing a building:

> [Silver], because he's got CCTV, sees this happening and thinks, 'Hello, we've got somebody "graffiti-ing"!' He starts thinking about sending in resources but I gets onto [the PLT Bronze] who immediately says, 'No, it's only chalk!' which he could tell because he'd already been stood there watching them. So, of course, I tell all this to [Silver] and, straight away, we opt for a low-key response because we know it'll wash off and, anyway, it always rains in Sheffield!' (Silver Negotiator/Co-ordinator)

It is evident from our interviews that the PLT Bronze regarded this intelligence-gathering role as one of his team's most significant contributions to the policing of the event: 'I actually think that we spent a good 50% of the time we were on duty interpreting things for Silver – saying 'No, don't do this, I'm stood here and I think it's unnecessary.' It was ultimately still Silver's decision but I genuinely feel that we gave him an additional set of eyes'.

One final example, taken from Saturday afternoon, nonetheless highlights some possible dangers and limitations inherent in this type of police liaison work. This concerns the incident in which the protester lit up a flare, scaled the barrier and was eventually arrested. Almost immediately afterwards, another demonstrator ignited a second flare, whereupon the PLT Bronze approached the individual concerned and quietly asked him to extinguish it in the interests of public safety. Bronze is adamant that at no point did he feel endangered – even when the front section of the crowd started chanting: 'Let's kettle the police! Let's kettle the police!' Nevertheless, he did not pause to argue when Silver gave the order to withdraw. On the following day, however, the merits of the decision were more thoroughly analysed:

> I went into Silver and watched the CCTV together with [him], and my conclusion was 'It didn't feel like it just looked on here!' I would never privately or publicly criticise [Silver] for pulling us out, but what he said was, 'I sat there watching it thinking "I don't know how to get you out of there safely, so you're coming out,"' which we did. What [Silver] and I ended up saying on reflection is that CCTV is just one view and that what we did provide throughout was an alternative perspective...and I can promise you that it's different to how you're likely to be perceiving it.' (PLT Bronze Commander)

The work of the PLT was both complemented and enhanced by the related efforts of a corresponding Social Media Team which, on the days of the demonstration, was located in the Silver Command suite, thereby ensuring that police communication processes were able to function as interdependently and harmoniously as possible. The following section outlines the nature and activities of the Social Media Team.

The police use of social media

SYP's decision to employ social media reflected the force's determination to learn from the recent experience of their counterparts in the MPS, and to build on lessons learned from their policing of student demonstrations in Sheffield the previous November. The student demonstrations saw the appointment, at relatively short notice, of a female inspector to the role of Social Media Officer (SMO), who was then given the responsibility of overseeing the social media activity during the conference.

A Social Media Strategy was drawn up in January 2011, which outlined the aims and objectives of social media use during the event. These included: maintaining public confidence; engaging with social media communities and potential protesters; and providing 'consistent and informed messages' to the parties concerned. The strategy involved the use of a range of social media (including the microblogging site Twitter, the social networking site Facebook, and local and national discussion forums) both during preparations for the Lib Dem conference, and on the days of the event itself.

Pre event

In the run up the conference the SMO worked for several months to build up as significant a Twitter following as possible:

> I wanted a very strong Twitter presence, I wanted to build up my following, because unless you've got the vehicle there's no point putting stuff out if nobody follows you, so I [got] involved with engaging with people and getting them to follow me. (SMO)

Tweets relating to the event began on 16 Feburary, with the SMO taking personal responsibility for maintaining the account, @SMOTweets (note that this and all other user names are pseudonymous), which was attributed to her as an individual, rather than corporately to 'South Yorkshire Police'. According to the SMO, this reflected a conscious decision to 'personalise' the messages in order to encourage engagement: 'I do think it needs a named individual, the people were engaging with me ... I think its success was the personalisation of it, but it doesn't need to be just one person'.

At this stage, Twitter was used to make users aware that regular updates regarding policing would be posted from the account, using the 'hashtag' #libdempolicing, and encouraging them to follow the account. These messages were deliberately upbeat and positive in nature. The SMO notes that 'We spent a lot of time on the tone of the briefings', and this tone was maintained throughout, as in the following examples (which, like similar online messages reproduced in this chapter, are verbatim and uncorrected):

> **@SMOTweet:** SYP are committed to providing a safe and enjoyable environment for all through their #libdempolicing. More details to follow.

> **@SMOTweet:** SYP acknowledges peoples right to protest peacefully and looks forward to the challenge the #libdempolicing weekend will bring.

This form of 'impression management' was complemented, in the week leading up to the event, by the Police use of Twitter to communicate logistical details about the official 'processional route', along with information about road closures, parking restrictions and potential travel disruption. Any direct queries were responded to, and an email address was provided where the SMO could be contacted. This information was also disseminated via Facebook and the local Sheffield Forum.

During the conference

On the days when the conference took place, the SMO worked as part of a team of four officers, committed to providing 'live time information' via a range of social media. In addition to monitoring these online sources, the team received regular updates from the PLT Bronze Commander regarding activities on the ground.

According to the SMO, the majority of the engagement during the conference itself took place on Twitter, which was used extensively. On the Saturday in particular, regular updates were posted (and 'retweeted' from sources on the ground) about the progress of the march, and the mood of the crowd, for example:

@SMOTweet: RT @BronzeTweet Latest: approx 5,000 #libdemconf protestors moving towards Barkers Pool. Loud, and good natured #libdempolicing

As in the days preceding the conference, a large part of the Twitter activity was devoted to keeping protesters and other members of the public updated in terms of such practicalities as the presence of any traffic congestion, and of the build up of numbers on the main protest site at Barker's Pool. In this final respect, in particular, Twitter feeds were used interactively to address any potential misunderstandings about the reason why the police were choosing to operate a gated barrier:

@SMOTweet: #libdempolicing - barriers at rear of Barkers Pool in place to ensure safety. Peaceful protestors will not be contained

@bella12: @SMOTweet #libdempolicing Will more ppl be allowed in if we move up?

@SMOTweet: @bella12 Its not about moving up, the Barkers Pool site safety limit has been reached. Peaceful protestors will not be prevented leaving

@bella12: @SMOTweet thanks for replying. If some of us leave, will you allow 'one in, one out' so others can come in?

@SMOTweet: @bella12 Yes, as long as numbers remain at a safe level. There is still capacity at the moment.

Tweets were also used with the intention of scotching potentially pernicious rumours and/or enabling the police to contradict dangerous or inflammatory public assertions or misperceptions. An obvious example of the former occurred when the SMO immediately intervened to quash the growing theory that police personnel on top of the John Lewis department store, situated directly opposite the protest site, were actually armed snipers: 'It came from the forum, ' she explained. 'I responded on the forum and proactively put one out on Facebook and Twitter, because I thought: "Firearms? That's got the potential to run quite quickly!"'

Easily the most contentious topic of all concerned online allegations that the police were eager and ready to implement the controversial containment or 'kettling' tactics routinely employed by the MPS. The SMO responded consistently to every public expression of concern or indignation by maintaining: 'South Yorkshire Police does not acknowledge kettling as an approved Home Office method of crowd control', and reassuring the sender that the gates to the rear of the protest site were there to ensure public safety and that anyone wishing to leave the area was entirely at liberty to do so:

@SMOTweet: #libdempolicing - barriers at rear of Barkers Pool in place to ensure safety. Peaceful protestors will not be contained.

@footyfan: @SMOTweet so what you're saying, in a roundabout way, is your starting to kettle people?

@SMOTweet: @footyfan SYP respects the right to peaceful protest but will intervene when the conduct threatens the rights of others

@footyfan: @SMOTweet Thanks for the reply, but are we likely to see the same kettleing tactics used here in Sheffield as was used in London?

@SMOTweet: @footyfan SYP does not recognise kettling as a crowd control measure. Have you seen a Police liaison officer in a blue tabard?

@footyfan: @SMOTweet once again, thanks for your answer. I'm sure that will set many peoples minds at rest (such as those who's family are there)

@footyfan: RT @SMOTweet: @footyfan SYP does not recognise kettling as a crowd control measure.

In this exchange @footyfan appears to react positively to the SMO's response, even retweeting the official response to his own followers. Some time later, when another Twitter user (who was not present at the protest) asks for information, prompting him to reiterate the message:

@nstudent: Who can we follow for updates about anti-Libdem conference protest in Sheffield? We are hearing reports of arrests and kettling.. #demo2011

@footyfan: @nstudent @SMOTweet: stated the following in the last hour: "SYP does not recognise kettling as a crowd control measure."

On this incident, the SMO notes that: 'I definitely think I took the wind out of his sails, and I think that's its key. Because it's live time, I think it's able to just take the momentum out of a potential issue'. In her view, Twitter provides SYP an opportunity to publicly refute any criticism, or to correct any false claims, thus 'defusing' any potential catalysts for conflict. The site is also potentially a powerful tool for disseminating a message via tweets and repeated retweets.

However, attempts to address accusations of 'kettling' were not met with an unequivocally positive response. A similar exchange (this time regarding the placement of barriers across the main shopping street, Fargate) took place with another Twitter user who responded more cynically:

@RadicalVoice: A kettle has formed in Fargate around protesters #ldconf #twitpic

@SMOTweet: What you refer to as 'kettling' is Officers trying to prevent disorder and damage while keeping peaceful protesters safe

@RadicalVoice: Kettling or containment; semantics – protesters are telling me they were peacefully demonstrating against tax avoiders @SMOTweet

His tweets of the following day suggest that he remained unconvinced that the barriers on Fargate did not constitute 'kettling'. Nevertheless, there is a hint of a more positive attitude to SYP's approach:

@RadicalVoice: The police did suggest 5000 protesters, but eventful and there was incident of kettling ("containment" police told me to call it)

@RadicalVoice: That's what I felt. They'll be calling kettle black next! I have footage, it was a kettle. Other than that, dialogue seems OK.

Reactions to the use of social media

It is obviously difficult to gauge the extent to which the use of social media contributed to the peaceful nature of the protest. The SMO's own impression - that her team's efforts - had helped to encourage a 'positive atmosphere' during the two-day protest was endorsed by the President of Sheffield Hallam University's Student Union, who was especially complimentary about the Twitter feed:

> It tended to accentuate the positive and was generally reassuring; and whenever any gossip started running round the grapevine, they were very quick to interject that 'There's been no arrests', 'There won't be any kettling', and other messages of that nature to help defuse any simmering controversy. It was very upbeat and positive, and it helped to clarify any confusion or misapprehension regarding their tactics, particularly in relation to kettling.... In fact, we tweeted back to them that we felt they were doing really good work, and that sort of friendliness soon became contagious.

This interpretation of events is also supported by the positive online response from Twitter users, one of whom explicitly drew a favourable comparison with recent events involving the MPS:

@ukcity55: @SMOTweets #libdempolicing found open dialogue reassuring today as a worried Mum. All sides benefit except Libdems. Are the MET watching?

@Bella12: @SMOTweets #libdempolicing went really well – thanks for helpful tweets + prompt replies. Open twitter dialogue with police the way fwd
(posted later in the day by the crowd member involved in the exchange regarding the capacity of the protest area)

The SMO considers the apparent success of this social media engagement to be due in part to SYP's decision to allow her to make Twitter posts as an individual, rather than via a corporate account, which she deems to be crucial in enabling the force to 'engage on quite a personable level'. In her view, the upshot of this was that 'We enhanced our reputation as a force willing to talk to people, live time, I think. ...And I think because we were well briefed, well placed, and had thought about it, it's very, very difficult to rage against an organisation that continually demonstrates it wants to engage with you.'

Conclusion

This chapter has highlighted the ways in which a commitment by South Yorkshire Police to using social media and a Police Liaison Team in their handling of a contentious political protest appears to have helped to create a policing environment in which elements of public disquiet were suitably assuaged, a spirit of police-protester trust and co-operation was cultivated, and inappropriate and potentially provocative tactical interventions were averted or discouraged.

The pervasiveness of mobile technology in today's society is such that it is virtually guaranteed that people are going to be posting online messages about the event right throughout the day in question. As our case study has shown, having an online police presence therefore gives the impression that the police are willing to engage with protest groups while also enabling them to contradict problematic public assertions and misperceptions (e.g. regarding 'kettling' or 'snipers on the rooftop'), establish the police perspective, and explain and justify actual or impending police actions. What our study also suggests is that, the more personable (and personalised) the police use of social media can be, the more effective it is likely to prove.

SYP's use of social media was complemented by the work of a specially constituted Protest Liaison Team, whose assiduous efforts in terms of outreaching protest organisers prior to the event and developing a healthy rapport with such leaders and their rank-and-file both prior to and during the event did much to ensure a peaceful demonstration. Such sentiments are endorsed by the representatives we interviewed of student and other groups opposed to government spending cuts participating in the protest. Our particular focus in this article on the role of police liaison officers in providing real-time intelligence to the remote Silver Command team has indicated how, by providing a complementary, and undoubtedly more intimate, perspective to the one presented by CCTV, such officers are capable of correcting dangerously refracted perceptions and improving the effectiveness and perceived legitimacy of tactical incursions.

The absence of any truly serious or sustained disorder outside the Lib Dem protest makes it impossible to glean from our case study any sense of the extent to which social media and the intelligence function provided by police liaison officers will continue to have utility beyond the onset of violence and confrontation. As we observed in the previous section, Silver's main priority, once this stage has been reached, will be on ensuring that his or her liaison personnel are safely delivered from the fray.

It would clearly be disingenuous of us to pretend on the basis of such limited evidence that the police deployment of social media and liaison teams offers a panacea for the control and facilitation of contemporary protest. What our case study and subsequent discussion of the policing of the TUC march does indicate, however, is that such human-centred approaches to the use of communication and surveillance technologies have a vital complementary function to play that can only help to ensure the effectiveness of more 'conventional' approaches to dealing with public disorder.

References

ACPO/ACPOS (Association of Chief Police Officers and Association of Chief Police Officers in Scotland) (2010). *Manual of Guidance on Keeping the Police.* Wyboston: Bedfordshire: National Policing Improvement Agency.

BBC News (2010). 'Nick Clegg regrets signing anti-tuition fees pledge', 11 November 2010. http://www.bbc.co.uk/news/uk-politics-11732787. Accessed 16 March 2011.

Copitch, G. & Fox, C. (2010). 'Using social media as a means of improving confidence'. *Safer Communities*, 9 (2), 42-48.

Greer, C. & McLaughlin, E. (2010). 'We predict a riot? Public order policing, new media environments and the rise of the citizen journalist'. *British Journal of Criminology*, 50 (6), 1041-1059.

Her Majesty's Chief Inspectorate of Constabulary (HMCIC) (2009a). *Adapting to Protest.* London: HMIC.

Her Majesty's Chief Inspectorate of Constabulary (HMCIC) (2009b). *Adapting to Protest: Nurturing the British Model of Policing.* London: HMIC.

Her Majesty's Inspectorate of Constabulary (HMIC) (2011). *Policing Public Order: An Overview and Review of Progress Against the Recommendations of Adapting to Protest and Nurturing the British Model of Policing.* London: HMIC.

Lewis, P. & Taylor, M. (2010). 'Student demos in Twitter age: no leaders, only chatter'. *The Guardian*, 24 November 2010.

Loveys, K. (2010). 'Come down from the roof please, officers tweeted'. *Mail Online*, 11 November, 2010. http://www.dailymail.co.uk/news/article-1328586/TUITION-FEES-PROTEST-Met-chief-embarrassed-woeful-riot-preparation.html. Accessed 16 March 2011.

Rosie, M. & Gorringe, H. (2009). 'What a difference a death makes: protest, policing and the press at the G20'. *Sociological Research Online*, http://www.socresonline.org.uk/14/5/4.html.

Stott, C., Gorringe, H. & Rosie, M. (2010). 'HMIC goes to Millbank'. *Police Professional*, 232, November 25, 13-17.

Chapter 14: Police Learning Strategies

Sérgio Felgueiras

Abstract European police cooperation needs to be underpinned by mutual understanding between the numerous police organizations that operate across the Member States. However, the very diversity of these organisations is a major factor that hinders this process. The complexity of the police activity, the importance of the protection of civil liberties and Human Rights and the demands of the operational necessity for trans-national police cooperation result in a requirement for new integrated police learning strategies to be developed and implemented. These learning strategies will impact on European police culture, on agencies learning strategies and on the resources to be allocated, as well as on the use of the new information and communications technology (ICT).

Introduction

One of the most complex activities of in contemporary societies is, undoubtedly, the policing of that society. Police activity must actively develop communities, protect citizens and ensure their security. The protection of citizens' fundamental rights must be central to the development of this activity. The policing activity needs also to fit within the scope of the development and acknowledgment of regional, national or supranational spaces. To this end the European Union has developed several policies to implement supranational policing to provide consistent freedom, security and justice.

Following the Lisbon Treaty, the European Union, through its European Council, approved the Stockholm Programme (see chapter 2). This established an EU security policy, which tries to balance freedom of movement, promotion of security and citizens' protection. This programme is based on certain politically established pillars, which address:

- The promotion of citizenship and protection of citizens in all European space
- The defence of citizens' fundamental rights
- The construction of a European space of justice supporting easier access to justice for all its citizens.

This chapter explores several issues and potential tools to address them that area vital to the implementation of this policy. The key ones being:

- Mutual trust among the various European actors. This trust needs to be based on the comprehension of the different legal systems
- A rapid adoption of the various policy tools focused on citizens' and companies' needs
- The definition of a systematic evaluation process to supervise the implementation of the defined policy tools of the programme whilst avoiding the duplication of processes
- The reinforcement of professional networks, the creation of common manuals as well as regional projects and the sharing of good practice
- The improvement of quality, coherence and an easier application of legislative acts that regulate matters such as freedom, security and justice. In the context of judicial cooperation, the principle of mutual recognition must be applied
- A better articulation and coordination among the various European agencies. These include: Europol, Eurojust, Frontex, the European Police College (CEPOL), the European Monitoring Centre for Drugs and Drug Addiction (EMCDDA), the future European Asylum Support Office and (EASO) the European Union Agency for Fundamental Rights (FRA).

As far as the implementation of the Stockholm Programme is concerned, the training of police personnel plays an important role for the construction of a European culture in the fields of justice and policing. For the European Union, it is essential to systematically encourage all professionals - who contribute for the construction of a space of freedom, security and justice - to receive continuous professional development (CPD) and training.

From the European perspective such training needs to systematically address the European dimension of relevant issues. It also needs to be implemented through the distribution of various training products such as: common curricula; exchange programmes; electronic platforms; sharing of good practice and the constitution of communities of practice.

Given the complexity of the European context, difficulties naturally arise when we try to move police training onto a European wide footing. Such European wide police training has to face national, regional, cultural, political, social, financial, legal and organizational differences that are hard to overcome. This chapter explores what should be the European strategy for the implementation of education and training programmes targeted to systematically overcome these challenges. Such a strategy should address training needs so as to support spirit enshrined in the Stockholm Programme.

The police function in 21st century

The resulting demands from the Stockholm Programme oblige us to rethink the police functions in the European space and to consider the common purpose of the different Member States of the European Union. As a starting point we need to understand the key features of 21st century policing.

Although it is difficult to find an universally accepted definition of policing, it can be characterized as a set of organized and developed functions to provide security, tranquillity and public order whether by individuals or by organizations.As Newburn (2008) states:

> "[it] involves organized order maintenance, peace keeping, rule or law enforcement, crime investigation and associated information brokering, which may involve the conscious exercise of coercive power" (p. 217)

In Crawford's opinion (2008) this concept has four important fundamental elements:

> "first, it entails intentional action or a purposeful condition; secondly, it involves the conscious exercise of power or authority by an individual or organization; thirdly it is directed towards rule or norm enforcement, the promotion of order or assurances of safety; and, fourthly it seeks to govern in the present and /or the future" (p. 149)

Traditionally, policing was seen as an activity of the functional monopoly of police forces. Presently, however, there is a tendency to consider police forces only as one of the actors, the law enforcement agencies (LEAs) that play a part in implementing policing. Supporting this position, Reiner (1997) argues that policing: "may be carried out by a diverse array of people and techniques of which the modern police is only one" (p. 1005). Following Reiner et al (1996) we can define policing as "the self-conscious process whereby societies designate and authorize people to create public safety" (p. 586). This way, security emerges as a key associated concept of policing. This position deserves consideration and Johnston (1999) affirms that:

> "policing may be defined as a purposive strategy involving the initiation of techniques which are intended to offer guarantees of security to subjects." (p. 586)

In conclusion and in our opinion, the policing concept presented by Reiner, not only resumes the debate on policing but it allows us to establish a relationship between this approach and the social complexity in which we live. In this way, the author considers that policing:

> "is an aspect of social control processes involving surveillance and sanctions intended to ensure the security of the social order. The order in question may be based on consensus; or conflict and oppression, or an ambiguous amalgam of the two, which is usually the case in modern societies." (Reiner, 1997, p. 1008).

The transnational dimension of the European space, its multidimensional diversity (social, cultural, political, financial and organizational), the increasing complexity of society, crime and police function, the permanent technological evolution and the continuous scientific developments are therefore factors that limit policy implementation. This situation makes policing one of the most demanding, dynamic and complex professions.

The demands of the police intervention need to be compared to other professions contributing to the law enforcement. Pais (2008, p. 15) argues that it is important to consider the difficult circumstances in which these professionals act. Police officers face adverse, and even violent, social conditions and individuals, some with challenging mental health issues, and constantly interact with vulnerable people who are often isolated from their familiar social environment. Under these circumstances these professionals are asked to find and re-establish the equilibrium in those situations. They are expected to overcome difficulties and to maintain their trust in themselves and in justice. In short, they are asked to manage the psychological impact caused by their involvement with cases. Only through education and learning can police officers improve their professional competences in the resolution of this kind of conflict.

During their life time, police forces have been obliged to find solutions allowing, on one hand, a certain level of homogeneity regarding police activity and on the other hand, to provide citizens with a high standard of security and in terms of their expectations as far as police responses are concerned.

As Wain (2008) notes:

> "a world marked by vertiginous change generated by rapid technological and scientific advance, which has redefined our economic challenges in global terms, created instability and dislocation in our lives, seen the advent of the information society and of a post-industrial landscape, and prioritised the culture of risk, innovation and performativity" (p. 104).

These changes oblige police officers to be updated in terms of their knowledge, procedures and techniques. This is a consensual position among police organizations. Van Beek et al (2005) affirm that:

> "a competent police officer is able to do the core activities of his or her job in a proper way. Because of our fast changing society police officers have to update their competencies continuously. Striking features of the police profession are taking responsibility and initiative" (p. 5).

However, limited operational resources do not allow police organizations to implement, in a systematic way, educational and training actions targeted to their police officers. Consequently, dilemmas arise among the main police organizations in terms of inefficient solutions versus limited resources or in terms of training needs versus capacity to promote education, training and learning.

Van Beek et al (2005) state that "police officers must be responsible for their learning during their whole career" (p. 5) and we believe that this indicates the tendency of police organizations to focus on self-learning approaches and methods. Obviously, these organizations cannot be alienated from the process, it is our belief that they should create the necessary conditions to allow and to encourage the self-learning of their police officers.

Needs and barriers in police learning

The goals of the Stockholm Programme associated with the complexity of police activity, oblige Police Forces to choose education programmes that encourage lifelong learning by their professionals.

Traditionally, in most European countries, it is possible to identify four different kinds of police training:

- Initial training
- Advanced training
- "Tailor made" training
- Lifelong training.

These approaches have supported two general requirements in police training. First, those relating to time of service and the need to be competent in the key professional practices deemed necessary for good performance in their role as police officers. Such competencies change over time.

However some factors encourage the permanent adaptation of police organizations to their own surrounding social and national environment. This adaptation is derives from the demands of the civil society and citizens, the contemporary extensive police exposure of police to the media, to continuous political and social changes, and to technological innovations. In the case of changes might be due to scientific developments (say in forensics) or to responses within police organizations designed to simplify, improve or reduce the costs of functions. In many cases it is a combination of some or all of those factors.

To this we need to add the European dimension. This leads police organizations to feel the need creating conditions where they are able to develop themselves in line with European policy goals. In order to really adhere to this concept, the different Police Forces have to realize that a European police model is essential to the development of both their organizations and staff. Training and learning are central to this reorientation of activity.

In the domain of police education and training, Police Forces face several challenges to the implementation of education and training programmes - as well as to changing such investment into advantages in police work. When addressing the theme of European policing in dilemmas arise and there are often barriers to this type of educational development within security forces. Some examples are:

- Global versus National versus Local, - namely the diversity of intervention environments such as varying legal, political and social contexts
- Human and material resources restraints
- The organizational culture and learning – for example an involving organization model versus a developed organization versus an apprentice organization
- When compared to operational activities, educational activities do not have autonomy

- There is no trust among communities of practice, education community and the scientific community
- The difficulty in creating learning environments that on one hand are interesting to professionals and one the other hand can work with the operational restraints inherent to the police activity
- The professionals' motivation to maintain interest in learning.

The issue of knowledge transfer and adult education provokes are huge challenges in and of themselves. This is no different with regard to the realization, implementation and evaluations of learning programmes in the context of policing. In the case of professional development we need to achieve outcomes in terms of behaviours as well as knowledge. As Colman (2006) notes such learning is:

> "any lasting change in behaviour resulting from experience, especially conditioning. The act or process of acquiring knowledge or skill, or knowledge gained by study" (p. 415).

In Europe, there is no systematic, concerted and scientific approach in the field of 'policing science'. The debate around what is police science contains a range of positions. However, in this chapter, we use the concept of police sciences that was presented by Romero et al (2009):

> "the scientific study of police as an institution and of policing as a process. As an applied discipline, it combines methods and subjects of other neighbouring disciplines within the field of policing. It includes all of what the police do and all aspects from outside that have an impact on policing and public order. Currently it is a working term to describe police studies on the way to an accepted and established discipline. Police science tries to explain facts and acquire knowledge about the reality of policing in order to generalize and also to be able to predict possible future scenarios" (p. 30).

Although there has been the establishment of the European Police Academy it did not derive from scientific research activities, though some steps were taken in order to:

- Characterize the state-of-art of in Police Sciences
- Create networks to facilitate intelligence exchange in this domain
- To make the dissemination of scientific research results easier, using them, whenever possible, in training actions
- Organize activities to promote international cooperation in the field of scientific research

In our opinion, this College must be the hinge element in all European police education promotion. This will, in the first place, begin to satisfy the needs resulting from the Stockholm Programme and, in second place, provide technical assistance to Member States in the area of police learning strategy and practice.

Teaching strategies versus learning

Presently, the existing debate on training is focused on the differentiation between teaching and learning. On this subject, Wain (2008) argues that:

> "the policy debate today is not about 'education' but about efficient and effective 'learning', about skills and competencies, about knowledge creation and management, and about learning to learn. It is about lifelong learning not about lifelong education." (p. 104).

According to Wain, the essence of this debate is related to the instrumental validity of learning as far as purposes, results and objectives are concerned. Depending on the circumstances, the instrumental validity of learning can occur, or not, within the scope the training activities.

The education and training strategies defined by any LEA depends on several specific factors in the police organization. These factors inclue: the organization itself and its culture; the police subculture; the needs identified by the organization; the available resources; time for the activity implementation and the period of time during which organisational change can be expectable to happen.

Within this we need to consider the kind of relationship between the organization and its employee. We can group the education and training strategies in three main categories.

1. First, it is possible to consider a situation where there is a focus on the organization – that is the training and education process is elaborated so that the employee is led through an assimilation process of culture, knowledge and of competences that the organization itself considers to be the most important. Consequently it is the organization that has all the responsibility and supervision of the process, providing the employee with a much reduced level of autonomy. In this category, training can be are limited to a certain period of time, given the permanent need of police organizations to orient their resources to operational activities.
2. Second, the police organization implements conditions so that its employee is autonomous in their learning process, encouraging in this way their self-learning. It is possible to extend this process for long periods of time, knowing that the main investment of the organization occurs before the process implementation. This allows learning to have an updated, permanent, sustainable and exponential effect, making possible the materialization of the concept of the 'learning organization'.
3. Third, it is possible to identify a hybrid system, where the two strategies are combined and where there is a sharing of responsibility during the learning period.

In our opinion, the essential reflection needed for the elaboration of a learning or training strategy goes through seven stages:

- Stage 1 - Identification, comprehension and a projection of the external social environment
- Stage 2 – based on the results of the Stage 1, it is possible to identify what kind of police and policing is adequate to that phase of Society
- Stage 3 – identification of the state-of art of sciences and technologies that are considered important to the development of the concepts, methods and techniques to be implemented
- Stage 4 –the definition of police competences necessary to the implementation of the kinds of police and policing that were identified in stage 2
- Stage 5 – reflection on the methods that should be used to measure and evaluate the identified police competences;
- Stage 6 – elaboration of the teaching or learning methods that allow the employee to assimilate the competences and techniques to successfully achieve tin any evaluations or tests
- Stage 7 – quality evaluation, a posteriori, of all the proceeding stages with regard to the formulation of learning or training strategies.

Learning methodologies

Learning methodologies play a vital role in a successful learning process, however, "a learning method is a method, not an aim" (van Beek et al, 2005, p. 6). Everybody has a different ways of learning; this means that there should be different approaches for different people. The implementation of a learning environment should consider the diversity of students' learning. In this sense, van Beek et al (2005) defend the need to create a diverse learning environment "to give students with different learning styles the opportunity to acquire the proper competencies for their profession" (p. 6).

There are several different available learning methods, which can be used in accordance with specific objectives. Van Beek et al (2005, pp. 38-39) identify: feedback; reflection; role play; mind maps; lectures; proposition play; discussions; assessments; question bins; for better or for worse; sorting outs; buzzings; self-study; sub groups; video feedback; learning with and from examples; gluing stickers; making a collage; quizes; and simulation games.

It is and strict requirement that police officers complete knowledge of of certain domains, principles, laws, rules, methods and techniques, so that the police activity can be professionally performed.

This reality obliges them to constantly update of knowledge. It is possible to ensure a permanent updating of knowledge since contents and actions are available and since there is a serious commitment from each professional party. On the one hand, the organization should encourage individual motivation; on the other hand, it should incentive the implementation of an added value knowledge chain.

As far as the domain of police methods and techniques is concerned, it is necessary that each professional develops their capacities throughout their working lifetime. Methodologies using partial or total simulation of the situation, the vision and analysis of real situations, the sharing of good practices are the indicated methodologies for this kind of learning. A good practice that that should be used in these situations can be summarized with the following:

- Train as you work, work as you train!

In conclusion, we can state that the choice of learning methodologies should be done according to the target group, organization and objectives promoting the quality assurance. The organizational culture plays a fundamental and transversal role to all this learning process in police organizations.

The new ICT role concerning police education

The use of the new ICT to support the teaching and learning activities has massively increased in the last decade. This reality is a consequence of the seemingly permanent technological change at present and requires constant monitoring. The incorporation of these new technologies in the world of learning needs a careful evaluation in terms of the various issues that we have been mentioned in this chapter, in particular, learning methodologies.

The use of the new information and communications technology in the learning area is not an end in itself. That is in any e-learning the main factor is learning and not the technological support that is used to deliver that e-learning. So the use of the technological support has to be in accordance with the learning methodologies. The specifications of police organizations are not an obstacle to the adoption of learning methods and techniques that use the new information technologies. The associated advantages to the use of the new information and communications technology allow learning content to be simultaneously available globally. This fact can be a value-added when it overcomes the territorial dispersion of the several police departments. This makes ICT based training a major opportunity for the development of European wide training and development programmes. Importantly ICTs allow us to create environments that encourage learning, namely, simulation environments (with manipulation of variables), contributing to the standardisation and repetition of proceedings, flexibility and agility (see chapters 6, 8 and 9). These technological platforms should be flexible so that each person is capable of learning according to their profile and style, following their own way in a structured and supported manner.

Conclusions

Learning has a vital role to play in the construction of a European space where justice and security are consistently supported and promoted. This is due to the fact that learning allows different approaches in the respective police organizations to become closer, facilitating the international police cooperation, which, in turn, contributes to build the pillars for the developing European police culture.

In the learning context, the European reality can be characterised by several different strategies from different origins. All these strategies are a challenge as far as the articulation, re-orientation and convergence of the multiple strategies targeted to the police learning are concerned.

Nowadays, the construction process of a European dimension to police learning faces challenges, which in our opinion are essentially the result of the local and national levels prevalence over those at a European level. The national resources allocated to the European process remain limited. This reality can be verified through the assessment of the level of performed actions at a national level to support the realization of cooperation activities. The national effort of each country is focused on national police learning strategies, which reflects the importance that national issues of sovereignty assume regarding Europeanization. However, some countries are themselves not able to implement a national strategy due to their own police organization. While the European solution is not presented as a reference in international terms, national investments will continue to be allocated to solve domestic issues.

By focusing on local, regional and national levels as opposed to a European level, the police forces neglect their officers in their education on transnational issues. This lack of European understanding contributes to the alienation of police professionals as far as cooperation activities are concerned. Given the transnational nature of today's organized crime and other criminal activity it is believed that police officers should be the focus of European strategies.

Relations based on trust are another key factor that deserve attention. These relations are a determinant factor not only to the international cooperation but also to the necessary articulation of learning and police activity in line with the results of scientific research. From our perspective, the process of incorporating of science results in police organizations should have three stages: to stimulate the scientific research applied to the police activity; to continuously update learning content and to validate operational decisions and actions.

In sensitive areas such as Human Rights, the police activity should be oriented to excellence, whether at the decision making process level, or at the police action level. The interdependence between decision and action is a daily reality for police officers, who patrol cities and it directly influences the police service quality.

The increase in quality levels in police activity is the consequence of continuous simple learning processes which are considered by police officers as a value-added for their Professional role. Besides the implementation of practice communities, realization and promotion of common manuals, sharing of good practice, and the application and promotion of European research projects results - it is fundamental to find a common approach to learning, which considers the self-reflection incentive, the different profiles and styles of learning and which is a value-added for all European police organizations.

ICT can offer the flexibility, exclusivity, interactivity and the speed that are demanded of learning programmes in a Professional context. However, the difficulty of their utilization depends on the production of content able to simultaneously associate profiles and styles of learning, knowledge and incentives for reflection, and support for lifelong self-learning.

The European Police College (CEPOL) presents itself as the main actor in the European police education scene and, in our opinion; it should develop into the European platform for police education and police learning. Obviously, it will have to pass through a process of development but the articulation of education actions, common curricula, e-library, the promotion of the scientific research results and its technological resources are a reference for European organizations. In short, every European strategy targeted to the police learning should focus on the future, privileging the self-education in transversal areas of the Member States, using the ICT to promote interactive content capable of stimulating the development of autonomous learning.

References

Bayley, D., & Shearing, C. (1996). The future of policing. Law and Society Review, 585-606.

Crawford, A. (2008). Plural policing in the UK: Policing beyond the police. In T. Newburn, Handbook of Policing (pp. 147-181). Devon: Willan Publishing.

Colman, A. M. (2006). A dictionary of psychology (2nd ed.). Oxford: Oxford University Press.

del Barrio Romero, F., Bjorgo, T., Jaschke, H., Kwanten, C., Mawby, R., & Pagon, M. (2009). Police sciences perspectives: Towards a european approach - extended expert report. Frankfurt: Verlag fuer Polizeiwissenschaft.

Johston, L. (1999). Private policing in context. European Journal on Criminal Policy and Research, 175-196.

Jones, G. (2001). Organizational theory (3rd ed.). Upper Saddle River, NJ: Prentice-Hall.

Newburn, T. (2008). Policing. In T. Newburn, & P. Neyroud, Dictionary of policing (pp. 217-219). Devon, UK: Willan Publishing.

Pais, L. G. (2008). A reinserção social no diagrama disciplinar. Ousar Integrar: Revista de Reinserção Social e Prova, 1 (1), 9-19.

Reiner, R. (1997). Policing and the police. In M. Maguire, R. Morgan, & R. Reiner (Eds.), The Oxford handbook of criminology (2nd ed., pp. 997-1049). Oxford: Oxford University Press.

van Beek, M., ter Huurne, J., van Vierssen, D., & Vinter, E. (2005). Palette for teachers, learning methods for use. Ubbergen: Tandem Felix publishers.

Wain, K. (2008). The Future of Education ... and its Philosophy. Springer Science+Business Media n.° 27, 103-114.

Chapter 15: Conclusions – Technology, Society and Law Enforcement Agencies

Simeon J. Yates

Concluding comments

The goal of this book has been to try and explore, through a range of examples, how the work of law enforcement agencies (LEAs) can be enhanced, developed or is being changed by contemporary information and communication technologies (ICTs). To this we have added the need for European or broadly cross-national cooperation in the fight against crime and terrorism. This is vital as crime and terrorism, as problematic and harmful social activities, are themselves supported in their transnational activity by the very same set of technologies. We have also sought to provide examples of how the strategic use of data, information, knowledge and intelligence – supported by contemporary information system solutions – provides a major opportunity for LEAs. As was noted in chapter 10 new forms of ICT for the support of investigations (see chapter 6), communication (see chapter 13), data capture (see chapter 7), training (see chapters 8 and 9) and also knowledge elicitation (see chapter 2) add to the complexity (see chapter 5) of the domains in which LEAs function. A systematic strategic approach to the management of knowledge by LEAs is therefore needed and, as chapter 11 clearly indicates, any lack of systematic strategic intelligence management has real and profound human consequences.

We have also sought to provide three levels of discussion. In section 1 we provided a more detailed description of the key elements of one solution to the above issues. In this case the Odyssey project which focused on the domain of gun crime. This provided more detailed explorations of: the challenges in creating such solutions; user needs and the theoretical reflection on the implications of implementation. Section 2 provided further examples of ICT based solutions to specific LEA challenges such as investigation, real time data acquisition, and training and community engagement. Section 3 moved to the broader question of the link between ICT and LEA policies and practices and the implications for LEAs of the impacts of ICTs on society. What general conclusions and themes can we draw from the chapters in this volume?

At the close of chapter 1 we noted seven issues that run through the volume:

- The use, development and management of data, information, intelligence and knowledge

  - All of the chapters in this volume have touched on this issue – ICT use is now an integral part of both policing and crime. LEAs must therefore develop robust Strategic Intelligence Management strategies (chapter 10) for the domains in which they operate. Both the strategies and the technologies they deploy need to address the transnational nature of crime and terrorism.

- The complexity of the social, cultural, political and legal landscape in which LEAs deploy new ICT solutions
  - The solutions, strategies and systems themselves are not solely technical. In fact the greatest challenge comes in changing the social, cultural, political and legal landscape. Systems such as the Odyssey prototype (chapter 1) can demonstrate the benefits of current and potentially beyond-the-state-of-the-art technology solutions. Yet the implementation of these solutions is both constrained and limited by current social context. This might be a lack of coordination and commonality in LEA practices, data collection or culture. Alternatively it might be a lack of legal frameworks which reflect the new realities created by ICTs in use by LEAs, citizens and criminals (see chapter 12). Yet it remains the case that the majority of the funding for research and development continues to focus on ICT based innovations and not on the social challenges.

- The manner in which new forms of ICT themselves change the social, cultural, political and legal landscape for users, citizens, LEAs and criminals alike
  - All the chapters have indicated that new ICT solutions are creating new contexts for the work of LEAs. In particular many new technologies are highly disruptive of existing practices. In many cases the challenges identified by projects such as Odyssey (chapter 2) derive not from the development of novel technical solutions but rather from understanding users and their social context. In fact given the raw commuting power and range of data, intelligence, and knowledge management tools already developed beyond-the-state-of-the-art may in fact be better evaluated in terms of our methods for understanding users and the disruptive impact of ICT than in the development of further ICT solutions.

- The desire by users and LEAs to best strategically use and manage the data, information, knowledge and intelligence they have
  - Throughout the volume it is clear that end users desire to make best possible and strategic use of the data they hold. The challenges are not therefore in persuading them of the usefulness of data, information, and management knowledge intelligence. Rather the challenges are around embedding such data use into the everyday practices of LEA activity

(chapter 6). There are two key elements to this. First, support for the training and education of LEA staff in the use of such data. Such training needs to be strategically planned and needs to be cognisant of the transnational context (chapter 14) but can also make excellent use of ICT solutions itself (chapter 8).

- The complexity and range of data, information, and intelligence knowledge available to contemporary LEAs
  - Despite their advantages ICTs also bring a 'tsunami of data' that may or may not be of relevance and use to LEAs. Dealing with this 'tsunami' and having the ICT, data and knowledge management 'literacies' needed to make best use of it remains a key challenge (see chapter 5). Not only do we need to configure new systems to help manage this, we also need to configure users to be able to know what this data can or is 'telling' us.

- The centrality of interoperability and standards to the utilisation of this data across national and organisational borders
  - This issue cuts throughout the volume. With regard to standards considerable work remains to be done in defining these and implementing them through policy actions within all the domains of LEA activity. In many areas of LEA work there are no accepted open standards for data capture, processing and representation in original and meta-data of key items. Nor are there accepted open standards for comparison, audit, and regulation of system usability, performance and reliability. This contrasts considerably with other domains (such as medicine) where such standards to support data exchange are becoming nationally and internationally established. Without progress on these fundamental issues the benefits of cross-border sophisticated ICT solutions to support LEA activity will remain curtailed.

- The importance of addressing the social, economic, political and legal issues as much as the technical ones
  - Crime and terrorism, however anti-social in their impacts are 'social activities'. Large organised crime groups and terrorists operate in a world of economic exchange, ideological and political action, media use and communication practices. LEAs also function within political and legal constraints and need to react to social pressures and the concerns of the citizens they protect (see chapter 4). ICTs and the strategic use of information and knowledge have key roles to play here too. They can help in engagement of LEAs with social and community solutions to specific issues (see chapter 9) or in their operational engagement with the public (see chapter 14). Having said this the experience of the Odyssey project is that greater and more detailed understandings of the social issues are needed not just to

better elucidate user requirements, but also to best understand the disruptive social and organisational impacts. Understanding these impacts, some of great benefit to LEAs and society others not, should be built into our research development agenda with regard to the use of ICT to support the prevention and detection of crime and terrorism.

Index

MIX
Papier aus verantwortungsvollen Quellen
Paper from responsible sources
FSC® C105338

If you have any concerns about our products,
you can contact us on
ProductSafety@springernature.com

In case Publisher is established outside the EU,
the EU authorized representative is:
Springer Nature Customer Service Center GmbH
Europaplatz 3, 69115 Heidelberg, Germany

Printed by Libri Plureos GmbH
in Hamburg, Germany